Kaust

The I of Philosophy

Thought and Redemption

palgrave
macmillan

The Power of Philosophy

Kaustuv Roy
Azim Premji University
Bengaluru, India

ISBN 978-3-030-07269-8 ISBN 978-3-319-96911-4 (eBook)
https://doi.org/10.1007/978-3-319-96911-4

Softcover re-print of the Hardcover 1st edition 2018

Cover design by Emma Hardy

This Palgrave Macmillan imprint is published by the registered company Springer Nature Switzerland AG
The registered company address is: Gewerbestrasse 11, 6330 Cham, Switzerland

… καὶ ἡ ἀλήθεια ἐλευθερώσει ὑμᾶς.
John 8:32

Preface

In old movie theaters, one could turn around in one's seat and see the hole at the rear wall through which the projector beamed, over the heads of the audience, torrents of colored light, hitting the screen out in front, creating scenes of wretched pain and intense Eros, of clichéd tenderness and scripted horror. Rays of light passing through celluloid and captured on screen were able to arouse various sentiments depending on the times, culture, and reception. Dust motes swirled, casually drifting in and out of the beams, indifferent to the events. As a child one found the colorful proceedings overhead almost as intriguing as the colored effects on the screen, at times more so. Much later, the recollection of this would serve as a good model for reflection on the general nature of that in which we are absorbed most of the time. Representations fill our mental horizon, but the invisible ontological mix that is the background stuff of consciousness remains obscure. We are glued to the images, but unlike the child of curiosity, are not particularly interested in or concerned about their source. Clearly, there is no 'hole-in-the-wall' from which images pour out in consciousness, nor yet beams of any discernible thing that visibly project thought. And yet the parallels are unmistakable. Somewhere in those similarities the idea of this book took birth. The human composite dances to the tune of thought, and yet has not the least idea of the true nature of its matrix. To claim that it originates in the chemistry of the brain or somewhere else is only to beg the question. It is not that the book attempts to discover the origin of thinking. Rather, it attempts to study thinking in a manner that philosophy has rarely done. Thought by itself cannot discover its own origin. But it can put itself under stringent observation such that gradually an intuition is developed toward a new perception and a readiness for disclosure. Thinking has been obsessed by the content of thinking; now thought is asked to look into its structure, which brings us to the door of origin. Then we can knock. And maybe the door is opened unto us. The book is an offering to the preparation for such a possibility.

Bengaluru, India

Kaustuv Roy

Acknowledgements

The author acknowledges institutional help received from Azim Premji University, Bangalore, in the production of the book. Acknowledgment is due to Chitra L. who has worked as research assistant on the project, read, and offered valuable suggestions.

Contents

CHAPTER 1

Introduction: Toward Philosophical Bilingualism

This book attempts a special kind of eidetic reduction—a phenomenological effort that goes beyond the epistemic and affective content of thought toward the singularity of its essential-embodied movement. The suggestion is that such reduction constitutes a unique form of philosophical praxis inducing a trans-historical relation with all that is. Praxis here refers not to the transformation of cultural content in thinking but in bringing about an inward mirror to thought with regard to its structural movement. The thesis proceeds from the observation that thinking takes itself for granted, and, for the most part, is focused on outer phenomena, rarely interrogating its own origin and character. This self-disclosure is vital if thinking is to recover its true bearing and potential, freeing itself from the limitations and one-sidedness that has become attendant upon it through history. For the accomplishment of this philosophical task, together with the building of an observation point from where to scrutinize the process of what is called thinking, the book turns selectively to the works of four major thinkers namely Heidegger, Schelling, Goethe, and Heraclitus, across a vast expanse of time, to carve out the vision of a transformative praxis beyond historical totality. The thread that links the above thinkers is their skepticism with regard to the conventional operation of thought and its implicit taken-for-grantedness. Each in their own way discovers something that would challenge the basic pre-suppositions, dualities, and limits within which thought operates. Each attempts to free thought toward attaining its true potential. The book proposes the notion of philosophical bilingualism as a way to take into account what is disclosed regarding the ontological character of thought

K. Roy, *The Power of Philosophy*,
https://doi.org/10.1007/978-3-319-96911-4_1

alongside its representational or symbolic content. The simultaneous consideration of these two aspects brings about within thought a new alignment with *what is*. Moreover, conditions press upon us to consider this not as an idle question but as an existentially urgent one, for thought in its conventional operation has brought about unending planetary crisis, even as it chanted of freedom, progress, and other talismanic incantations. Philosophy cannot remain silent to this spectacle, nor can it absolve itself of responsibility, since the problem of thought-made suffering must also be the central philosophical problem. It is against this mandate that the present attempt is made toward praxis.

"The alpha and omega of all philosophy is freedom." Thus wrote Schelling in a letter to Hegel in 1795.[1] The question immediately arises: Does the possibility of philosophical freedom, that is, attaining existential renewal by means of serious engagement in philosophy, still exist? Or has philosophy long been reduced to just another formal academic pursuit, recapitulating old debates or adding to scholarship in remote realms? Is there left to us a *doing* of philosophy, or rather, can philosophy do something with us? Some like Theodor Adorno seemed skeptical of the possibility. In the introduction to *Negative Dialectics*, Adorno wrote: "Philosophy remains alive because the moment of its realization was missed."[2] In other words, humanity failed to attain to philosophy at the very moment when it was ripe for existential and phenomenological realization. Now it merely lives on as a formal discourse, alive only because it did not come to fruition. However, assuming that Adorno was speaking from the standpoint of redemption, can the moment of realization of freedom be truly lost? For, must not freedom be implicitly understood as a blossoming free of the category of time? If time as a category were allowed to interfere with freedom, then it would no longer remain free. If that be the case, then philosophy as the search for freedom is not permanently compromised, since the ontological 'now' cannot be lost in the temporal progression of history. To be free (of time) is a ceaseless struggle; it is not some finally realized or realizable state. Moreover, by freedom we do not mean here something abstract and immensely generalized, but a concrete onto-phenomenological susceptibility that can be discovered corporeally by

[1] Devin Zane Shaw, *Freedom and Nature in Schelling's Philosophy of Art* (New York: The Continuum Publishing, 2010), p. 1.

[2] Theodor Adorno, *Negative Dialectics* (New York: The Continuum Publishing, 1973), p. 3.

the subject through, and in spite of, the relentlessness of history. And the present book will argue that just as the Fall of Man, or the temptation of history, is a daily occurrence, the possibility of freedom is implicit in each existential moment.[3] Freedom is thus trans-historical and it is ontological. It is not the attribute of something pre-existing, but the phenomenological composite awakened to its own temporal and spatial composition. It is not the mere product of social conditions or privileged epistemic content of thought, nor is it a function of the politics of time. The postulation here is that this redemption is realizable not as experience but as transpersonal turning-toward-being by anyone and no-one, implying that "anyone" who dares approach this becomes "no-one" in the process since s/he goes to the (spatio-temporal) root of experience itself. Thus is philosophical potential realizable in its most radical and acute form.

However, there is a dual necessity that attends upon such phenomenological inquiry into philosophical freedom since it is an active process: one must directly participate in it rather than see it in the mind's eye in a detached, representational manner. First, there has to be the willingness to question and set aside existing conceptual categories and organizing schemas. The inquiry into ontological freedom demands learning to think anew, and that means to sacrifice the existing entrenched image of thought. And second, the "thinker" must be prepared to become phenomenologically the object of its own careful study in a no-holds barred manner. To clear a path for an approach to the realization of these goals is part of the aim of the present volume. A hermeneutics of thought is attempted that combs the process of thinking itself rather than the content of thinking.

But let us go to the beginning of the story briefly with respect to the present age in the West. We have to, *prima facie*, establish the connection between philosophy and freedom on our way to eidetic reduction. In what mode does freedom become the central philosophical problematic

[3] To consider the Fall of Man only in mythological terms is to forgo the chance of realizing that myth is substantiated in each living moment, which is, in fact, why it achieves the status of enduring myth. The possibility of redemption is built into each moment just as is the possibility of Fall. The relation between evil and freedom is one of the most significant areas of discussion in philosophy and a major contributor to this discussion is F.W.J. Schelling whose ideas form an important part of the present volume. A more recent thinker to be drawn to this problem is Ivan Illich, see *Rivers North of the Future: The Testament of Ivan Illich* (Toronto: Anansi Press, 2005). Illich, like Schelling before him, argues that the possibility of Good and Evil arise simultaneously. Both terms are to be understood ontologically and not morally.

in the eyes of the moderns?[4] Let us turn to German Idealism and see how the problem begins to take shape within an opposition between subject and object. Schelling, for instance, along with much of modern Western philosophy, inherits the problem from Kant, or rather, derives it within the particular Kantian framing of our relationship with the world in which we find ourselves. But while Schelling breaks free of the Kantian schema and manages an incredible feat taking German Idealism beyond itself, much of Western philosophy remains contained within the hardness and definitude of the Kantian legacy. While Schelling breaks open the very opposition between Mind and Nature (subject and object) that was taken for granted within idealist conception, the opposition becomes the key background assumption for much of Western thought. Returning to Kant, what follows in the next few paragraphs might seem to be something of a harsh and hasty assessment of Kant's vision. But I beg the reader to bear with me as it becomes necessary to pay attention to the crucial phrases and turns in Kant's argument that initially frames my problem here. To do otherwise is to let the thing off the hook amid an array of divergent positions within scholarly debate. Confrontation with Kant becomes inevitable in a project such as the present one which envisages the possibility of phenomenological transcendence, or thought going beyond itself. By no means is this the only confrontation—ultimately thinking must be made to confront itself from multiple directions, as we shall see. With due regard for Kant's concern for what it means to be human, the choking off of the possibility of transcending or superseding a state that could plausibly be regarded as a transitory phase in the existential duration of a species being, and has been regarded as such in important traditions, is one of Kantian philosophy's limiting legacies. That humanity's self-understanding as constituting an implicitly "arrived" state is not problematized in Kant is one part of the concern; that the question of self-referentiality inherent in any self-description is not problematized is another part of the issue; that the possibility of an anarchic rejoinment to the existential infinitude is put out of prospect, is yet another part of the difficulty. A species being that has little comprehension of its origin, neither has any idea of the reason for its presence, nor has come to terms with its eventual ending, may

[4]Among the monists or *Advaitins* of the East, on the contrary, "freedom" is not a separate philosophical problem but the very *telos* of human life. *Moksha* or *Mukti* are among the terminologies often used to describe a state that is free of mental turbulence, representational activity, and hence of duality. All intermediate states are seen as unreliable and wrought by *Avidya* or ignorance.

not rightfully make categorical claims about its true relations with the world. It can only be helped to do so in eschatological or transcendental terms that exceed the ordinary frame. It cannot do so solely in logical terms no matter how carefully construed; there is an attendant incompleteness that is part of thought itself when it turns to reflect upon object relations. Besides, the turbulence within consciousness cannot be got rid of by putting the lid of reason on it—its source is deeper than reason can fathom—neither can the expansion of formal rationality in society produce reasonable humans who are in grasp of the innate nature of their thinking. This much needs to be admitted no matter how bothersome it appears at first glance. The appreciation that neither reason (science etc.) nor non-reason (faith etc.) *by and of themselves* can give a satisfactory account of existence and its interrelations is part of a humility that has never been adequately inaugurated in consciousness. We have not been helped to become philosophically "bilingual," building the necessary dialectical bridge between the two sides—reason and non-reason—leaving both to claim exclusivity on either side of the opposition at different points and within different "emancipatory" regimes in history. But here I am guilty of running ahead of the narrative.

To get back, Kant's central problematic is to philosophically demonstrate a reliable and consistent cognitive bridge between the perceiver and perceived. Kant tries to accomplish this with the humanism and anthropocentrism typical of the eighteenth century. There is even, one might be tempted to add, a peculiar innocence that seems incredible today after more than two centuries of reason's charge. Consider the following passage from Kant's first *Critique*:

> Reason must approach nature with the view, indeed, of receiving information from it, not, however, in the character of a pupil, who listens to all that his master chooses to tell him, but in that of a judge, who compels the witnesses to reply to those questions which he himself thinks fit to propose. To this single idea must the revolution be ascribed, by which, after groping in the dark for so many centuries, natural science was at length conducted into the path of certain progress.[5]

[5]Immanuel Kant, *Critique of Pure Reason*, trans. Norman Kemp Smith, 2nd ed. (New York: Palgrave Macmillan, 1929), p. xxvii. In passing it is worthwhile to note that the previous centuries are seen as "groping in the dark." It is not clear how Kantian reason is able to arrive at such a massive synthetic judgement and overwhelming generalization about the past. Besides, in this very judgement is presaged a view that sees nature as something lying around to be optimized by human activity.

First, "reason" itself is assumed to be supra-natural and unproblematic. The imagery is telling. Standing apart from nature in magisterial attitude, reason must interrogate what is not reason. Nature is to be likened to a witness for cross-examination. The magisterial voice "compels" nature to reveal itself in accordance with the questions posed to it. Thus the human mind is the "judge" who does not need to listen, but only demands answers that it sees fit to ask. The matrix of finite determinations is pre-established by which "nature" is to be known and treated. This "nature" apparently does not include the nature within, and of, the human. Hence there is no place for organic intuition, or invitation to the disclosure of self-nature by means of attentive resonance. The "judge" is external to the situation, an objective arbiter. And finally, this ideology of knowing, wherein nature is barred from offering any metaphysical hint of its own, is equated to "certain progress." A "revolution" of anthropomorphic objectivity is envisioned. There is an unwitting and blissful irony in each line; in the attempt to map out a kind of freedom through representational and epistemic activity alone, such a view ends up trapping the human in a self-made instrumental-utilitarian relation with all that is. *Man comes up against his own image in nature.* In religion, man was made in the image of God. In reason, nature is re-made in the imagery of Man. Thus we receive from Kant a certain model of thinking that would become dominant in the centuries to come. With the best of intentions, the stage is set for future conflict.

Witness yet another passage from the same text:

> When Galileo caused balls, the weights of which he had himself previously determined, to roll down an inclined plane; when Torricelli made the air carry a weight which he had calculated beforehand to be equal to that of a definite volume of water; or in more recent times, when Stahl changed metal into lime, and lime back into metal, by withdrawing something and then restoring it, a light broke upon all students of nature. They learned that reason has insight only into that which it produces after a plan of its own, and that it must not allow itself to be kept, as it were, in nature's leading-strings, but must itself show the way with principles of judgment based upon fixed laws, constraining nature to give answer to questions of reason's own determining. Accidental observations, made in obedience to no previously thought-out plan, can never be made to yield a necessary law, which alone reason is concerned to discover.[6]

[6] Ibid., p. 20.

Isolating cause and effect and systematically producing nomological structures through which nature is subsequently viewed is the path to illumination. Following a structured, consistent line of questioning no doubt produces a useful body of knowledge. But it is a double-edged sword as feminist philosophers have pointed out.[7] Questions come out of presumptions and world-views that pre-condition the nature of the answers received. A different kind of questioning may lead to focus on a different quality of the world. In other words, world-making through knowledge is never a neutral process. There is no recognition of this vital point in the above passage or the writing that follows. The sovereignty of Measure must be stamped upon what is receivable as legitimate knowledge. Nature is that which is produced, or presents itself, within human representational schemas and measurements. Judgments based upon "fixed laws" alone are the true gateways to the discovery of nature. Reason's ability to pre-determine nature's pathways and force it to yield "necessary" laws are to be extolled. A releasement is sought in deterministic principles which in time will become one of the great obstacles to seeking a new relationship with the world. Through this very over-determination, Kant ends up laying the ground for a series of oppositions such as "appearance" and "things-in-themselves," subject and object, from which his own theory will be unable to find a way out when it came to the larger ethic of existence. For the latter, Kant will have to rely on transcendental idealism, or speculation at best, to derive the notion of freedom. In other words, the problem of freedom emerges in Kant through the very nature of his theorizing, and although he posits the "Idea of Freedom," Kant cannot get to it phenomenologically, pushing it instead to some ideal domain.

Given the drift of his thinking, it is also not surprising to find in Kant an almost religious faith in mathematical reasoning as the sole mode of reliable disclosure of the empirical. The structure of finite mathematics may be seen to present itself as a series of tautologies or equations (left hand side = right hand side) and their internal elaborations. Fitting nature within mathematical formulations and finding surprising symmetry and order within previously unknown relations is certainly useful, but a case of limit-thinking arises when we become accustomed to solely this manner of viewing "nature." For instance, science or its mathematical

[7] See, for instance, the works of Evelyn Fox Keller, Sandra Harding, and Karin Knorr Cetina.

formulations can tell us very little about the psyche or consciousness itself, and yet it is precisely the invisible tensions and torsions within consciousness that are the ultimate determinants of the course of societal life, and, in turn, the source of the questions directed at nature. Besides, almost every culture holds in its bosom the source memory of an anarchic continuum to which it credits its incipient insights. In the attempt to delineate what it means to be human—its judgments and obligations—this aspect can hardly be forgotten. Taking our eyes off the background to focus only on objects of cognition thus produces the errors of a truncated reality masquerading as the whole. But for Kant only that part of the "doctrine of nature" could represent science proper which could be formulated within the formal structure of a priori cognition. An intuitive science, for example, would contradict this foundational approach since it would vary depending on the level of intuition or attunement attained. Kant wrote:

> I maintain that in every special natural doctrine only so much science *proper* is to be met with as mathematics; for... science proper, especially [science] of nature, requires a pure portion, lying at the foundation of the empirical, and based upon *a priori* knowledge of natural things. ... To the possibility of a determinate natural thing, and therefore to cognise it *à priori*, is further requisite that the intuition corresponding *à priori* to the conception should be given; in other words, that the conception should be constructed. But the cognition of the reason through construction of conceptions is mathematical. A pure philosophy of nature in general, namely, one that only investigates what constitutes a nature in general, may thus be possible without mathematics; but a pure doctrine of nature respecting *determinate* natural things (corporeal doctrine and mental doctrine), is only possible by means of mathematics; and as in every natural doctrine only so much science proper is to be met with therein as there is cognition *à priori*, a doctrine of nature can only contain so much science proper as there is in it of applied mathematics.[8]

Mathematics is seen as the purely formal and rigorous structure on which the possibility of a "determinate natural thing" can be mapped adequately. In other words, only the innately mathematical structure of reason, the admittedly "pure portion," can apparently intuit the a priori

[8] Immanuel Kant, *The Metaphysical Foundations of Natural Science*, trans. Ernest Belford Boax (London: Cambridge University Press, 2004), Preface.

conception of a natural thing. Viewed from a certain angle, this does not seem unreasonable: that a supremely self-consistent structure such as mathematics or first-order logic should ultimately appear as the consistent "inner" language of phenomena that can viably disclose "determinate natural things" does not *prima facie* seem to offend the sensibilities. But overwhelming investment in accuracy and the concern with the *a priori* in disclosure do not in the end necessarily guarantee the full range of experience in its wholeness. In fact, there is the possibility that the mathematical straitjacket could leave out of the reckoning other more intimate, gentle, and native ways of understanding *what is*.

Additionally, it is not unreasonable to say that the harder thought attempts to grasp the determinate thing through the *a priori* categories, the more it gets detached and alienated from the restless undulations of *what is* (which is now objectified). In other words, the gentle resonances or the sensibility of what Goethe called "delicate empiricism" are lost through the loss of the connection with the anarchic continuum. Moreover, existential irony includes the possibility that the very success of a thing turn out to be its own enemy, which might haunt this aggressively mathematized form of thinking. The heightened promotion of logical certainty, with the corresponding loss thereby of the ability to maintain a tentative relation with the Unknown, pushes thinking to become isolated. It no longer remains a true instrument of inquiry, becoming instead a vehicle of its own peculiar mode of apprehension. Thus it turns out that this very determinative edifice gives rise to the central problematic of modern philosophy both at the conceptual as well as at the phenomenological level—the opposition between objectivized nature and the perceiving subject, or the division between the observer and the observed. That which started out promisingly in the Enlightenment project as expansion of certain sensibilities toward a reasoned and reasonable life, gradually assumed the proportions of an insoluble problem with implicit consequences for the particular reality it bred.

Briefly, to recollect, the problem appears in this manner. The Kantian formalization of nature turns it into a system of ironclad laws which are conceptualized by means of the cognitive categories brought to bear upon an otherwise unknowable reality. But this formulation immediately gives rise to another conceptual difficulty. The perceiving subject (human cognition) cannot be deemed to be outside of nature and therefore must itself be subject to the same determinism. How then can a fragment of nature (the perceiving subject) detach itself and acquire the spontaneity and freedom to reflect upon nature, or, which is the same thing, bestow upon it the cognitive categories needed to self-consciously reflect upon it? In other words, how is it possible to fit the transcendent subject within a deterministic nature? Simply put, having reduced nature to a system of laws, Kant was stuck with the problem of explaining his own and others' subjectivities that seemed to transcend determinism. It introduced a dualism that has plagued philosophy ever since. The problem of consciousness could not be explained through transcendental idealism other than as background assumption.

Kant himself offered the most unconvincing and contrived solution to this problem. In the third *Critique*, Kant suggested that besides law-boundedness, nature also produced self-determined organisms that could contemplate themselves. This explanation merely begged the question, and being somewhat disingenuous, did not impress thinkers of the late eighteenth and early nineteenth centuries such as Fichte, Hegel, or Schelling. But of the three, only Schelling was willing to admit the possibility that *rational* reconciliation of freedom and necessity, or mind and nature, may be inherently impossible. In other words, Schelling envisioned the possibility that the Kantian project central to German idealism—the need to ground reason in an Absolute—was somehow flawed or misdirected. Thus we find the early Schelling rethinking nature and metaphysics away from Kantian formalism as well as Hegelian negation both of which were along the lines of age-old system-building efforts. I shall work on Schelling's position at length in Chapter 3 and show its importance for the present project of seeking out the possibility of another kind of (redemptive) thinking. Suffice it to say here that Schelling along with a few others began taking steps beyond Idealism and in a phenomenological direction that would be crucial for later developments in modern philosophy. Thus we have in Schelling, Hölderlin, and Goethe a threesome that attempts to turn the "night of the Absolute into day for knowledge" using a vast repertoire of poetic sensibility, art, metaphysics of revelation, and a new form of experiential with-it-ness.[9] In other

[9] Schelling writes: "For most people see in the essence of the Absolute nothing but pure night and cannot recognize anything in it; it shrinks before them into a mere negation of difference, and is for them something purely privative, whence they cleverly make it into the end of their philosophy…I want to show here how that night of the Absolute can be turned into day for knowledge." F.W.J. von Schelling, *Collected Works Vol. 4*, trans. Peter Heath (Cambridge: Cambridge University Press, 1985), p. 403.

words, phenomenological freedom and lived truth were begun to be approached not from the angle of logic alone but as intersections of various existential dimensions including the esthetic.

The methodology of the present book can be said to be in the direction of hermeneutic phenomenology. Thus there are two terms involved, hermeneutics and phenomenology; let us take up each of these in turn. First, among its many meanings, what is the idea of the hermeneutical that is intended here? In order to answer this question I shall turn to the hermeneutic philosophy of Martin Heidegger who was singularly responsible for renewed interest in this methodology, to try and recollect some essential elements of the method. According to this viewpoint, hermeneusis is the returning again and again to the point of concealment of things:

> If the question of being is to achieve clarity regarding its own history, a loosening of the sclerotic tradition and a dissolving of the concealments produced by it is necessary. We understand this task as the destructuring of the traditional content of ancient ontology which is to be carried out along the *guidelines of the question of being*. This destructuring is based upon the original experiences in which the first and subsequently guiding determinations of being were gained.[10]

First, we have to be concerned with "loosening of the sclerotic tradition." A system becomes sclerotic when it loses plasticity through doctrination, and the essential flows within it become restricted by a corresponding hardening and loss of flexibility. Traditional philosophy's obsession with systems and absolutes has led to sclerosis in the sense that the living questions of being, lived relationships, and ontological disclosures have been overshadowed or lost in the fixation on grand formalisms or on semantic analysis. Hermeneutics contains the possibility of shaking philosophy free of the sclerotic condition by dissolving or decalcinating the necrotic deposits and helping to reconstitute the elements within the ontological flows, achieving thus the *status of being*. Second, such a task is to be carried out by returning to authentic and living questions of being-in-the-world. In other words, the "traditional content of ancient ontology" needs to be deconstructed and freed with reference to the

[10]Martin Heidegger, *Being and Time*, trans. Joan Stambaugh (New York: SUNY Press, 1996), p. 20.

emergent and ever-new problem of current being. Heidegger discards the Hegelian approach of teleological dialectics for the method of hermeneutic destruction in relation to the principle of subjectivity. And third, in order to make metaphysics relevant again, ontology and hermeneutics must be thought together. That is to say, such a task is to be carried out by taking into account the source experiences, or disclosures, of what-is, in order to return to the status of authentic life. In addition, this return must be transparent: "The tradition that hereby gains dominance makes what it transmits so little accessible that initially and for the most part it covers it over instead...it bars access to those original wellsprings out of which the traditional categories and concepts were in part genuinely drawn. Indeed it makes us wholly incapable of even understanding that such a return is necessary."[11] The source events of cultures, as well as the intuitive and traditional elements of our understanding that were drawn from these, are covered over and hidden from sight by the dominant discourses making it difficult to access the original wellsprings of being and esthetic insight. A dimmed view shorn of the direct luminosity of experience and filtered through doctrinal and institutional biases robs us of the full existential potential of the *numinosum*. For instance, within Christendom, the complex of *anamnesis*, the sacraments, and the Eucharist derived from the source experiences have been covered over by theological discourse and religious politics and need to be visited hermeneutically in order to re-consider their living significance.[12]

[11] Ibid., p. 19.

[12] "The eucharistic *anamnesis* is not a mere spectacle; nor is it a mysterious phenomenon to be wondered at. It is participatory. However, discussion of the Eucharist has been, and continues to be, a focus of controversy with regard to both theology and practice, becoming a sign of pain and division. Indeed, the Churches' understanding of *anamnesis* has not been unproblematic, with interpretations ranging from notions of re-immolation to bare memorialism, in which different kinds of objective and subjective realities have been prioritised. These extreme views are neither adequate nor accurate. It is against this background that that a renewed engagement with the concept of *anamnesis* has the potential to make a constructive contribution to eucharistic theology, which underpins mission. Jesus' words of institution are the starting point for the Eucharist, but its potential is broader than that...The sacramental act of *anamnesis* draws the Church into a transformative encounter with the risen Christ in the present. This occurs within the context of retrospection and anticipation. On the one hand, successive Eucharists connect the Church to Christ's life, death and resurrection, the culmination of God's saving acts in history focused on the Last Supper. On the other hand, through participation in the Eucharist the Church is called into the mission of God – building his Kingdom – which comes to fulfilment at the eschaton. *Anamnesis* has the capacity to facilitate the reintegration and reinvigoration

What is more, the frozen culture often prevents us even from recognizing the *need* to return to these sources. We must recognize the urgency of such recuperation; the urgency releases a new quality in thinking. Herein lies the direction of the major effort we must undertake here.

Further, Heidegger adds with emphasis: "*All ontology, no matter how rich and tightly knit a system of categories it has at its disposal, remains fundamentally blind and perverts its innermost intent if it has not previously clarified the meaning of being sufficiently and grasped this clarification as its fundamental task.*"[13] When we have sidestepped the question of being, that is, overlooked ontology, and busied ourselves with description, representation, analysis, ordering, and the like, we have betrayed the true philosophical quest, no matter how sophisticated our terms and categories, or our conceptual understanding of phenomena. To return to the source problem again and again, that is, to the attempt to shed light on the nature of our being, is the fundamental philosophical task at all times, which alone provides a new direction to thinking. In order to split open the settled system and think again, the question of what-is must be approached in a hermeneutic manner, shedding the images and presumptions that get built up in each cycle.

Next, let us turn to the question of phenomenology; this is intimately linked to the central question here of redemptive thinking as it resurrects the moments of inter-being obscured by convention as monadic encounter (subject dealing with object), and therefore trapped in the attitude of business-as-usual. Phenomenology is precisely the existential and philosophical shock that cuts past the business-as-usual mode of being. Going back to the Greek source of the word is helpful here.

> The expression "phenomenology" can be formulated in Greek as *legein ta phainomena*...Hence phenomenology means—to let what shows itself be seen from itself, just as it shows itself from itself. That is the formal meaning of the type of research that calls itself phenomenology. "Phenomenology" neither designates the object of its researches nor is it a title that describes their content. The word only tells us something

of our conception of the relationship between the historical, sacramental and ecclesial embodiments of Christ, and to do justice to the past, present and future dimensions of the Eucharist." Julie Gittoes, *Anamnesis and the Eucharist: Contemporary Anglican Approaches* (New York: Routledge, 2016), p. 2.

[13] Heidegger, *Being and Time*, p. 9.

> about the *how* of the demonstration and treatment of *what* this discipline considers. …Now what must be taken into account if the formal concept of phenomenon is to be deformalized to the phenomenological one, and how does this differ from the common concept? What is that phenomenology [lets] be seen? Manifestly it is something that does not show itself initially, something that is concealed, in contrast to what initially and for the most part does show itself.[14]

Phenomenology does not objectify its interest nor supply it with attributes from the outside. Rather it is a process of discovery through empathic identification open to the flows and resonances that emanate from the source itself. Thus phenomenology is a method of inquiry that takes its cue from the "things themselves" with questions and procedures prompted by the latter.[15] What is it that phenomenological method allows us to see? It reveals to us aspects of the phenomena under consideration that are initially covered up or not ordinarily visible in relation to those that are obvious. It also brings to awareness things that are so visible as to be non-noticeable.[16] In short, phenomenological inquiry is thus a distinctive inter-counter that gives rise to distinct co-emergence of patterns that moves the total situation from an initial position to a more densely disclosed one giving access to its ontological character. It is easily distinguished, say, from methods such as those identified with nineteenth- and twentieth-century positivism which administers a will-to-knowledge.[17] All inner attitudes and alignment with categories need to be bracketed in order for that which is concealed to come to spontaneous self-disclosure. This is not an all-at-once procedure but one that needs to be carried out again and again. The entire perceptual mechanism needs to be cleansed of habits and images that interfere with what is.

[14] Ibid., pp. 30–31.

[15] To give an example of a contrasting approach, a social-scientific investigation into violence against a particular social group would begin by generating objective standards of violence, identifying victims and victimizers and so on.

[16] With respect to the invisibility of the supremely visible, Aristotle says: "Just as it is with bats' eyes in respect of daylight, so it is with our mental vision in respect of those things which are by nature most apparent." Aristotle, *Metaphysics Bk 2, 993b*, cited in Martin Heidegger, *What Is Called Thinking* (New York: Harper and Row, 1968), p. 110.

[17] At the heart of positivism lies a coldness that attempts to reduce the tumult of life to a set of laws and well-defined formulas.

Ultimately the phenomenologist's attempt is simply to be in the path of the emanation of raw being from the things-in-themselves, without the mediation of categories. But this is not to be understood as some 'power-packed' experience between observer and observed, but as a merger into that flow itself. Such merger does not produce mere effective knowledge, but enhances the depth of inter-experiential space, or the true space of a non-totalized livability. It produces existential quality, a word that has more or less disappeared from technological consciousness.

Next let us put together the two terms 'hermeneutics' and 'phenomenology.' Hermeneutic phenomenology or phenomenological hermeneutics is thus a form of disclosure that returns to the point of concealment both from the subjective and the objective ends. *Neither end is privileged* since the method is interested in revealing the conditions of possibility of experience itself. Setting aside the conventional ways of framing the experiencer as well as the experienced, it attempts to generate a topological understanding of combined "going through." "Both terms characterize philosophy itself, its object and procedure."[18] Together, methodologically, the elemental complexes are returned again and again to the *origo* in order to unearth not the 'what' but the 'how' of things in a demonstrable manner. It neither privileges nor takes the experiencer for granted but looks closely at the inter-experiential exchanges that reveal that which has remained undisclosed either from the beginning or become concealed over time due to other historical processes.

Then the next question to be asked is: toward what kind of disclosure is this method devoted in the present volume? In order to answer this question certain sweeping observational statements will be made that might appear unjustified at first glance. Nevertheless, the melancholy that grips the earth despite unprecedented material accomplishments presses upon us these observations. Further, these observations lead us not to further despondent criticism or helplessness but to put philosophy to work toward the possibility of a radical transformation, or philosophical praxis. This becomes absolutely essential at a time when time itself does not bring us any closer to an emancipated life, rather only to the deferment of catastrophe in world and ecological relations. There is no longer any collective belief in the emergence of a reasonable society; indeed, there is not even agreement on what constitutes a reasonable society. Instead, there has

[18] Heidegger, *Being and Time*, p. 34.

come about an increased fragmentation in the cognitive apparatus or psychic-material process that we call thinking with which we ought to be philosophically concerned. It is a desultoriness such that as soon as thought starts to think (other than in the domain of technology) there is an odor of staleness. An examination of thinking reveals the familiar grooves in which it has settled and which have become the *zeitgeist* of the age. In the present age, this staleness manifests itself in a major way in the technologization of all aspects of being as Heidegger has noted in *The Question Concerning Technology* as well as in *What Is Called Thinking*. No significant problem is allowed to be articulated other than in technologistic-instrumental terms. Where difficulties arise we suspect a particular line or content of thinking, we do not question or doubt the process of thinking itself.

Besides, even if the stage of doubt is reached, the constitution of the doubter remains transcendental and out of reach of questioning. This self-legitimation of thought is the very negation of reason as it was understood by the Pre-Socratics who gave the word 'reason' its substance. The process of thinking seems to have become numbed to the point where we are unable to change the direction of thinking even when the action of thought has patently brought nothing but disaster.[19] Thought has operated with the "as if"; it is always *as if* things were getting better. Thus the piety of thought has become all-comprehensive; in starting to think we seem to immediately cross a threshold or overstep something, a move that compromises what is yet to come. In other words, we have lost all freedom of thought; that is to say, we have lost the ability to direct thought in non-coopted or non-technologized directions. It is here that we must turn to the question of redemptive thinking with which we began the present inquiry. It is argued that now the prime task of philosophy is to inquire into the nature of thinking itself and not merely into the content or character of particular projections and systems of thought. We have to uncover the original purpose of thought. As a corollary then, will it not be reasonable to demand that we inquire into the mystery of the thinker at the same time and not accept the *cogito* as unquestioned background presence? And finally we have to ask: is there a redemption in thinking that is thinkable, that is, can thought move toward salvation, or at least make preparation for such an event?

[19] It is hardly necessary to catalogue the various aspects of the man-made eco-psychological catastrophe that we face today.

It is clarified that the present work is not yet-another criticism of modernity and technological civilization, nor is it interested in conceptual distinctions between modernity, modernism, and suchlike. The critique of dominant contemporary modes of thinking is only a point of departure. Essentially, the problems identified here with regard to the process called thinking could be raised at any point in the history of thought. Although the crisis in thought is not related to any developmental juncture, the intensity of the present crisis is unprecedented due to the fact that the tolerance limits within nature have been repeatedly breached by human societies, and the reactions of thinking have in turn been more and more reactionary, thus raising the profile of the present conflict inwardly and outwardly.

To continue the explication on the phenomenological method, as we noted earlier, the latter entails not the objectification in thought as representation, but the subtle corporeal grasp of the emanation-perception between two ends—observer-observed—of an experience-event. During his extensive investigations into natural phenomena, Goethe realized that every new phenomenon when "well contemplated, opens up a new organ of perception in us."[20] In other words, the pro-prioceptive spectrum is definitely extendable, depending on how much we open ourselves, corporeally and phenomenologically. This claim and its substantiation is important for the present work and hence we labor toward this end here. The careful contemplation of thought *qua* thought, and not as the representation of something else, opens up new modes of perception in us. Philosophy has for the most part concerned itself with what has presented itself in thought. Rarely has it problematized the *res cogitans* itself, implicitly accepting the Cartesian position, and inordinately fighting shy of such an ontological inquiry. And yet, it might be that herein lies the root of much that bedevils humans and their projects; it might be that the very unit of thinking—the division by which thought goes forward from one thought to the next—is problematic. It might even be the case that isolated thinking (attempting to decode existentials solely through mental effort) has led humans into a philosophical and existential *cul-de-sac*. Thinking creates a sophisticated bubble and thinks of it as an independent reality, and when the actuality creaks and groans, and life itself shrivels in several

[20] J.W. von Goethe, *Scientific Studies* (New York: Suhrkamp, 1988), p. 39.

dimensions, thought merely extends the bubble without critical examination. Hence, for a reality check, it is imperative now to engage in:

> the development of a (participatory) practice—the chiasmic intertwining of a way of seeing with a way of acting with a way of think-ing, all from within an embedding of ourselves in a living way in the same surroundings as the relevant phenomena so that we too allow ourselves to be responsive in a spontaneous bodily fashion both to them and to them in relation to their surroundings. We need to enter into the kind of engaged relationship that consists in an active interplay of activity in which, by our going out to meet them in this way and that, moving both up close and away, looking from this angle and that, and so on, so that, as [David] Bohm (1965) puts it, 'the structure of his environment is, as it were, gradually incorporated into his outgoing impulses, so that he learns how to meet his environment with the right kind of [anticipatory] response.'[21]

It is highly doubtful whether till date humans have truly developed an adequate and wholesome response to the world which they occupy. At least philosophers such as Spinoza and Nietzsche did not seem to think so. Rather, the self-conscious human seemed to have moved increasingly toward alienated existence than consciously deepening modes of participatory existence. Correspondingly, the historical attitude for the long part has been an oppositional human-versus-world rather than a participatory being-in-the-world. For this, the existing mode of disembodied thinking is responsible to no small extent. Single-minded intent must give way to active, corporeal engagement—looking this way and that, including into thought itself. And unlike solving logical or abstract problems, the answers or understandings here are not going to be forthcoming immediately but with sustained engagement, and not until there are fundamental changes in the direction of our sensibilities and expectations.

The sensation of thought inquiring into itself is a novel one. It requires an entirely new set of participatory practices, a new and "delicate empiricism" in the language of Goethe, that necessitates an insertion of ourselves and our subjectivities into previously enclosed

[21] John Shotter, "Goethe and the Refiguring of Intellectual Inquiry: From 'Aboutness'-Thinking to 'Withness'-Thinking in Everyday Life," *Janus Head*, 8(1), 2005, pp. 132–158.

and opaque processes.[22] When thought, which habitually remains a taken-for-granted, unconscious tool, is forced to become conscious of itself, a sea-change occurs, and the "outgoing impulses" are now modified through the incorporation of this new set of awareness of inner movements. This change, as the present work will argue, is of singular philosophical importance. We are now presented with a simultaneous inside-outside perspective that results in a kind of perceptual strangeness distancing us from the conventional modes of organizing experience. We can begin to see that the learning involved here is independent of the subjective or epistemic content of thought. It is instead concerned with the ontological structure of thinking itself in general. This is a very significant move in philosophical thinking and the doing of philosophy.

The learning involved is aimed at destroying the imperviousness, and taken-for-granted ways of thinking. Such scrutiny, as will be discussed later, endows the commonplace with a new significance. All our existing organizing ideas undergo a kind of transformation resulting in each relation gaining a trans-personal import.

> Our everyday ways of thinking are a mystery to us. How is it possible for us to see directly, in the unique, particular circumstances we encounter, certain opportunities and impediments to the actions that uniquely matter just to us? How is it that we can recognize friends and loved ones merely from the sound of their voices on the telephone, or recognize just from other people's facial expressions as we talk to them their reactions to what we are saying? How can we come to know our way around so well inside familiar surroundings? What is involved in our acquiring specialized skills and sensitivities in mathematics, music, carpentry, literary criticism or art criticism, in discriminating shades and hues of colors as a painter, etc., etc. How, when presented with a mathematical proof or a case in a court of law, do we recognize that what we have witnessed is in fact a proof? How do we, in hearing a piece of music, seeing a painting, or in reading a text in philosophy, say, see important 'connections' between it and aspects of our lives? How, in our speech and writing, do we recognize just the right word to use in a particular context? How, for that matter, do we recognize the stream of sounds coming from a person's mouth as meaningful speech? How, as any kind of practitioner, do we recognize what the material of

[22]The full quote is: "There is a delicate empiricism which makes itself utterly identical with the object." Goethe cited in Shotter, ibid.

> our practice is, how to move about within in, and how to choose with any surety what it seems best to do in a particular situation before us?[23]

Does the author mean immanently mysterious or that we are conscious of the mystery? While it is true that all perception, recognition and the systematic, impeccable respond-ability are *mysterious in themselves*, it would be an error to think that these are "a mystery to us" in the sense that we feel or acknowledge this mystery.[24] In fact, the real enigma is that these are no longer perplexing to us, and the everyday is quickly reduced in consciousness to a humdrum containing none of the mystery that is their actual quality. We would be living in a differently ordered, esthetic, and sensitive world if we actually grasped and lived the mystery of the very processes of our perceiving and becoming. Their arising in thought and eventual subsidence would then be the main focus of our pedagogic relation with phenomena. Part of the hermeneutic effort of the present volume is to return us phenomenologically to the source of this mystery beyond mystification, leading to a philosophical praxis.

But if there is a mystery greater than perception itself then it is the apparent entity that perceives. At least thinking can be established to some extent physiologically in terms of nervous activity and so on. But who or what is the thinker that seems to organize experience and direct thinking? If one cuts open the brain, one might find the organic substratum of thought, but there is no equivalent substratum of the thinker to be found. Descartes grounded all thought in the *res cogitans* and set further speculation to rest by diktat (*ergo sum*). But to assume that a thinker stands behind thinking is as intellectually preposterous as it is to assume that a tornadic entity stands behind a tornado. Nevertheless, such a spurious logic continues to hold firm in the cultural imaginary across societies, and frontal assaults on the thinker or the self are never very successful. The commonsense perspective, which is another term for the unexamined life, holds on to the naïve view of the thinker, despite rejection by specific religio-philosophical traditions, as well as by master thinkers such as Spinoza and Nietzsche, who find no evidence of such agency. In sum, at the lowest level of psychic existence, the commonsense self has tremendous hold, and while theoretical

[23] Shotter, op. cit., p. 132.

[24] Cognitive psychology as well as neurosciences have been at pains to reduce perception to the mechanical model.

sophistication might dismiss the thinker as hallucination, it does nothing to dislodge it at the intuitive or phenomenological level. This does not philosophically improve the situation. It is only by means of a careful phenomenological and hermeneutic exploration that we begin to get an insight into the production process of the thinker, and the relation between thinking and the thinker. The physicist-philosopher Ernst Mach, who profoundly influenced Einstein, notes:

> Our greater intimacy with this sum-total of permanency, and the preponderance of its importance for me as contrasted with the changeable element, impel us to the partly instinctive, partly voluntary and conscious economy of mental presentation and designation, as expressed in ordinary thought and speech. That which is presented in a single image receives a single designation, a single name.[25]

The central issue relates to the question of permanency. Obviously, there is a certain durability and organic continuity to the physical body. But there is much more to the construction of the psychological self than mere organic continuity. The body is introjected and mentally represented as an "inner daguerreotype" and given a unitary designation and image. A residual memory seems to accompany the image-entity in its perambulations giving rise to a peculiar sense of psychological permanency that is further fortified by recognition and encouragement within social mores and contracts. The obverse side of the social contract is the self-contract. Although the fact is that memory itself undergoes continuous additions and deletions, there is a lingering sense of ineradicable permanency and the feeling of a constant nucleus. Clearly this residuum has much to do with the question of freedom and redemption that will be discussed later in the appropriate section. The psychic fraud that we enact keeping the body at the center of that which is called "normal life" must be studied with great care in order to find out whether there are "holes" through which the true situation seeps out. Speculative knowledge of actuality is not even remotely enough; breaking through must necessarily be phenomenological. Philosophers of the West are generally loathe to speak of this since it might carry the contagion of mysticism and thus contaminate their purely cerebral speculations.

[25] Ernst Mach, *The Analysis of Sensations*, trans. C.M. Williams and Sydney Waterlow (London: Dover, 1959).

However, the present volume sets aside this fear and seeks to bridge the separation between the psychical and the intellectual, or between the head and the heart. For it is precisely in this separation that human thinking has lost its bearing.

Then the next thing to be considered is the relation between the two more or less occult processes that are ironically taken for granted—the relation between the process of thinking and the production of the "thinker" or the agent. This metaphysical relation is central to the book's search for a redemptive quality or energy through philosophical and hermeneutic engagement. Are thinking and thought two distinct phenomena and reside in the psychic-material system side-by-side? Or are they part of the same process? If it is the latter, then why do they seem manifestly different—experiencer distinct from the flow of experience? How does one part "become" the controller and another the controlled? Is the controller a sovereign essence? The philosophical investigation into these questions lead us deep into territory where the strange nature of thought is begun to be disclosed. The division in the psyche between thinker and thought is carefully evaluated for its implications for human freedom and emancipation. With a question mark hanging over the nucleus of continuity (agent), the issue of freedom becomes, more properly, a negative one of phenomenological awareness of the process of slippage into bondage, or mythically, Fall, in one word. Phenomenological exercise opens up the hallways of thought to unsentimental scrutiny, demystifying its "sacred" representations in every direction.

The hermeneutic learning toward new thinking visualized here takes us back through history to those sites of insurrections of thought that irrupted suddenly to disclose the hitherto covered-over truths. It is the submission of the present book that Pre-Socratic thinking such as that of Heraclitus is one such site of insurrection where we are helped to think anew. Placing themselves at the material edge of thought, thinkers such as Heraclitus went beyond the conceptual or epistemic content to delve into the ontological matrix. Speaking of the singularity that was the source of awareness, Heraclitus was simultaneously addressing the inside and outside of thought. He returned to the ontological boundary hermeneutically to secure from therein a resurrection of being of which he spoke in elliptical and aphoristic terms. There is no other language in which the boundary qualities can be expressed adequately, certainly not within the conventional oppositions and images of thought. In this connection, the profound silences of Heraclitus are legendary.

Often times he countered his contemporaries in studied silence, famously declaring that he had learnt all there was to learn by looking into himself (a silent process).[26] Heraclitus writes: "There is one wisdom, to understand the intelligent will by which all things are governed through all (*En to sophon epistasthai gnomen e kybernatai panta dia panton*)."[27] True knowledge of the principles that guide the universe is wisdom, but this wisdom does not lie in acquiring more and more knowledge about phenomena. Rather it lies in grasping or entering into the nature and substratum of thinking itself as a medium of finite determinations. This understanding is not representational (i.e., does not lie in epistemic content or symbolic substance) but consists of a leap into the material underpinning of knowing itself. In other words, one must ride knowledge, much in the manner in which Einstein, as a boy, wanted to ride a light beam (the light beam can bring no information to the rider about the phenomenal world, but only about itself as revealer). To crack open the form of thought, and not be seduced by content, *that* is the "single thing" that discloses—revealing the innate structure of all mental formations as well as that which might lie beyond all formations. This single thing works through everything (*panta dia panton*). Thinking comes to the edge of its own materiality, and leaps-into-itself as it were, grasping the root cause, making representational knowledge secondary.

Freedom or the Unbounded is not disclosed in thought, for thinking is always manifested in cultural and material conditions. The Unconditioned cannot be revealed in the conditioned. It cannot be disclosed in thought except in-so-far as being intuited from afar as the formal background condition of its possibility. Rather, thinking might be acknowledged as an off-shoot of the movement of the Unconditioned as it works through the elements. But the question arises, if thinking is a *pro-jection* of the Unconditioned, then can the pro-jected conceivably recoil or retreat self-consciously to the point of its pro-jection? In other words, can the conditioned substance in-fold and revert to the threshold of the Unconditioned in voluntary abnegation? For it is only in the ceasing of the incessant activity of the content of thinking (multiplicity) that insight into the matrix of unitary wisdom (freedom) become a real

[26] "I have inquired of myself," Fragment 80 of Heraclitus, in George T.W. Patrick, *The Fragments of the Work of Heraclitus of Ephesus on Nature* (Baltimore: N. Murray, 1889), p. 6.

[27] Ibid., p. 18.

possibility. Hence the supreme philosophical importance of understanding the general nature of thought as movement of content that is discussed in the following pages.

To summarize then:

- These pages have a single overwhelming purpose, which is to show that philosophy can lead us to a philosophical shock that is beyond the semantic formations and meaning structures, beyond concepts and systems, toward a readiness and preparation for redemption.
- Contrary to the commonplace view that one cannot do much with philosophy, this book argues that philosophical insight can literally turn the psychic-nervous life inside out and give us an unexpected view of ourselves.
- The book contends that a special kind of redemptive power accompanies the ontological (structural) understanding of thought.
- This "power" is not conceptual power born of political understanding such as that, for example, claimed by critical thinkers; in other words, it is not epistemic or cultural in nature, nor is it mystical.
- This "power" is also not the power of agency as is commonly understood but is orthogonal to individuality and agency.
- Rather, this power of insight is derived directly and phenomenologically from the formal/structural understanding of thought as a movement of content (symbols, representations, concepts, etc.).
- This power becomes available through philosophical engagement in tracking the vortex of psychic substance that we ordinarily call thinking. This power is freedom from the known.
- Philosophical engagement indicates a series of deconstructive steps through which we get closer to the mysterious thing that we call thinking and the substance that thinks.
- Beginning with Heidegger's search for Being, the book travels backward in time through Schelling, Goethe, and all the way to the Pre-Socratics in search of a redemptive power that lies at the outer edge of thought.
- The redemptive power is of a character different than that of the Hegelian march of Spirit, and is experienced in retreating to the point at which the psychic individuality in the form of division between thinker and thought (experiencer and experience) arises in each conditioned agglomerate. In other words, the freedom discussed here is ontological and not historical or developmental; it is

the same at all times and all points of history. To make a distinction, the Hegelian "World Spirit" is systemic, speculative, and teleological. The insight born of the self-knowledge of thought is anarchic, non-dialectical, and phenomenological. This is not to deny the legitimacy of other kinds of movements including the dialectical, and redemptive action as envisaged here does not exclude such possibilities and potentialities. The world is plural and multiple; accordingly the attitude here is that of the inclusive 'And' rather than the exclusive 'Or.'[28]

- The power of ontological freedom does not inhere in the "overcoming" of finite determinations or confronting one set of pre-conceptions by a different set, but lies in grasping the material process of their formation.
- The self-knowledge of thought that gives rise to philosophical bilingualism—awareness of content plus awareness of form—allows ordinary consciousness to transcend the commonplace opposition between the "inner" and the "outer."

As far as the chapter divisions are concerned, each chapter attempts to inquire into a particular aspect of the habituation of thought, and invoke possible conditions for breaking out of the taken-for-grantedness, and onto a more intimate phenomenological plane. For instance, Chapter 2 on Heidegger goes into the basic question of the nature of thinking itself from where we must begin this inquiry. What stirs and how? What is it that provokes thought to think? What might have been the original imperative? These are the key questions here. The reflexive "I" or "we," that must be simultaneously put under critical scrutiny, is forced to reflect on this basic problem. From where does thought emerge and into what space and time does it project itself? In its present form, thought has reduced itself to logistics for achieving techno-logistical aims.[29]

[28]To give an ordinary example, a conscious intervention in bodily crisis need not exclude the possibility that the body might be implicitly seeking homeostasis in a different way. The objection must be to single-track thinking that totalizes.

[29]Let us turn to Max Weber for a critical understanding of the logistical form of thought and calculative rationality: "The general result of the modern form of thoroughly rationalizing the conception of the world and of the way of life, theoretically and practically, in an intellectual and purposive manner, has been that the more this type of rationality has progressed, from the standpoint of an intellectual articulation of an image of the world, the more [other ways of thinking] have been shifted into the realm of the irrational." Max Weber cited in Anthony Carroll, S.J. "Disenchantment, Rationality and the Modernity of

Is it conceivable that the original intent of thought as movement in a certain matrix was different? Can ontological investigation throw light on this original intent of thought? What now will make thought think about itself, that is, turn its attention on itself? If thinking does not originate with us, how can thinking now recover the intent of ancient thought? The onto-theological preoccupation of thought through the centuries hides the true relation of thought with the origin. How may it be possible to go beyond the onto-theological preoccupation? Besides, there is another fixation of thought with which one must contend, namely, historicizing. The preoccupation with historicizing and producing universal history is an obsession of the present age. The attempt in thought is to get a complete anthropological picture of the world. But we know that the universal project of history creates its own object, that is, generates its own object of study through the very lens-apparatus that it uses. It does not reveal anything about the true significance of world-existence or its destiny. No real answer about the nature of thinking is therefore to be found in history.

We discover within the ambit of the above path of intense questioning that there is no easy or ready answer to any of the above questions with regard to thinking. We can only be under way with an attentive inquiry, and observe with a firm and unsentimental reserve. Thought has gathered immense amounts of information about the world, and yet, Heidegger insists, that we have not even begun to think, that is, face what urgently needs to be thought. In fact, thought seems to always escape what truly needs to be thought. Therefore, the essence of thinking remains out of our sight and grasp. In order to understand

Max Weber." With the expansion of managed societies and extensive bureaucracies in a Weberian sense, alternative visions of the world have been thoroughly sacrificed. Thought becomes the logistical tool of this instrumental rationality that makes humans forget other ways of thinking and being. This one-sidedness drew the following lament from Weber in the *Protestant Ethic*: "No one knows who will live in this cage (*Gehäuse*) in the future, or whether at the end of this tremendous development entirely new prophets will arise, or there will be a great rebirth of old ideas and ideals, or, if neither, mechanized petrification, embellished with a sort of convulsive self-importance. For the 'last man' (*letzten Menschen*) of this cultural development, it might well be truly said: 'Specialist without spirit, sensualist without heart; this nullity imagines that it has attained a level of humanity (*Menschentums*) never before achieved'." Max Weber, *Protestant Ethic and the Spirit of Capitalism* (1992), p. 182.

and realize this counter-intuitive position, we need to do some radical unlearning, which is to renounce the arrogance of thought and the off-handed confidence that comes from growing and living perennially within thought-colonies. The unlearning takes us beyond the one-track thinking that has become the character of thought over the centuries. This has produced a peculiarly sterile wasteland that Nietzsche had warned us about. Thinking from within thought, Nietzsche was not fooled by the activities of thought or its social pretensions and preoccupations. Nor was his writing yet another critique of culture. According to Heidegger, Nietzsche's *Zarathustra* represents a "written scream" about the one and only thought to which thinking needs to return and yet fails to do. The onward march of thought, without looking back at its own ontological matrix, thus becomes nothing other than conceit. And precisely because of this, the human remains "as yet an undetermined animal." The Nietzschean *ubermensch* is not some inexplicable or fanciful 'superman' as is often erroneously portrayed in the literature, but the human carried beyond her/himself to a fullness that can only come to be when thought subjects itself to itself. In modernity, freedom is (mis) understood as the unmooring of thought, and not as the phenomenological return of thought to its source. Freedom is mistakenly sought to be achieved through the finer and finer elaboration of, and differentiation in, the content of thought and not through the hermeneutic leap onto the ontological structure of thinking. This chapter orients us in the direction in which thinking needs to move in order to be underway toward what might be termed as redemptive thinking.

Chapter 3 moves rearward (temporally) from Heidegger to Schelling. Why backward to Schelling? In a movement that symbolically parallels the pushing back of thought onto its antecedents, the temporal order throughout the book is reversed, pushing thought back on itself and onto prior reflections on this key question about the ontology of thought. It also points to the position here that with respect to thought, being itself the medium of its own reflection, there is no philosophical or psychological evolution. Thought as psychic substance cannot evolve, notwithstanding the apparent changes in content-image; it merely goes round and round in its own circuit, maintaining the same problematic in new forms through the ages. In other words, in thinking, there is no incremental or cumulative change with respect to itself through time, and the problem of thinking remains the same, notwithstanding changes in epistemic content. Only sudden breaches or leaps are thinkable that keeps us under way to a new potential in thinking. Schelling helps disclose the conditions for such a leap, as do some others that were before him such as Goethe, considered later in these pages, who help prepare thought for a readiness to make this recoil. Schelling begins by asserting that philosophical reflection only has negative value: *Philosophy must of necessity presume an original parting between phenomena and essence, because without it there would be no need to philosophize.* Hence, a primordial wholeness or essence must be presupposed in which there is no role for thinking. Thought comes to be relevant only when the elemental wholeness or essence is disturbed, lost, or goes out of view for obscure reasons. In turn, redemptive thinking or freedom would imply regaining an intuitive awareness of, or a partial brush with, the original wholeness.

What then are phenomena and how is thought able to bring itself in cognitive relationship to these? Ontological freedom must be thought from the perspective of these basic relations. For Schelling, phenomena are nothing but *disequilibria* in systematic attraction and repulsion that tend to form spatial concentrations. An ontological deflation occurs in the original departure from primordiality that produces forces of attraction and repulsion. Matter is therefore intense activity of a certain kind rather than something inert, in the same way as mind is activity (of thought). Hence, matter or phenomena, exist in a reciprocal relation to so-called Mind or consciousness. This reciprocal relation of mind and matter forms the basis of Schelling's Nature philosophy, as distinct from the Kantian in which the Cartesian subject is in a one-sided relation with Nature. Each determinate 'particle' carries within it its own element of mind or consciousness. No particular form or level of organization of matter is privileged, or seen to uniquely possess sensibilities associated with consciousness. Nor is there anything that can be said to be inert. Due to well-entrenched perceptual prejudices and inattention, humans tend to see 'objects' as given or presented to consciousness for they see the relation from one side only. Redemptive thinking involves a *negative effort* to admit the other side of the relation. In other words, we have to break out of the habit of perceiving ourselves as integral self-presence, and instead carry out the task of phenomenological disaggregation producing the intuitive awareness of sub-aggregates. From this emerges a new relation between observer and observed. In actuality, the collection of symbols and representations that cognition designates as objective 'Nature' faces continuous extinction (death, for instance) at various levels of disaggregation, and makes its reappearance as yet other aggregates.

But as the civilizational process takes hold, the divide between the two levels of matter-mind aggregate, namely, subject and object, hardens, and a special phenomenological effort is required to gain small breakthroughs in perception toward the actual relation between the two.

But for Schelling it is necessary also to reverse the perspective and look at our relation with the world from the standpoint of the Absolute. The project of redemptive thinking is inaugurated only when both perspectives—from differentiation to essence as well as from Absolute to relative—are simultaneously realized. The pulse of finitude that emanates from the Absolute, which forms the basis of time as thought and experience, also contains the totality. It is due to this moment that all that is subsequently manifest must of necessity be *sub specie aeternitatis*, or carry within them always the principle of eternity. The Absolute cannot be broken down into parts but is reproduced in each difference-moment. The specific state of transition or passage of essence into form gives unities their individual characteristic. All "presence," for Schelling, is thus always a relative presence. Schelling here profoundly departs from the Kantian schema, foregrounding the transcendental or the Absolute as the sole measure of being. While for Kant, cognition is a positive act of knowledge, for Schelling, by contrast, all of our sensory knowledge is only a privation, arising out of the denial of essence. Ontologically, thought is an inter-being that is neither form nor essence but a passage or a transition phenomenon. Each instant thought runs through several states such as "tranquilizing," "alienating," "entanglement," "turbulence," "anxiety," and so on, to borrow some useful categories named by Heidegger in *Being and Time*. These transitory states need to be kept always under close observation without attempting to interfere. It is thus that thinking comes to realize its essential emptiness and begins to lose attachment to its projections and introjections. Redemptive thinking is therefore an ontological realignment with 'what is.' The proclivity of thought to separate itself from the world and then consider its effects on the world is now seen as an error because it necessarily involves *objectification of that which in truth is not an object*. The commonsense beliefs about "progress" and "development" turn out to be shadows and reflections in an anthropological hall of mirrors. Unlike modernists who imagine an enlightened social world that has left behind the religious frame of reference, Schelling contemplates a "final development to religion" that overcomes the opposition between essence and relativity. To keep us underway toward redemptive thinking the contemplation of the

Absolute or essence requires a humility or stillness in thought that belies the extreme cogitation that is the hallmark of life based on continual differentiation in thought.

In Chapter 4, we move to the poet-philosopher-naturalist Johann Wolfgang von Goethe whose work aims principally at achieving a profound change in the direction of thinking in its relation with the world. At the core of the present project is the invitation to a change in the direction of thinking. The notion with which we will be particularly concerned here is Goethe's construction of "delicate empiricism." Goethe teaches us to move from the "objective" fact or datum toward an empathic relationship with all that is in which 'cold data' is always already theory. Further, the distinct observer who is conventionally placed outside the process of observation thereby appears to be the consequence of wrong viewing and a certain mento-psychic indolence. In other words, the 'observer' is not a positivity, but rather the product of curtailment of the sensibilities. A small variation in the recuperation of available sensibilities would, in this view, result in a phenomenologically different relation between observer and observed. In this qualitatively new relation one can briefly glimpse the window to freedom. A complementary epistemology to conventional scientific practice thus becomes available here that might be termed as conscious-process-participation, which focuses on direct intuitive knowledge of the world, something denied by Kantian epistemology. The idea of participation in the Goethean framework comes out of Goethe's insistence that complete isolation of the object was not possible, and the esthetic dimension necessarily entered all observation. For Goethe, in living nature, each thing "happens" in connection with, or arises against, a background of totalities. Isolated experiences are misguided representations. Thus Goethe embarked upon an investigation into the process of engagement in order to develop a methodology for conscious participatory experience. With a certain phenomenological effort, the participating consciousness places itself within the draft of the phenomena and their continuities beyond. Here, the privileging of the observer comes to an end and along with that ends the narrow intentionality of the human. The implications for thinking are clear. All along, thought has become used to segregating, framing, postulating, and shaping, imagining that it is acting on an independent outside. With an expanding intuition, the inside-outside relation is recast along very different lines. Besides, there is another significant implication of the recasting of the inside/outside relation: there is a gradual overlap of the ontological and the epistemological. The sense of freedom is a creative production in this emerging unity of perception.

For Goethe, the study of form is the study of transformation. Taken into the consideration of thought, thinking must study its constant morphing into other thoughts. The principal study of thinking must be the engagement with its own morphology. Here there is a blurring of what is and how thought thinks about what is, since the subject of both is thought itself. What enters the picture is the esthetic, something deliberately left out in the conventional scientific discourse about the objective world. To claim that esthetic intuition was a valid way of judging the mysteries of nature was anathema to scientific thought. But to Goethe, to leave out the esthetic dimension in the adequate consideration of the fact was to remain in ignorance about the place of the intuitive in disclosures about the world. The immanent or the deep inner connections between phenomena could only be disclosed in properly awakened intuition. Thinking is merely another organ of apprehension just as the other senses, and its work consisted in becoming aware of the affinities that necessarily existed between tendencies in nature: "There is necessity, there is God." The esthetic, according to Goethe, is nothing other than the secret principles of nature inscribed in intuition that are realized in the awareness of a *beauty-within-necessity*. Realizing this necessity in thinking introduces the redemptive in thought, or rather, it puts us under way toward a phenomenological salvation.

Art, therefore, to Goethe, was just as objective as science, only representing a different mode of apprehension of necessity. Goethe was not interested in art or science for their own sakes but was after the revelation of necessity that required the *presence of both*. The one-sided pursuit of science or art gave rise to dangerous illusions about what is. To Goethe, philosophical poesy was about ontological correspondence with the macrocosm. And therefore, this meant, essentially, that it was the poetic sensibility that made sense of nature's "sullen jangle," and the task to group phenomena into "rhythmic dance" whereby meaning appeared was the supreme task of the esthetic dimension. In Goethe's *Faust*, we hear the desire of the protagonist "That I may detect the inmost force/ Which binds the world, and guides its course." Faust is fed up of the dry, second-hand knowledge of thought, and desires instead to gain direct ontological truth about the world that emancipates (lifts the spirits). Thought is in possession of knowledge but gains no wisdom or intensity of being thereby. Here we find the most powerful indictment of thinking as mere knowing. Emancipatory thought or redemptive thinking must turn its face away from fragmentary knowledge and toward essence. Faust realizes that the will-to-knowledge toward the fragment is death. It is in turning to face what thought has for so long turned away from that there is a glimpse of freedom. The turning toward the immediate present (the now) is the manifestation of Presence, something free of all content, and yet full of "impulse, mystic and divine." Faust strikes a deal with the Devil that will allow him direct and continuous insight into the workings of the world. This "deal" can be read as an allegory about the technological pact of thought that attempts to uncover the secret of life and death. Goethe shows this to be an enormous error. No such deal, or technologization of being, can be ultimately fruitful. Thought must instead give up the constant gnawing toward glory, and simply be under way toward comprehending its ontological structure, thereby becoming open to the possibility of Grace.

In Chapter 5, we take up the next major figure considered in this book, namely Heraclitus of Ephesus. Goethe's Faust would have had no need to look to the Devil for deliverance if he had proper acquaintance with Heraclitus. For the latter is the ultimate ontologist who discovers all truth by looking into his being. While for Kant, "We are acquainted with nothing except our way of perceiving them, which is peculiar to us…," for Heraclitus there is a unique category called "wisdom" (*σοφόν*) that is apart from mere ways of perceiving phenomena. When we permit ourselves to forget about this category we betray ourselves and others who follow us. It is wisdom that allows thinking to turn back toward itself and once more contemplate essence. Nevertheless, Heraclitus is a difficult philosopher. The aphorisms are dense and susceptible to multiple interpretations. "Heraclitus hints rather than reveals, makes unremitting demands on our intellect, patience, and efforts, and refuses to easily yield the extraordinary brilliance and individuality of his thoughts, rapt in their oracular expression."[30] By means of cryptic and oftentimes mystical insights Heraclitus lays bare the folly in the existing categories of thought exalted by other philosophers in an uncompromising manner. Heraclitus begins by asserting that "We should let ourselves be guided by what is common to all. Yet, although the Logos is common to all,

[30] Ava Chitwood, *Death by Philosophy* (Ann Arbor: University of Michigan Press, 2004), p. 93.

most men live as if each of them had a private intelligence of his own."[31] But what is common to all? Is there something common to all? Is not every strife in the world about the differences in perception and the privacy of intelligence? And yet Heraclitus claims that there is something common to all and that we must be guided by that common intelligence. Obviously that common intelligence cannot reside in the content of thought which is particularized; thinking is a process of endless differentiation and opposition. On the other hand, the ontological medium in which thought cogitates has necessarily to be the same, and it is this medium that is common to all, and its intuitive awareness the only salvation for thought. To give a crude analogy, each wave in the ocean is different but the medium in which the waves rise is the same. That which is common to all is the background elemental-consciousness shared by all. Humans go about oblivious to this background consciousness (*logos*), attentive only to the content of each particular thought-wave. Thereby we perceive only differences and not unities; we experience doubt and uncertainty, and not clarity or steadiness. In an astonishing philosophical *tour de force*, Heraclitus cuts through all the civilizational pileup and cultural debris, products of differentiation in thought, to show in one single stroke the basic error of thought. To attempt to derive *phronesis* from and on the basis of thought waves is akin to building structures atop ocean waves. Thus, when we proceed in life heedless of this basic denominator that underlies all of experience, we have no real understanding of the things we meet in daily life. Phenomenal life can only be understood correctly when we simultaneously pay attention to the condition of its possibility, that is, the common background, or universal intelligence, or what Heraclitus terms as *Logos*. Otherwise, everything in experience appears as torn pieces of ephemeral clouds in the sky, with no fundamental relation to any other thing, and no intrinsic connection to our lives. We flounder in a sea of factoids and part-phenomena that overwhelm us with their oppressive fragmentation and tedious march. That is not to say that we can ignore the content of thought-experience or phenomenal knowledge, but to observe that the thread that connects all of experience does not inhere in experience itself. At one level this must be obvious: meaning or totality is always a meta-experience and cannot be captured in any particular phenomenal occurrence.

[31] Heraclitus, Fragment 2.

The incredible thing, however, is how humans (including philosophers) have managed to obscure this basic fact and proceeded as if things could be otherwise. It is also to be noted that if we grasp the essence of this fragment (no. 2), all the rest of the known fragments can be seen as elaboration in multiple directions and planes. In other words, the essence of the Heraclitean position is revealed in a single aphorism at the inception. One is reminded of a great sage in the Indian tradition, namely, Patanjali, author of the famed *Yogasutra* written circa second century CE (some date it even earlier). Here too coincidentally in the second aphorism, Patanjali says, *yoga* is mind-formation restraint (*yogaḥ cittavṛtti nirodhaḥ*); that is, yoga consists in restraining mental formulations or representations. The 194 verses (*sutras*) that follow can be seen as the elaboration and practice of what has been indicated at the very outset. Returning to Heraclitus after this brief excursus, the universal quality or common intelligence gathers force in intuition when thinking acknowledges the necessity of it, and begins its journey toward it. This (ontological) movement is the same under all situations, and in all beings, that is, it is independent of context-content, and hence common. Epistemic difference is thus balanced by ontological sameness. It is this union of apparent opposites that for Heraclitus is wisdom. Personal intelligence or one-sided apprehension of the world of particulars cannot bring about this wisdom. Every other observation about the world is subservient to this order of wholeness that is available to the seeking consciousness, albeit with considerable phenomenological struggle. Heraclitus is puzzled by the fact that humans no longer seek this wholeness or are turned away from it. Instead they seek wisdom in the world of particulars and are inevitably frustrated by it.

The journey begins in these pages with Heidegger, posing the question: what does thought disown or turn away from? Moving in measured philosophical steps, reversed in the order of time, through Schelling and Goethe, we reach Heraclitus in whom we find the clearest and most direct expression of the answer to this question. Thought turns away from what is common to all and instead chooses to look at the world from the perspective of privatized and differential intelligence. It looks for salvation in the mass of details (objective knowledge) gathered from the world of phenomena and derives causal laws that fit the data. But phenomenologically the unfulfillment, fragmentation, conflict, and violence continues unalleviated. For all the sophistication of mental processes and representations, the contact with the essence remains impossible, which alone is redemptive. A different thinking therefore becomes necessary. Consequently, the exploration in these pages are devoted to the reorienting of thought toward what needs to be thought most urgently.

Chapter 6 returns to the beginning, and ponders thought's relation to time. Thought breeds more thinking toward a 'what-ness,' it's justification lying in thought itself. At the same time, thinking interprets itself, and the interpretation constructs the present or the mental representation of time at the social level. This production Heidegger calls "public time." The public time appears endless and masks the inevitability of private death. The continuity of thought is thus born of public time. Vulgar temporality prevents thinking from seriously contemplating its organic ending. Equally, it also obscures the perception of a primordial time, *Kairos*, distinct from common progression, or *Chronos*. The singularity that otherwise has the potential to bring recoil and quietude in thinking is prevented. Time as progression rolls on generating the phenomenon called world history. The question arises: Can the grip of *Chronos* be broken? For a breakthrough to be glimpsed in phenomenological temporality it would be crucial to depart from the narrow, one-sided secular order of things that breeds time as experience as well as experience in time. It would be necessary to peer instead into the 'non-chronic,' such as the messianic time-of-the-now present in, for example, the Pauline testament. Here time decomposes into *Parousia* or Presence, that is, into a non-progressive, non-sequential sequence of nows. What lies beyond has no name but is pure experience, an indeterminateness normally abhorred by thought. This radical discontinuity is *Pleroma*, always present at the ontological edge of thought. The possibility of freedom is thus present in each decomposed moment.

Toward the development of intuition and maturation of the above sensibility, and the direction of its deepening, the present chapter makes an excursus into the Book of Koheleth or *Ecclesiastes*. The piety of thought and its vanities are relentlessly attacked in this text till the pseudo-grandeur of thinking is brought to its knees. Verse after verse testifies to the essential emptiness of all the designs of thought till thinking is forced to face itself stripped and denuded of all its categories and camouflage. The work of thought is seen as "vapor" as everything returns to its source: "The wind goeth toward the south, and turneth about unto the north; it whirleth about continually, and the wind returneth again according to his circuits. All the rivers run into the sea; yet the sea is not full; unto the place from whence the rivers come, thither they return again" (*Ecclesiastes* 1.6–1.7). Further, it reminds us of the futility of private intelligence or determination of thought in the face of the "King" or the messianic force that had always already accomplished its task: "And I turned myself to behold wisdom, and madness, and folly: for what can the man do that cometh after the King? Even that which hath been already done" (*Ecclesiastes* 2:12). For, Koheleth seems to imply, thought to distinguish between wisdom and folly it would have to transcend itself; it cannot do so from within itself, or even repeat adequately that which had already been accomplished. In other words, thought is repetition; it cannot discover anything radically new. The new is always at the outer edge of thought, in its essence. The new is not something of the future, nor of an unprecedented moment come upon by thinking. The new has already happened, in the very instant when thinking was born. But the timeless new was left behind when thinking jettisoned it in order to march ahead along its own projections.

Chapter 7 looks at some of the characteristic postures of thought that keep thinking oriented away from itself and toward the manufacture of different levels and layers of self-delusion. Distinct from the rest of the book, this part is written in a propositional style with accompanying explanations. The key focus here is the process of introjection resulting in the inner picture (daguerreotype) or the self-image of thought. The techno-poieisis of thinking populates the "inner" environment with phantasms that are superimposed on the experiential flow to set up the reality dialectic within the precinct of the daguerreotype. In other words, the deliria of thought mixes with the materiality of the environment producing ceaseless agitation around a pseudo-nucleus of continuity. Just as the earth's motion around the sun gives rise to the apparent plane of the ecliptic against the background of the stars, the ceaseless motion of thinking produces the peculiar inner plane of a 'psycho-dialectic' that supports the nucleus. The ontological inquiry is an effort to study this plane of production carefully such that adequate self-disclosure occurs to, and within, thinking. It is only by means of self-disclosure that a transformation begins toward a preparation for redemptive thinking.

Finally, turning to criticism, a book like the present one raises many questions, especially since an attempt is made to open an unusual line of inquiry into philosophical thinking. It presents difficulties not only of communication but also of content. One way to anticipate possible misgivings, misunderstandings, as well as communicative problems is to refer to the initial criticisms offered by an expert reader at the manuscript review stage. Although the final form of the work incorporates many of the suggestions, and attempts to respond to the objections, some of the initial comments (and responses) might still continue to usefully connect to questions and basic concerns that might possibly come up in the judgments of other readers as well. Therefore I present below, in a paraphrased form, some of the important remarks received initially, followed by the author's responses, with the note that the thrust of these observations have had their say in the text proper, at relevant places, and whenever it was useful or pertinent. The sole purpose of this inclusion, a risky maneuver, is to improve communication with the reader.

- "The author is somewhat vague about just what this goal [redemptive thinking] is; it is uncovering 'essence,' providing the 'door to the real', transcendence, awaking the 'soul force' to guide us, etc. It would be helpful to spend a little more time explicating this positive goal. What is this real or essence?"

The goal of redemptive thinking is a radical transformation in thought whereby thought is not only engaged in representational thinking, but begins to have an intuition about its formal (structural) and phenomenological aspect. But, before we go on, the idea of 'transformation' itself is in need of clarification. Conventionally, transformation in the present context is taken to mean a (desirable) modification brought in some element or group of elements. This is not what transformation means here. In the view taken here, thought is always already a modification. The task is to realize the nature of this modification leading to a *katargesis* or deactivation. This leads us to understand at the intuitive level the formal structure of thinking, not its content. What is the use of grasping the formal aspect of thinking? The argument here attempts to show that it orients us toward the essence of thinking that is very different from the usual content of thought. Why is that necessary? The need arises from the recognition that today there is a crisis in thinking that has been in the making for some time. The political, ecological, and personal challenges that face humanity today bear testimony to this fact. All usual attempts at rearranging the content of thought have mostly failed at the level of action in bringing about general well-being and emancipation. What is necessary is a complete re-evaluation of our ontological being, and that means understanding thinking at a deeper level, since it is in thinking that the intentionality and direction of human efforts is mostly reflected.

- "One gets the sense that this idea is rather influenced by the Buddhist doctrine of No-Self: discovering one's self-nature and the idea of emptiness. I would like to hear more about the relation to Buddhist thought."

The central idea of the book concerns the possibility of a deep and direct engagement with a transformative process that is at base unmediated and independent of any particular system of thinking. The surrounding philosophical treatment from several angles helps to clarify and deepen the intellectual intuition necessary to approach thought at the ontological level. It is not necessary to see it as linked to Buddhist doctrine in particular. Nevertheless, notions such as *anatta* (no-self) and (*sati*) mindfulness may resonate with the ontological investigations carried out here, just as the discussion might attract certain notions (for e.g., *neti neti*) in a very different tradition such as *Advaita Vedanta*. While being eclectic, the approach has been also minimalistic, skirting past the various traditions, and yet remaining true to philosophical inquiry, in order to remain singularly focused on praxis. A word here about Praxis: it is not about end-gaining, nor is it about personal emancipation. Praxis aims at freeing thinking in a transpersonal manner out of which the fundamental social unit might undergo a change and therefore act differently. This also makes the book distinct from "new-age" literature in that the latter is mostly about end-gaining, personal, and psychic expansionist in nature. Praxis has nothing to do with spiritual materialist adventures. It is serious philosophy put to work in a careful way in order to understand the ontological principles on which we stand from moment to moment, think, speak, and act.

- "A general concern is that, as with so much continental philosophy, the work is written at such a high level of abstraction that it can seem far removed from any concrete practical ends."

Abstraction is necessarily a character of philosophy, but the present work also has praxis in mind. It is not directed only at pure scholarship but at the possibility of transformation in thought by reconsidering the action of thinking. Throughout the book the emphasis is on the development of intellectual intuition or a new organ of perception as put forth by Goethe and substantiated in Schelling's work. The effort returns again and again hermeneutically to a general four-pronged phenomenological labor: *noesis* (intellectual intuition), *kenosis* (voiding the conventional categories of perception including temporality), *katargesis* (progressive deactivation of modification and differentiation), and *epekteinomenos* (straining forward without intentionality). The critical understanding of the process of thinking as it thinks its way through life is aimed at producing conditions that aid the intuitive process, leading to philosophical insight that can literally turn existence inside out esthetically (as thought looks from the outside inwards). The book argues that a special kind of redemptive power awaits the ontological (structural) understanding of thought. However, one must be willing to be open to such an intensive inquiry, be a participant inquirer in order to fully gain what the book has to offer. This is part of the hermeneutic phenomenological method. "The concrete practical end" must surface in an inter-relational space between word and thought.

- "To take one example of excessive abstractness, the author declares that thinking produces difference. But this seems flatly untrue; just as often, thought recognizes similarities, sameness. Isn't part of the problem of modern culture not excess differentiation, but excess homogeneity, standardization? In any case, it would be useful to see concrete discussion of how this actually plays out in the modern world or recent history."

Here difference must be understood in ontological terms. Even in copying a thing or, say, a piece of art to the last detail, there is a difference, since, at the very least, the copy occupies a space other than the original. Plato writes of the problem of the simulacrum: the simulacra duplicate the *Idea* and yet are different. A thought, when it takes off from a prior thought, has created a space of difference, even when it is tending toward (cultural) homogeneity. Modernity displays the production of homogeneity as noted by Adorno in his comments on the "Culture Industry," nevertheless, the similar is not the Same, ontologically speaking. In other words, representational thought is always a copy, and a copy always incorporates difference, even where that difference is a mere repetition. That is to say, thought is always differentiating. Otherwise it would be still. This problem has been discussed by the

French philosopher Gilles Deleuze in his well-known work *Difference and Repetition*.[32]

- "[The author] attributes all suffering to human excess, which again seems flatly false. Much suffering is due to nature (disease, drought, natural disasters), and one cannot reasonably claim that all evil is due to human wrongdoing, even if much of it is)."

The understanding of suffering in the present work is specifically with regard to the range of man-made or thought-made suffering, and not related to natural disasters. It is the kind of (produced) suffering identified by Theodor Adorno (*Negative Dialectics*) and Hannah Arendt (*The Human Condition*). It is not necessary to include here so-called natural disasters simply because they are, conventionally speaking, "natural," meaning that they relate to endless transformations of matter in which the human is not a privileged category. But self-consciousness of thought cannot claim the "innocence" of nature, as its actions are selective, committed, and intentional. In other words, although, ontologically, thought is not excluded from nature, its self-consciousness and possibility of choice-making confers on it a fundamental ethical responsibility. We cannot absolve thought of ethical obligation by drawing attention to natural calamity.

- "Personally, I would also question why the author focuses the idea of redemption merely on 'thinking.' To me, this embraces an unfortunate (Cartesian) dualism between thinking and action. Where is the discussion of redemption [in] action?... We are not merely thinking beings, and redemption should be primarily a matter of action, or of thought as it guides action."

Let me refer the reader to para 2 of Chapter 3: *In order to appreciate Schelling's theory of reflexivity and its central relation to our problem, we must acquire a rudimentary understanding of his metaphysical theory of nature and mind. For only then we shall be able to surmise the basis of his comprehensive rejection of Cartesianism together with the notion of pure subjectivity, and begin to appreciate the essentially non-dual cognitive world*

[32] Gilles Deleuze, *Difference and Repetition*, trans. Paul Patton (New York: Columbia University Press, 1995).

he inaugurates instead. The discussion that follows shows clearly why this work has no interest in the Cartesian split. Second, the idea (and task) of redemption is not being attributed to thinking alone. There is also redemption through Grace and by other means not discussed here. The point being made here is that *thinking is in need of redemption.* That means the image of thought that thinking has operated with in a forward movement in time has not critically interrogated itself sufficiently to understand its ontological source. There is no Cartesian dualism at all being suggested between thinking and action. In fact it is emphasized that *redeemed thought is action.* Redemption cannot be "primarily a matter of action" as the reviewer suggests, since the very need for redemption arises with the Fall (i.e., variance with what-is, or disorientation from essence, etc.). And the Fall, whether understood mythically, rationally, or esthetically, is primarily cognitive (rejection of necessity). Pure action on the other hand, such as planetary movement or heliotropism, without the intervention of thought, cannot be the subject of redemption. The epistolary effort of the Apostle Paul demands a supreme cognitive effort to change the image of thought that is an important sacrifice (action). Even the voluntary change of name from Saul to Paul, in the biography of the Apostle, reflects this change that is thought and action at the same time.

- "A concern I had was one where we get the strange idea that thought is a "material movement," whatever that means...don't remember anything in the book that shows how thought is matter, nor do I think it likely one could show such a thing."

Etymologically, the word "matter" comes to us from PIE *mater* and Sanskrit cognate *matṛ* meaning mother. The connotation is source, or cause, or origin. In saying that thought is a "material movement," the implication is that it is a movement of the origin or an originary matrix that is not directly available to thinking itself. From Schelling and Spinoza one can gather that this movement (of thought as form) is *sub specie aeternitatis* or under the principle of eternity, meaning that thought as form is a pulse of essence. To give an ordinary example, a radiation wave through space is a formal and originary entity without content till it interacts with a receiving apparatus of some kind producing phenomena (content). In a similar manner, thought as representation is only a secondary phenomenon in this schema. Here it is important that an effort is made to jettison the commonplace meaning of the word "matter" or "material" and the image of the solidly tactile that these signifiers evoke. In the event that at some node, thinking, all of a sudden becomes open to phenomenological inquiry, directly and intimately, becoming its own object of study, it would begin to feel itself as a pulse or a distinct sensibility within mento-corporeality. This is the closest to materiality that thinking might get.

The "dialogue" above is obviously nowhere near an exhaustive one with regard to the range of difficulties that a reader might have with the text, nor can such a (comprehensive) thing be envisaged. A more humble effort is one which attempts to set the stage by clarifying some basic parameters surrounding the text that might aid in comprehending what is to come, avoiding needless misconstruals between reader and text, smoothening the path for the real dialogue. Thus it stands in the same relation as a clearing does to the surrounding forest.

A few more things need to be clarified here. First, with regard to the title of the book: what is this "power" of philosophy? This is not the "positive" power of knowledge as expansion of the mental corpus and the epistemic limit of its activities. Rather, the self-knowledge of thought is negative knowledge or *negative power* of philosophy. The negative power is not additive or incremental; it attempts to loosen and thaw the existing image of thought that has exclusively taken hold of the human, even defined the limits of the human. The assumption here is that it takes considerable phenomenological labor—looking and sensing this way and that—for this new "negative" sensibility to arise. The phenomenological labor central to this negative philosophy (which, in reality, is more positive than anything else in terms of its invitation to engage with what is) requires an unsentimental disinvestment in the historical build-up of thought. This in no way undermines the positive achievements of thought or threatens its underpinnings. Rather, it demands an alternate (ontological) vision that allows the human to change frames when necessary, avoiding ontological crippling. It introduces a "bilinguality" in philosophical thought extending the possibilities of the human toward realizing potential. Just as the command over a second language allows one to transcend the epistemic-cultural limits of one language without condescension, philosophical bilingualism allows us to escape the historical limits that thought has brought upon itself. Thus the positive power of philosophy is augmented by a negative power. This negative power, as must be obvious to the reader, does not belong to anyone (as distinct from positive power). Although the starting point into its inquiry might appear to be the "individual," it is neither discrete nor individuated. Instead it exerts an archetypal pressure on relationalities by lifting the oppression of ontological misconceptions.

Next, a small note on the approach to *oeuvre*. In traditional scholarship, the later views in the work of a scholar are often implicitly privileged and seen as trumping the earlier views. In other words, the later view is seen as the more mature one. This is not necessarily the stance of the present book unless it relates to something explicitly rejected by the same writer (such as in the case of Ludwig Wittgenstein who rejects his own views presented in the *Tractatus* in a later work). For instance, an important notion in the work of the early Marx is *Gattungswesen* or "species being," another is *Entausserung* or "alienation." Both these terms more or less disappear from the later Marx. Similarly the early Heidegger, in *Being and Time*, for instance, differs from the later Heidegger as appears in *Introduction to Metaphysics*. This change in the approach to the central problematic is sometimes referred to as *die Kehre*, or "the turn" in Heidegger's thinking. The attitude of the present author is that we must deal with each notion or insight on its own terms, affording each the necessary critical space without imposing a totality on the *oeuvre* from the outside. Besides, such a totality is against the framework of the present book in that it militates against the spiritual anarchy that is at the heart of negative philosophy. To assume that a unified presence covers the length of a life and can be made to speak for any part of it, is, in terms of this view, a philosophical error. Again, this is not to say that those who prefer the later views of a scholar over the earlier ones are wrong. The case is only made for the possibility of another attitude.

Finally, one must distinguish between philosophical praxis and individual liberation. Eastern philosophies are mostly directed at self-realization or going beyond phenomenal life to an Absolute realization. But philosophical praxis is not aimed merely at individual liberation (whatever that might be) but at producing a livable reality that is free of contradiction. In other words, it is aimed at producing a richer here-and-now in which each existential node realizes its temporality and the horizon in which it arises. This is not individual; the so-called individual is itself a by-product of the activity of thinking. Hence, it is immaterial as to where and what are the entry points to this praxis. The significant thing is to establish that the possibility exists and enriches the world.

References

Adorno, Theodor. *Negative Dialectics*. New York: The Continuum Publishing, 1973.

Chitwood, Ava. *Death by Philosophy*. Ann Arbor: University of Michigan Press, 2004.

Heidegger, Martin. *Being and Time*. Translated by Joan Stambaugh. New York: SUNY Press, 1996.

Heidegger, Martin. *What Is Called Thinking*. Translated by Fred D. Wieck and J. Glenn Gray. New York: Harper and Row, 1968.

Kant, Immanuel. *Critique of Pure Reason*. Translated by Norman Kemp Smith, 2nd ed. New York: Palgrave Macmillan, 1929.

Kant, Immanuel. *The Metaphysical Foundations of Natural Science*. Translated by Ernest Belford Boax. London: Cambridge University Press, 2004.

Mach, Ernst. *The Analysis of Sensations*. Translated by C.M. Williams and Sydney Waterlow. London: Dover, 1959.

Patrick, George T.W. *The Fragments of the Work of Heraclitus of Ephesus on Nature*. Baltimore: N. Murray, 1889.

Shaw, Devin Zane. *Freedom and Nature in Schelling's Philosophy of Art*. New York: Bloomsbury, 2010.

Shotter, John. "Goethe and the Refiguring of Intellectual Inquiry: From 'Aboutness'-Thinking to 'Withness'-Thinking in Everyday Life." *Janus Head* 8(1) (2005): 132–158.

von Goethe, J.W. *Scientific Studies*. New York: Suhrkamp, 1988.

von Schelling, F.W.J. *Collected Works Vol. 4*. Translated by Peter Heith. Cambridge: Cambridge University Press, 1985.

CHAPTER 2

Heidegger and the Pathless Land

How or why does Heidegger figure in this project of philosophical redemption? Where or when does he allude to freedom through any form of emancipatory activity? He does not, indeed, he would not, within the framework and in relation to the task that he sets for himself. Such a question seems to hinge too much on conscious exercise of responsibility and intervention, neither of which plays an explicit role in his work as a whole.[1] Besides such a venture seems to carry the flavor of an Eastern attitude of liberation etc. which Heidegger avoided. It is clear at the outset then that pilgrims will part according to destination, and there would come a point at which the present project must go beyond the Heideggerian perspective and prepare to walk on in the company of yet others.[2] But that is well ahead at this point, and the importance of Heidegger's discussion of being is of central importance here that

[1] This early declaration is to allay the suspicion of Heideggerians and reassure that the author does not intend to drag Heidegger in a direction that his thought does not go, and yet recognize the centrality of his thoughts with regard to the present project.

[2] This is elegantly described by the philosopher Giorgio Agamben in the following words: "whenever we interpret and develop the text of an author in this way, there comes a moment when we are aware of our inability to proceed any further without contravening the most elementary rules of hermeneutics. This means that the development of the text in question has reached a point of undecidability where it becomes impossible to distinguish between the author and the interpreter. Although this is a particularly happy moment for the interpreter, he knows that it is now time to abandon the text that he is analyzing and to proceed on his own." Giorgio Agamben, *What Is an Apparatus? And Other Essays*, trans. David Kishik (Stanford, CA: Stanford University Press, 2009), p. 13.

K. Roy, *The Power of Philosophy*,
https://doi.org/10.1007/978-3-319-96911-4_2

prepares the ground for exploration in the development of philosophical bilingualism. Let us recollect a few things about Heidegger's early project, and then construct its relation with the current mission. Let us begin by noting that Heidegger's problem in his early work *Being and Time* is the very problem that haunted the early philosophers: the problem of the articulation of Being. The articulation of Being necessarily involves thinking, but *thinking of a very different kind* with no epistemic content or historical image, something that we too must develop in these pages.

> The question touched upon here is hardly an arbitrary one. It sustained the avid research of Plato and Aristotle but from then on ceased to be heard *as a thematic question of actual investigation*. What these two thinkers achieved has been preserved in various distorted and "camouflaged" forms down to Hegel's *Logic*. And what then was wrested from phenomena by the highest exertion of thought, albeit in fragments, has long since been trivialized. Not only that. On the foundation of the Greek point of departure for the interpretation of being, a dogma has taken shape which not only declares that the question of the meaning of being is superfluous but sanctions its neglect. It is said that "being" is the most universal and the emptiest concept. As such it resists every attempt at definition. Nor does this most universal and thus indefinable concept need any definition. Everybody uses it constantly and also already understands what is meant by it. Thus what troubled ancient philosophizing and kept it so by virtue of its obscurity has become obvious, clear as day, such that whoever persists in asking about it is accused of an error of method.[3]

A philosophical doctrine has taken shape which regards being as the most universal (general) concept and hence indefinable. In other words, it is against the absolute generality of being that other concepts are arrived at, and hence itself is empty. Although true at some level, Heidegger clearly does not accept this tack, and feels that modern thought singularly lacks a proper discussion of being, or rather, an adequate formulation of the formal structure of the question of being. Modern thought concerns itself with *ontics* (objectified elements or modes of being), that is, with the "onticization" of being, but not with what makes entities intelligible as entities. What follows in *Being and Time* is an in-depth exposition of the intelligibility of *Da-sein* in terms of its temporal and spatial structure and the nature of its relation with the world-at-large.

[3] Martin Heidegger, *Being and Time*, trans. Joan Stambaugh (New York: SUNY Press, 1996), p. 1.

Out of this lengthy discussion comes two vital questions "Is there a way which leads from primordial time to the meaning of being?" and "Does time itself manifest itself as the horizon of being?"[4] These questions are left open in the book, for, as Heidegger says, the book is only a "beginning" and a "preparation" to help us get "underway." But to help us get underway toward what? We have forgotten, or turned away from Being, or the question of Being of beings. Although Being is what allows entities to be intelligible as entities, we take this insubstantial ground of possibility for granted, and no longer wonder about what it is that allows us to be.[5] We are dazzled by all the external projections before us. We do not ask, for instance, what makes thought possible, or, what is the medium in which the peculiar phenomenon called thinking arises?[6] Instead, we focus on the technological thrills, and the various games of truth that thought spins out, and perceive the totality of these as an independent reality that is solely worth our attention. To put it figuratively, we are mostly taken up by the branches and foliage, and no longer strive for awareness of the root. Where the question of the "root" is even brought into view, it is technologized, such as, for example, in relation to questions of cognition-perception. Modern philosophy, for the most part, has set aside the question of Being as too abstract, and has become absorbed in semiotics or logic. One might even say that philosophy since Kant is embarrassed by the notion of metaphysical wisdom (*Sophos*), replacing it by the problem of judgement, and the question of liberation-redemption today seems remote and antiquarian. Rather philosophy

[4]The full quote is as follows: "The existential and ontological constitution of the totality of Da-sein is grounded in temporality. Accordingly, a primordial mode of temporalizing of ecstatic temporality itself must make the ecstatic project of being in general possible. How is this mode of temporalizing of temporality to be interpreted? Is there a way leading from primordial *time* to the meaning of *being*? Does *time* itself reveal itself as the horizon of *being*?" Ibid., p. 398.

[5]Being must not be understood as some higher order entity or ultimate ontological ground waiting to be discovered. That would be in line with the old onto-theological doctrines that Heidegger repudiates. In other words, there is no metaphysics of Presence in Heidegger. Being is always disclosed in beings, but not coincident with the onticity of any particular being. The capitalization of being as 'Being' merely helps to keep the latter in mind.

[6]From the previous note, we can say that the relation of thinking to Being is merely the relation between a specific onticization (in response to the world and the "they") and the ontological generality.

prefers debates on logic and semantics that do not go beyond the existing frameworks and categories of ordering experience, and for the most part avoids ontological questions.[7]

Nevertheless, the present work cannot sidestep these questions, for these are directed at the very heart of, or have as their true stakes, the possibility of redemptive freedom, and indeed help us get underway. These questions are not commonplace questions that can be, or are meant to be "answered." Rather, the 'question' here reflects the *quaestionem*, its Latin root, implying a 'seeking' or an 'inquiry' into things that must be sustained. *Prima facie*, how does the relation of being to time have a bearing on the question of redemption? First, the reconsideration of being as a philosophical problem forces thinking back onto itself, as it cannot be resolved through facticity. The requisite for a revolution in thought is a new plasticity that can only come through the wonder of being. Also the appearance of the sensible, including (the phenomenon of) the self that speaks, is a construct in time, and therefore, in a sense, *is* time. Thought cannot organize perception, including self-perception, without temporal coordinates. Loosely speaking, each cell, for instance, in the organismic coordinate, has a preceding state, a now-state, and a succeeding state, collectively giving rise to a phenomenological temporality that is lived time. If such be the case, then an inquiry into radical freedom must of necessity inquire into the coordinates onto which experience is mapped as a first step in understanding the possibility and limit of thought-experience. To give an example, ordinarily the future is understood as a yet-to-come openness in time. But bringing time under a Heideggerian lens, the meaning of future is seen as a coming toward-oneself; it is a turning of Da-sein toward its own being, that is, a contraction toward death.[8] This radically

[7]Although the present work begins with a critique of the Kantian position, it is fair to admit that the schism between epistemology and ontology goes back before Kant. In fact, there are in Kant, moments of ambiguity, especially in the third *Critique*, where he seems to admit the possibility of an emptiness-experience (pure time and space) that borders on transcendence. However, these openings are not taken seriously, and the followers of Kant do not elaborate on this point as well, choosing to remain on the categorical path to certainty.

[8]Michael Roubach notes: "In primordial temporality, the future is the basic temporal 'dimension': it is in terms of the future that the present and past are understood. However, the future is not "a 'now' which has *not yet* become 'actual,'" as it is usually understood, but is characterized as anticipation: "Anticipation makes Dasein *authentically* futural" (SZ 325). The meaning of "future" is "[coming] towards-oneself," it is the move toward oneself that is made by evincing what Heidegger calls "resoluteness" (SZ 329), namely, by

alters our vision of what time means between now and the future (or the next instant). The illusions stitched together through the reference to an apparently unlimited "public time"—a concept discussed later in this chapter—are disturbed and forced to yield to the existential and phenomenological truth of time. Negative philosophy is the operation of philosophy to break down the false accretions and sclerotic traditions that have worked their way into perception. We might even find that the removal of errors of perception is all that is needed for praxis rather than some positivity.

Equally important for us here is something that Heidegger calls "primordial time." What is the nature of this primordial time and what is its connection with the present problem? Heidegger does not derive his notion of primordial time from some religio-aesthetic order of eternity or anything like that. Rather, primordial time is seen as the vision of a moment in which the past, present, and futurality of a being come together. In other words, it is an experience in which the usual divisions in the temporal order disappear. In what sense can the past, present, and future come together? The problem is actually the other way around. We must inquire into the authenticity of that which creates this temporal division in the first place. Thinking records something which betokens its past, as having-been, and from that reference point, imagines or projects or anticipates a future. To begin with, this much may be loosely admitted as thesis, that the temporal structure is in reciprocal relation to the emergent (psychological) nucleus that, in turn, helps maintain this division, making it a 'natural' horizon from where to determine existential locus with respect to others. In other words, the having-been offers

Dasein's authentic self-disclosure (SZ 296). This future is characterized as "towards-oneself" because it separates Dasein from other entities by turning Dasein toward its own being, toward its death, a separation that requires resoluteness. Heidegger's basic characterization of the future is, therefore, anticipatory resoluteness (SZ 326). But if, in primordial temporality, the future is basic, what is the meaning of the past? The meaning of the past in primordial temporality is "having-been-ness" (*Gewesenheit*). The past is understood through the future, because it is revealed through Dasein's relation to its own death, its future past-ness. As "having-been-ness," the past situates Dasein and enables Dasein to encounter that which is given in its environment (SZ 326). Dasein's temporality as a whole, Heidegger tells us, is 'the unity of a future which makes present in the process of having been.'" Michael Roubach, "Heidegger's Primordial Temporality and Other Notions of Time," in *Cosmological and Psychological Time*, eds. Y. Dolev and M. Roubach (New York: Springer, Cham, 2016), p. 265.

a basis for the nucleus, which, in turn, strengthens the temporal division. The uncritical consciousness begins to see itself in terms of a past, present, and future. Thus a horizon arises wherein the sensible or *pragmata* appear *as contingent phenomena* to the apparently invariant locus of observation. That is to say, everyday self-consciousness becomes the vulgar link between time and becoming. But "primordial time" remains differently related to Being as the past-present-future distinction is collapsed. There is a singularity that overwhelmingly *IS*. The discussion in the following pages will gradually unfold the phenomenological relation between being, hermeneutic disclosure, and philosophical redemption. Briefly, generating a preview of the Heideggerian position that brings to light the thesis of the present work: a disclosure occurs in the exercise of thinking wherein thought becomes its own object of inquiry disclosing to itself its true relation to time and being. For this unusal exercise, I mostly rely on Heidegger's later work namely *What Is Called Thinking*.

To turn thinking back on itself then, we have to first ask: what is it that poses the question (about the nature of thinking), or rather, how are we called upon or enabled to raise the question in the first place? In other words, how does a specific thought become the theme or subject of thinking? Since to "call upon" also means to invite or call into presence, what calls into presence, in the present instance, a critical reflection on thinking? For what calls upon us to think in the first place, may not be different from that which invites us to wonder about thinking itself. To put it differently, *how does thinking re-turn to its original undertaking*? Let us proceed from the opposite direction. In order to examine the possibility or otherwise of thinking in the direction of reflecting upon thought itself, let us find out about the things that mesmerize and stand in the way of such reflection. What prevents thought from becoming aware of the nature of itself as a patterned activity or a structural movement in emptiness, between two existential moments?

It is not difficult to see that one major smokescreen is the continuous inner traffic of verbal-images, incessant representations, and will-to-action that produce a sense of continuous becoming. We must observe this activity and ask about the ontological nature of the constituents of this voluntary/involuntary verbal stream. When the inner babble, or thought traffic, which is the lowest common denominator of commonness, is momentarily examined, what do we find? What are these waves that rise and fall away each instant? How shall we categorize this language of the inner torrent? First, with respect to speech in general, Heidegger points out:

> To speak language is totally different from employing language. Common speech merely employs language. This relation to language is just what constitutes its commonness. But because thought, and in a different way poesy, do not employ terms but speak words, therefore we are compelled, as soon as we set out on a way of thought, to give specific attention to what the word says.[9]

Commonplace use of language is instrumental; it deploys language as a set of terms in order to overcome a situation and thereby attain certain ends. Just as a signal-man is not particularly concerned with the signal per se but about the directed-toward-ness of the signal, common speech uses words without specific awareness to achieve a desired goal of communication. This means-to-an-end attitude defines the common use of language. Words become things-to-hand employed reflexively as habit. The inner speech too is subject to the general nature and quality of this deployment. What is the thrust of such deployment? Heidegger speaks of the "They" or the generalized other from which initially the sense of "I" or an apparently enduring nucleus is derived.[10] The nervous internal chatter is thus directed at an intangible "they." This obscures the primary nature of the word and obstructs the possibility of giving careful attention to what the word says, because the focus is on the amorphous and ubiquitous "they" that seems all important. But when we set out to think seriously about thinking, we have to pay a great deal of attention to the word, for thought often shapes itself in the word. We have to teach ourselves to speak words as they were meant to be spoken and not as mere terms strung together. This gives the spacing necessary to observe the thought-word. We have to *think* with the word as it moves in us, feel its texture, and be aware of its ambiguities and its depth. For us, the net result is a *slowing down*. The usual employment of language is to speed up things, to bring things to a closure, whereas, the careful use

[9] Heidegger, *Being and Time*, p. 128.

[10] Heidegger observes: "Initially, "I" "am" not in the sense of my own self, but I am the others in the mode of the they. In terms of the they, and as the they, I am initially "given" to "myself." Initially, Dasein is the they, and for the most part it remains so." *Being and Time*, p. 121.

of words is a slowing down of the tempo of things that bring into view the hidden wellsprings of thought and the spaces between thoughts. Disclosure is thus deceleration toward praxis.

Besides, the careful, and sensitive use of words can bring into light the philological pathways that disclose the co-development of thought and the word. Taking etymology seriously:

> The Old English *thencan*, to think, and *thancian*, to thank, are closely related; the Old English noun for thought is *thanc* or *thonc*—a thought, a grateful thought, and the expression of such a thought; today it survives in the plural thanks. The "thanc," that which is thought, the thought, implies the thanks...Is thinking a giving of thanks? What do thanks mean here? Or do thanks consist in thinking?[11]

Here the etymology, which might be considered to remain as a trace within the word, reveals a secret-sacred aspect of thought. In inquiring into the structure of thought, the close assonance between thinking and thanking is revealing. Did thinking originate in a kind of thanksgiving? Is the purpose of thinking primarily to offer gratitude toward its own self-nature? If future is a turning-toward-being (death), is authentic thinking the horizon for the appearance of being? Are we staring at the possibility that thinking at its root, that is, at the origin, is the movement of a form of *agape*? Philology gives a clue to a new direction of inquiry. Something more than the means-ends relation is at stake here, something rather mysterious with regard to the ontological essence of thought. It indicates further that thinking could be its own nourishment as distinct from the image of thought as logistics and representation that culminates in its correspondence with an extrinsic object or an action.

But thinking should also be ordinarily regarded as signifying the movement of memory in the sense of recall or remembrance, should it not? Again, etymological or philological understanding comes to our aide:

> "Memory" initially did not at all mean the power to recall. The word designates the whole disposition in the sense of a steadfast intimate concentration upon the things that initially speak to us in every thoughtful meditation. Originally, "memory" means as much as devotion: a constant

[11] Ibid., p. 139.

> concentrated abiding with something—not just with something that has passed, but in the same way with what is present...the gathering of the constant intention of everything that the heart holds in present being.[12]

The Avestan *mimara* "mindful," and the Greek *merimna* "care," are close cognates of the word memory. At the least, there is a hint that the word memory initially meant much more than mere recall, gradually drifting away to signify something more superficial and mechanical. Memory brings up not the picture of mechanical remembrance, although that might be one of its functions, but a gathering upon the heart of the sum of existential significance in our present, a concentration, as it were, of distilled worth of present being. Consequently, one could say that thinking imbued with such a character of memory becomes a form of devotion, an offering that amounts to "thanks owed for being."

But to whom or to what does thought give thanks? Thanks are owed to the possibility of thinking, to the supreme possibility of thought itself. The words indicate a realm beyond speech from where the ancient word is projected. Implicit in thinking is an obligation to think back to the source of thinking or giving thought to "what is most thought-provoking."[13] What is most thought-provoking is the possibility of thought itself. In the very stirring of thought, implicit in it, there is already the principle of what is to be thought. Hence thanks well up in the ontological attainment of thought. When initially thought moves, it moves with the innate knowledge of why it moves. It is to this unity of things that thanks are due, to this fullness that is full of the potentiality of thought. It should not be confused with the representational or epistemic content of thought.

> When the transaction of a matter is settled, or disposed of, we say in Alemannic dialect that it is "thanked." Disposing does not mean here sending off, but the reverse: it means to bring the matter forth and leave it where it belongs. This sort of disposing is called thanking.[14]

[12] Ibid., pp. 140–141.

[13] Martin Heidegger, *What Is Called Thinking*, trans. Fred D. Wieck and J. Glenn Gray (New York: Harper and Row, 1968), p. 4.

[14] Heidegger, *Being and Time*, p. 146.

Each time thought moves, a wholeness is activated that must be brought back to its resting place. This returning to origin is thankful disposal. The movement of thought gains its legitimacy from this possibility of returning to the wholeness of the nature of things, each time, every time.

But how can we know of this origin, how do we point to it? To understand this we have to recognize or acknowledge the nature of a being.

> If we are to think of man not as an organism but a human being, we must first give attention to the fact that man is that being who has his being by pointing to what is, and that particular beings manifest themselves as such by such pointing.[15]

For long, rational thinking as well as scientific anthropology has reduced the human to the biological and classified it along with other organisms. But we are not just humans, rather we are human *beings*, and the human is distinguished from the mere organism by the fact that their being is pointed to the what-is, or toward Being. The very nomenclature says so. The being of the human identifies itself, attains their being by being pointed to the original Mystery of being. This however does not mean that all beings are self-consciously beings in the above sense; it simply means that they have the potential of attaining fullness of that which is attested to by such pointing.

> What gives us food for thought we call thought-provoking. But what is thought-provoking not just occasionally, and not just in some given

[15] Ibid., p. 149. Further, Heidegger distinguishes an organism and a being thus: "Man can be conceived as an organism, and has been so conceived for a long time. Man so conceived is then ranked with plants and animals, regardless of whether we assume that rank order to show an evolution or classify the genera of organisms in some other way. Even when man is marked out as the rational living being, he is still seen in a way in which his character as an organism remains decisive—though biological phenomena, in the sense of animal and vegetable beings, may be subordinated to that rational and personal character of man which determines his life of the spirit. All anthropology continues to be dominated by the idea that man is an organism." Ibid., p. 148.

> limited respect, but rather gives food for thought inherently and hence from the start and always—is that which is thought-provoking per se. And what it gives us to think about, the gift it gives to us, is nothing less than itself—itself which calls on us to enter thought.[16]

Entry into thought is the self-knowledge of thought, which is the greatest gift that thought gives to itself. What provokes thought into putting the question to itself about a certain possibility of itself—about thinking itself—moving away from the usual inventory of images, semantic content, exercise of will, or modes of action? The engrossment with thought ontologically is a "rare thing." In other words, how does thought turn away from logistics and habitual preoccupation, making a 180 ° turn to face itself in the manner of an eyeball turning inward in its socket? To the reasonably alert mind, reality is confounding and one's own thinking contradictory.[17] In a novel exercise, thought awakens to its own erotic principle—ideal food for thought—and enters into contemplation to ask about that which appears normally impenetrable—itself.[18] What is most thought-provoking gives us this gift; rather it is a "gift" that it gives itself; for only by means of a non-instrumental, non-habituated, spontaneous gesture is such a thing possible. It is by means of a gift that thought reaches into its own nature to look into the question of thinking that frees life as a gift. Hence the realization of the status of gift is the important thing:

> This gift, which gives to us what is most thought-provoking, is the true endowment that keeps itself concealed in our essential nature... We *are capable* of thinking only insofar as we *are* endowed with what is most thought-provoking, gifted with what ever and always wants to be thought about.[19]

[16]Heidegger, *What Is Called Thinking*, p. 121.

[17]"I returned, and saw under the sun, that the race is not to the swift, nor the battle to the strong, neither yet bread to the wise, nor yet riches to men of understanding, nor yet favour to men of skill; but time and chance happeneth to them all." Ecclesiastes 9:11. The fact that the world is not logical in this simple and direct manner ought to alert the minimally watchful of a different order of things.

[18]In the *Symposium*, Plato suggests that eros is a *daimon* that can contribute to the understanding of truth, in helping us to participate in beauty as ideal form. It is in a related sense that the word is used here, and not in its usual understanding in literature or in psychology.

[19]Heidegger, *What Is Called Thinking*, p. 126.

Thought is capable of thinking only to the extent that it is ontologically furnished with what deserves to be thought about, which is its own inmost nature. Thought's own inmost nature provokes it to think about what is most worthwhile to think about, which is itself. The gift consists of the innate possibility of a sudden departure from content (semantic or verbal traffic), when thinking penetrates itself reflexively. A crude example might serve usefully: a ripple on the surface of a waterbody might appear to have content (water), but in reality it is only a pulse, different from content.

What does this have to do with the power of philosophy? Philosophical power or redemption, in this sense, consists in the fulfillment of the true potential of thought. It resides in a kind of philosophical bilingualism which is the simultaneous awareness of the inside and outside of thought, its content as well as structure. To recall, in its normal disposition, thought is directed at experience, using time as an apparently unlimited openness to a not-yet. But the thinking-thanking relation leads us to an unsuspected and fresh perspective, deepening the intuition regarding the primary nature of thought, and to the authentic demand placed on it. Through the following pages, the meaning of being underway will be found in the growing participatory awareness of all that was taken for granted and the minutiae of everyday consciousness that has been placed beyond the need for continuous close examination. It is hermeneutic because there is no once-for-all conclusion to be reached in the manner of logical or deductive propositions. It teaches us that thinking must be Janus-headed, facing simultaneously inward and outward, toward experience *and* origin. Why? Each posits a limit for the other: experience is put in perspective through the unity of the origin, that is, the origin emancipates experience from the danger of fragmentation and monadic isolation, and experience, in turn, allows the noble possibility of the entity to emerge.

But this also points to a disarticulation in the nucleus of continuity, for the imaginary center cannot entirely survive this two-headed necessity. The nucleus born of time is predicated upon a one-directional pseudo-continuity. The two-way necessity introduces a deep dissonance in the nucleus. It is the beginning of a deep deconstruction. The continuity founded in thankless thought—all thanking is a form of closure through *dis*-closure—is thus called into question. Besides,

> [the] gathering of recalling thought is not based on a human capacity, such as the capacity to remember and retain. All thinking that recalls what can be recalled in thought already lives in that gathering which beforehand has in its keeping and keeps hidden all that remains to be thought.[20]

Thinking-thanking relation is thus not an attribute or capacity of the societal "individual." It is *prior* to the individual. It is already given in thought as potential, kept in-gathered, to flower when conditions beckon. Redemptive thinking gives birth to a new image of thought that is ontologically appropriate, which is that in the very act of thinking we ***participate*** in primeval thought. Thinking does not originate in us; it is not *my* thought. This is a singularly important realization for it creates a viewing distance. It makes listening to the ancient stream that precedes us, of which we will have more to say later, key to further discovery. Besides, it introduces a vision of thinking that is beyond semantic content. Instrumental capacity to retain and recall, which is one part of thinking, may be individuated and associated with specific beings, but the facing-toward-origin that is encoded in the very possibility of thought is not necessarily individuated, that is, it is of the form of a transpersonal passage (as we will find in Schelling in the following chapter).

Unfortunately, the history of formal thought begins in the denial of this transpersonal element. Formal thought acquires its form in amnesia of its origin.

> In fact, the history of Western thought begins, not by thinking what is most thought-provoking, but by letting it remain forgotten...The beginning of Western thought is not the same as its origin. The beginning is, rather, the veil that conceals the origin—indeed an unavoidable veil. The origin keeps itself veiled in the beginning.[21]

The beginning itself is a departure from origin. For Plato, prior to birth, the soul is at the origin, in full self-knowledge. At organic birth, a veil is drawn, and thereafter, in epistemological terms, all knowledge

[20] Ibid., p. 150.

[21] Ibid., p. 152.

is a partial remembrance or recovery of what remains hidden in the origin.[22] It is possible that there is in the above quote an allusion to this Platonic theory and why Heidegger refers to the veil as "unavoidable." Nevertheless, the history of Western thought with its focus on formal systems is a movement away from phenomenologically looking back at the origin.[23] The "beginning" must not, therefore, be confused with the "origin." For Heidegger, the *beginning* of Western metaphysics connotes the reduction of the divine to the "God of the philosophers," and this is what he calls the onto-theological preoccupation throughout the different epochs of the history of metaphysics. The beginning "conceals the origin" because the theological abstraction stands in the way of actually looking back at the origin, even distracts us from the obligation of inquiring into the origin—the origin being what is most thought-provoking or what calls upon us to think in the first place.

We have to concede that until now we have not said anything positive or concrete about thinking or about redemptive thinking other than mostly in negative terms of what it is not, or at best, about the context of its (im)possibility. This is because the question of thinking has

[22]In *Phaedo*, Plato develops his theory of *anamnesis*, in part by combining it with his theory of Ideal Forms. First, he elaborates how *anamnesis* can be achieved: in *Phaedo* Plato presents a way of living that would enable one to overcome the misleading nature of the body through *katharsis* (Greek: κάθαρσις; "cleansing" (from guilt or defilement), "purification"). The body and its senses are the source of error; knowledge can only be regained through the use of our reason, contemplating things with the soul (*noesis*). Secondly, he makes clear that genuine knowledge, as opposed to mere true belief (*doxa*), is distinguished by its content. One can only know eternal truths, for they are the only truths that can have been in the soul from eternity. Plato, *The Collected Dialogues of Plato*, Bollingen Series LXXI (Princeton: Princeton University Press, 2005).

[23]Heidegger: "If we recollect the history of Western–European thinking once more, then we will encounter the following: The question of being, as the question of the being of entities, is double in form. On the one hand, it asks: What is an entity in general as an entity? In the history of philosophy, reflections which fall within the domain of this question acquire the title ontology. The question "What is an entity?" [or "What is that which is?"] simultaneously asks: Which entity is the highest [or supreme, *hochste*] entity, and in what sense is it? This is the question of God and of the divine. We call the domain of this question theology. This duality in the question of the being of entities can be united under the title ontotheology," cited in Iain Thomson, *Heidegger on Ontotheology: Technology and the Politics of Education* (Cambridge, UK: Cambridge University Press, 2005), p. 13.

to be problematized in a full-fledged manner and cannot be disposed of quickly. Moreover, we have to understand at this juncture and even more widely what thinking as understood here does not and cannot accomplish. Heidegger is blunt in pointing this out:

> Thinking—more precisely, the attempts and the duty to think—is now approaching an era when the high demands which traditional thinking believed it was meeting, and pretended it had to meet, become untenable. The way of the question "What is called thinking?" lies even now in the shadow of this weakness. The weakness can be described in four statements:
>
> 1. Thinking does not bring knowledge as do the sciences.
> 2. Thinking does not produce usable practical wisdom.
> 3. Thinking solves no cosmic riddles.
> 4. Thinking does not endow us directly with the power to act.[24]

This helps us to say in uncompromising manner what is *not* power of philosophy as construed here. Let us meditate on the first statement: thinking does not bring knowledge. This appears to be counter-intuitive, but thinking must not be confused with knowledge generation or the production of epistemic culture. Science doubtless brings knowledge (in the selection and arrangement of facts), but as we have seen, the foundation of science is grounded in metaphysics; it cannot be otherwise. And metaphysics, in turn, has become seriously limited since it is not facing toward origin. If we hold philosophical bilingualism as the primary obligation of thinking, then by that criteria science does not think. For similar reasons, other sources of human knowledge are not able to think as metaphysics itself is barred from thinking. Next let us turn to the second assertion: thinking does not produce practical wisdom. Thinking as it is being conceived here is not geared toward solving everyday problems. Rather it is directed at throwing light on that medium in which problem formation occurs in the first place. Thought in its capacity to be used as a tool for action or directed upon experience gives rise to practical wisdom. But redemptive thinking is not to be directed upon experience. It seeks, instead, its own ontological ground.

[24]Heidegger, *What Is Called Thinking*, p. 159.

The third statement says thinking does not solve cosmic riddles. Riddles do not arise by and of themselves; they are framed within a cosmological framework whose foundations are in metaphysics. In other words, something presents itself to the sensibilities as a riddle because the logic of the system is not yet able to reconcile the various parts. This effort at reconciliation may form part of thinking in its fragmentary outward movement but plays no part in its looking back toward the origin. And finally, consider the last proposition: thinking does not endow us directly with the power to act. Civilization's incessant activities and technological business demands of thought powers of action. Yet, the obligation to think supersedes all the cravings for new powers to act that are demanded of thought. The technologization of being and thinking does not truly reveal the power of thinking but conceals it even in revealing.[25] That is to say, the exteriorization of thought as technology and as technical power to act is in the ultimate sense a withholding, and never a final revealing. Thought's redemption remains in looking into itself, into its own origin and self-nature, and for this it needs to free itself from ceaseless outer action.

The idea of thinking as somehow related to logistics goes all the way back to the Greeks who saw its essential character as *logos*. But, at the same time, the Greeks were not unaware of the profound ambiguity in the vital sources of thinking, and so why did it turn out that the determination of the essence of thinking came to be placed in the *logos*?

> [The] one and only thing that is decisive for what even still for us constitutes the basic character of thinking—the λέγειν of the λόγος, the

[25] "In an important later work, 'the Memorial Address' (1955), Heidegger seeks to take his audience performatively through a "turning" whereby they come to recognize that although technology is ubiquitous, its meaning remains mysterious. He believes recognizing that the ontological impact of technology remains concealed even though our worlds are saturated with technological devices, and thus that *technology reveals itself in a way that conceals its meaning*, helps facilitate the crucial insight that enframing *is* the way "being as such" reveals itself for us—viz., by "concealing" or "withholding" itself (as we noted with respect to his analysis of "earth"). "Where the danger is, the saving power also grows," then, because that which makes possible our technological understanding of being—and every other understanding of being (without being exhausted by these successive understandings of the being of entities)—is a pretheoretical source of intelligibility which simultaneously elicits and defies full conceptualization, a "mystery" which, Heidegger thinks is key to understanding ourselves otherwise than in the terms established by enframing's reductive ontotheology." Thomson, op. cit. p. 74, footnote 57.

> proposition, the judgment—is that call by which thinking has been called, and is still being called, into its long-habituated nature... What is it that destines our nature to think according to the λόγος, that directs it there, and there turns it to use?...The doctrine of thinking is called logic because thinking develops in the λέγειν of the λόγος. We are barely capable of comprehending that at one time this was not so, that a calling became "needful" in order to set thinking on the way of the λόγος into the λέγειν.[26]

Logos has been reduced to one aspect only. The contemplation of being is fullness of the logos. But thinking takes birth in the verb λέγειν of the λόγος, in a move that is already a movement away from being. A fallenness is suggested. Heidegger's assertion brings to mind Parmenides who says that "One should both say and think that Being is." If we merely *say* that Being is, then thinking slips from its true calling and develops into the *logistikon* (becomes a worldly instrument). In other words, repetition in language is not the actuality of being; it is entry into the domain of use or instrumentality. This is the proposition or "judgment" form of thought as Heidegger puts it, suggesting a worldliness into which thinking has long settled and become habituated; so much so, that today it has become almost impossible for us to think that thought might have a different calling.

But none of this can be established historically, in the sense of determining a precise historical moment of its occurrence when thinking began to be considered in a certain way. In fact, although it is a historic question, to consider it historically itself maybe a philosophical blunder.

> The more completely our thinking regards itself merely in terms of its own comparative written history, and historical in *this* sense, the more decisively it will petrify in fatelessness, and the less it will arrive at the artless, fateful relation to the calling by which thinking has been directed to the basic character of the λόγος...Our age rages in a mad steadily growing craving to conceive history in terms of universal history, as an occurrence.[27]

[26] Heidegger, *What Is Called Thinking*, p. 164.

[27] Ibid., p. 166. This and the paragraphs immediately preceding and succeeding directly contradict Iain Thomson's assertion that "Heidegger did not believe that our technological understanding of being could be transcended through a phenomenological practice disconnected from sociohistorical reality." Thomson, op. cit., p. 74. Heidegger puts his faith in the deepest questioning of thinking, which is definitely phenomenological practice, and one that is unconnected with the sociohistorical.

There can be no history of Being, or the turn away from Being; it is not to be fixed in time, for it runs parallel to time itself. In a sense, time itself is the product of the turn. To temporalize it is to lose the sense of destiny in which it is implicated. The Greeks distinguished between *Chronos* and *Aion*. *Chronos* is the temporality of the ontic or the particulars of finitude. It is to the latter that being belongs. The preoccupation with historicizing and constructing universal history is a mark of the present age. There is an overwhelming sense that if we put together all the varied histories, from the Mongols to the Mayans, from the Assyrians to the Aztecs, we will get a complete anthropological picture of the world. In actuality, this world or universal history creates its own object, meaning that it generates its own object of study. It does not reveal anything about the true significance of the world or its destiny. All the world-historic "voyages" with which the present age is obsessed will not disclose to us the nature of thinking, its origin, or why we are called upon to think in the first place.

Instead it is in the trans-historical reflection on the question 'what calls on us to think' that we may understand our "essential mission," that is, the true mission at the origin of thought. From here we take the cue to develop the other mode of thinking—outward and simultaneously facing toward origin—necessary for the integral freedom that we intuitively seek and for which we turn to philosophy.[28]

> The way of thinking cannot be traced from somewhere to somewhere like a well-worn rut, nor does it exist as such in any place. Only when we walk it, and in no other fashion, only, that is, by thoughtful questioning, are we on the move on the way. This movement is what allows the way to come forward....Thinking clears its way only by its own questioning advance. But this clearing of the way is curious. The way that is cleared does not remain behind, but is built into the next step, and is projected forward from it.[29]

[28] It must be made clear that redemptive thinking as an active possibility is not specifically found in Heidegger. Rather Heidegger offers the notion of "enigmatic solitude." This solitude is not something solipsistic or sentimental but a getting underway in order to open ourselves to the aloneness of being. For the praxis of philosophical bilingualism, the author must look beyond Heidegger and to elements in Schelling and Goethe that are to follow in subsequent discussions.

[29] Ibid., pp. 169–170, text rearranged.

There is no pre-existent way; rather the attention to the way itself opens the way. Attentive questioning keeps us on the move and it is only when we are on the move that the way comes forward to meet us. The phenomenological attitude of careful search clears the way forward, but the clearing is not left behind as some cleared path, but taken forward into the next step progressively, hermeneutically. Such is the *pathless land* of hermeneutic thinking. One cannot see the next step until one has taken the preceding step, and so on. When we get thus involved with thinking, we are not formulating ideas or indulging in concepts, but simply being underway with only the question with which we set out as our way forward. This is also not about looking for quick solutions that we seek today; in fact, in this kind of inquiry there are no answers in the conventional sense. *We are* part of the "answer" inasmuch as we are part of the question; in other words, our becoming in the way is the "answer" if at all such a term is applicable here. Here the reader must be invited to make a special effort to leave aside the traditional mode of intellectual inquiry wherein the inquirer remains distinct from the act of inquiry more or less in the manner of an outsider looking in. Here the outside is the inside, and the inside the outside. Once we are underway, the line between inquirer and inquiry gets blurred, since it is thinking that is looking into itself, a peculiar phenomenon distinct from the habitual situation of thought thinking about the world.[30]

When we call upon ourselves in this manner, that is, call upon ourselves to take heed and wonder about getting under the skin of thought, it shows up in three ways:

> One which thinking must go before all other ways; one to which thinking must also pay heed as it proceeds; and one which remains impassable to thinking. The calling calls thinking to the crossroads of way, no way, and wrong way. But the way of thinking is of such a kind that this crossroads can never be crossed by a once-for-all decision and choice of way, and

[30] "Today, when we know much too much and form opinions much too quickly, when we compute and pigeonhole everything in a flash—today there is no room at all left for the hope that the presentation of a matter might in itself be powerful enough to set in motion any fellow-thinking which, prompted by the showing of the matter, would join us on our way." Ibid., p. 171. Hence there is the need for invitation to participate and take steps in the way of the inquiry.

> the way can never be put behind as once-for-all behind us. The crossroad accompanies us on the way, every moment.[31]

The emergent path before us reveals a strange intersection of a triple necessity—the necessity of traversing a *choiceless* path, of considering the path itself as the *destination*, and of acknowledging the presence of the *Unthinkable,* or the limits of thought, or that which cannot be pulled into the domain of thinking as it has operated thus far. This intersection can never be put behind us once and for all, as having been dealt with, but instead it accompanies us each moment that we are underway. We learn here the most important lesson about what it means phenomenologically to be thinking. Each moment becomes independent of all the other has-beens; there is no carryover, since memory as recall is of no use in the disclosure of the living present. To put it differently, contrary to the cumulative character of epistemic or representative knowledge, there is no accumulation, and yesterday's insight is not today's wisdom.

Moreover, none are exempt—the writer, reader or anyone else in the dialogue—from inquiring *directly* into the problem of what it means to carry the obligation to think phenomenologically each moment. Putting philosophy to work here makes it incumbent on each one to participate in some degree, and experiment with all that has been thrown up in the present discussion. Only then there is a deep dialogue that takes us progressively away from our existing image of thought; otherwise, the inquiry degenerates into a mere reading or "conversation." With regard to this distinction, Heidegger notes:

> Every interpretation is a dialogue with the work, and with the saying. However, every dialogue becomes halting and fruitless if it confines itself obdurately to nothing but what is directly said—rather than that the speakers in the dialogue involve each other in *that* realm and abode about which they are speaking, and lead each other to it. Such involvement is the soul of dialogue. It leads the speakers into the unspoken. Each conversation is a kind of dialogue. But true dialogue is never a conversation. Conversation consists of slithering along the edges of the subject matter, precisely without getting involved in the unspoken.[32]

[31] Ibid., p. 175.
[32] Ibid., p. 178.

The hermeneutic path is essentially a continuous dialogue that is concerned not merely with the *said*, but thrusts itself against the *unsaid*, the unspoken, in attempting to reach the Unthought. To remain confined within the spokenness does not amount to a true dialogue. Whereas conversation nibbles at the outer edge of the issue, remaining merely at the verbal level, the task of dialogue is to lead us beyond the bounds and confines of existing frameworks of thinking whose parameters have been set up culturally through habit. Besides, in a dialogue we learn to use words with great care breaking them out of their daily routine use that has numbed their reach and meaning. To draw an example from Sanskrit, the principal language of Indian philosophy, the *ṣabdá* or "utterance" has a primordial resonance of its own even before attribution of meaning. Spoken correctly, the *ṣabdá* emanates a characteristic quality (as in the chant) that is its own redeeming power. With sensitivity and focus we attempt to recover the inner "radiance" that once accompanied and illumined the spoken word. This happens once we enter into the language of thinking, that is, the language in which thinking needs to be thought, as distinct from thinking about things.

Besides, it is to be noted that this kind of dialogue is not just a matter of interest. There is plenty of casual interest in philosophy within the ambit of what modern man understands as interesting. The present interest is not of that order.

> Interest, *interesse*, means to be among and in the midst of things, or to be at the center of a thing and to stay with it. But today's interest accepts as valid only what is interesting. And interesting is the sort of thing that can freely be regarded as indifferent the next moment, and be displaced by something else, which then concerns us just as little as what went before.[33]

Things appear as interesting only to be displaced by something more current, more exciting or impactful. Interest is thus confused with what is interesting or that which holds attention for a time. Interesting-ness is measured on a comparative scale that ranks what is more or less interesting or what is no longer interesting. Thus the representational content of thought is always undergoing assessment in terms of what is worth keeping in view and what may be discarded. In this manner modern man keeps with the times. But the preoccupation with the content of

[33] Ibid., p. 5.

thought, as we have seen earlier, is not the indication of thinking as it is being construed here. Redemptive thought is not a passing interest nor a movement from topic to topic along with the shift in intellectual fashion or cultural preoccupation. It could be imagined as a lifelong passion of thought. This question of thinking and what it means to think has not changed at all from antiquity.

And thus again, Heidegger returns hermeneutically to assert that we have not even begun to think, and it is possible that man has acted too much on every whim of thought but thought too little about thinking itself.

> What is thought-provoking, what gives us to think, is then not anything that we determine, not anything that only we are instituting, only we are proposing. According to our assertion, what of itself gives us most to think about, what is most thought-provoking, is this—that we are still not thinking. This now means: we have still not come face to face, have not yet come under the sway of what intrinsically desires to be thought about in an essential sense. Presumably the reason is that we human beings do not yet sufficiently reach out and turn toward what desires to be thought.[34]

What is most interesting is that despite the antiquity of the problem we have still not begun to think, that is, not begun to seriously interrogate thought itself. It would seem to be the most obvious thing to do, but it has not been done, in general. For example, there is no remote hint of this in the social endeavor that goes by the name of education. In other words, the essence of thinking is still out of our grasp. Is it the case then that it is a matter of human tardiness and that this situation can be remedied by taking appropriate steps? Heidegger answers in the negative and says that the fact that we are still not thinking is not only because "man does not yet turn sufficiently toward that which, by origin and innately, wants to be thought about…[but] rather stems from the fact that the thing itself that must be thought about turns away from man, has turned away long ago."[35] A certain intrinsic quality that illumined thought-at-origin, cast its glow on the word, has remained turned away, and hence thought, in terms of *legein*, flounders in darkness. But being is not a positivity, that is, an ontological entity, nor some *theos*, that can

[34] Ibid., p. 7.

[35] Ibid.

abandon or turn away. That would be contrary to all that has been said. So what is this turning away? Being is not a positivity; nor is it a negativity. To a conditioned finitude (an ontic activity/entity) this is painful, since it is habituated to the exclusivity of presence or absence. It is not attuned to an in-between, to a simultaneous non-this and non-that. This in-between non-substantiality "turns away" in the sense that the eros of pure suffering no longer comes to our aid. This creates the paradoxical situation that we can have the profoundest of thoughts and yet remain out of contact with the essence of thought, which is not thought at all in the sense of image or representation. Besides, this turning away is not a historical event, meaning that it cannot be located in time; it cannot be fixed historically. Rather it has always been so in a general way. The essence always remains turned away until a specific attempt is made to awaken to it, to "light the lamp," again as it were.[36]

What does it mean to "awaken" to it? It means that there is no incremental "bridge" to redemptive thinking, but one must "leap" into it. There is an unbridgeable hiatus between all that humans consider as thinking and what is being considered here as the essence of thinking. Therefore the most important thing we can do from the point of view of praxis is to "radically unlearn" what we have become accustomed to consider as thinking. To be underway, one must drop the image of thought that we have so long harbored. The essence of thinking, in its very withdrawal, draws us toward itself. "Our essential nature already bears the stamp" of this withdrawal. We are (unknowingly) drawn toward this immense phenomenon of withdrawal. We become a pointer or a sign of that profound withdrawal. In a sense human existence is nothing but a void that "points towards what withdraws."[37] This might sound mystical or mythological in its sweep and tone. But the opposition between mythos and logos itself is part of the fallen-ness or turning away of the essence.

> The *mythos* is that appeal of foremost and radical concern to all human beings which makes man think of what appears, what is in being. *Logos* says the same; *mythos* and *logos* are not, as our current historians of philosophy

[36] "And the sin I impute to each frustrate ghost/ Is the Unlit lamp." Robert Browning, "The Statue and the Bust," *The Collected Poems of Robert Browning* (New York: A&L Books, 2011).

[37] Heidegger, *What Is Called Thinking*, p. 9.

> claim, placed into opposition by philosophy as such; on the contrary, the early Greek thinkers are precisely the ones to use *mythos* and *logos* in the same sense. *Mythos* and *logos* become separated and opposed only at the point where neither *mythos* nor *logos* can keep to its original nature. In Plato's work, this separation has already taken place. Historians and philologists, by virtue of a prejudice which modern rationalism adopted from Platonism, imagine that *mythos* was destroyed by *logos*. But nothing religious is ever destroyed by logic; it is destroyed only by the God's withdrawal.[38]

Part of the prejudice we have to give up as we get underway is the sharp distinction drawn in modern thought between *mythos* and *logos*, or between myth and reason. The distinction was not there in this form in early Greek thinking. *Mythos* could indicate speech and thought just as *logos* could. The distinction, if there was one, was in respect of temporal scale. *Mythos* was the "gathering of recollection" with reference to the origin or source of things, that is, something which necessarily kept the source in view. By letting ourselves become oblivious of the source events of cultures we become blind to the real nature of things of which we are a part. *Mythos* and *Logos* are thus, metaphorically, the anode and cathode of existence, the one becomes empty without the other. Modern rationalism's penchant for dismissing *mythos* and consequent amnesia is one reason why we are unable to read the sign that we are, that has been from the beginning, the sign that points to the withdrawal of the essence.

For this reason, although we are subjected to, and go through, certain forms of relatedness to the age in which we live, we are unable to determine what it is exactly that we are going through. We muddle along under the invisible patina of the peculiar prejudices of our time, long used to the shadows under which we labor.

> Neither the industrial workman nor the engineers, let alone the factory proprietor and least of all the state, can know at all where modern man "lives" when he stands in some relatedness or other to the machine… Neither Hegel nor Marx could know it yet, nor could they ask why their thinking, too, still had to move in the shadow of the essential nature of technology; and so they never achieved the freedom to grasp and adequately think about this nature. Important as the economic, social,

[38] Ibid., p. 10.

> political, moral, and even religious questions may be which are being discussed in connection with technological labor, none of them reach to the core of the matter. That matter keeps itself hidden in the still unthought nature of the way in which anything that is under the dominion of technology has any being at all. And that such matters have remained unthought is indeed first of all due to the fact that the will to action has overrun and crushed thought.[39]

The real picture is hidden from thought. The essence of technology is not technological as Heidegger repeatedly points out. Even the greats such as Hegel and Marx could not really decode the true nature of the technological age which had begun to assume dominion. Hegel attempted to think his way past thought by positing the World Spirit and offered the dialectical engine as the historical machine of emancipation. Marx directed thought toward uncovering the nature of the reductive and oppressive producibility of Capital and its resultant contradictions. Both took the forms of active thought for granted, and although their thinking was a strong response to the age, they could not transcend it or penetrate to the source. Today there is a lot of discussion about technology in cultural and political terms, but none of these succeed in reaching the core of the matter which still remains unthought. The excessive concern with action and the commodity relation has crushed all possibility of thinking; we no longer even look toward the unthought or retain an intimation about it. All discussion remains within the technological doability of things, and their efficacy or otherwise. The entire culture speaks with one voice; such is the absolute state of planetary technicity. There is "one-track" thinking that leaves no room for an altogether different kind of questioning.

At the same time, we must not imagine that a lofty or scornful dismissal of this one-track thinking and one-sidedness is all that is required of us to overcome its effects and escape the power of reductive homogeneity. "On the contrary, the point is to discern what weird, unearthly things are here in the making."[40] There is need to pay careful attention to the monstrosities that are under preparation in the name of technological progress, which are made to look harmless and quite acceptable for public consumption. We must carefully look at the manner of their

[39] Ibid., pp. 24–25.

[40] Ibid., p. 25.

naturalization and study the processes of mindlessness that are called upon to acculturate the social imaginary toward their accommodation. However, it would be an error to construe the present discussion as yet another negative appraisal of this era, a typical critique of the rationalist, technological age. Nor is the reference to what is thought-provoking to be grouped with those commonplaces that evoke the ordinary sense of the grave and worrisome.

> When we say "thought-provoking," we usually have in mind immediately something injurious, that is, negative. Accordingly, a statement that speaks of a thought-provoking time, and even of what is most thought-provoking in it, is from the start tuned in a negative key. It has in view only the adverse and somber traits of the age. It sticks exclusively to those phenomena that are good for nothing and promote every form of nothingness—the nihilistic phenomena. And it necessarily assumes that at the core of those phenomena there is a lack—according to our proposition, lack of thought.[41]

If we proceeded along the assumptions of lack we would be completely off the mark here, for what is being presented under the rubric of what-is-most thought-provoking is not another chorus about the "decline of the West" or "civilizational failure" or something of a similar tune. In fact what is being suggested is that we could be on our way to thinking, underway to the prospect of redemptive thought not as a concept or idea but as a revolution from within thought, which is not technological, judgmental, or propositional. Again, this must not be perceived in the spirit of new-ageist invitation to individual emancipation. Rather, the careful investigation of thought is a serious philosophical and multi-dimensional task that is not to be reduced to the individual or personal plane. The task is to develop an intuition within thought that balances the sensible with the intelligible. In other words, thinking has so far remained within the precincts of the sensible; it has now to unearth the meaning of *intelligencing the world*; intelligence is moved from the status of a noun to an action that is beyond the individual. This is neither easy nor impossible, neither hopeful nor hopeless, neither pessimistic nor optimistic. It simply is putting philosophy to work: the need for thinking to think thought and become thankful in the process.

[41] Ibid., p. 29.

To be sure there have been times when a rare and original warning has been sounded from within the depths of thinking that was not a mere assessment or condemnation of the age. Nietzsche issued such a philosophical cautionary to the world in the famous words: "The wasteland grows: woe to him who hides wastelands within."[42] At a time when no one doubted the grand narrative of the "Ascent of Man" and progress was the watchword of the Western nations Nietzsche struck the opposite note. Why? Nietzsche was thinking from within thought. He was not fooled by what thought was doing, or how effective it was, or what the civilizational glow was telling him. Neither was his intent in the opposite direction of being a prophet of repentance. Prophets foretell events in time but Nietzsche was not a prophet in that sense. Now after more than a century of wars, holocausts, and planetary destruction, one might look back and say Nietzsche was right. But Nietzsche was not foretelling of things to come, of events in chronological time, nor was he interpreting history. He would have been right *even if none of the above had occurred*, and societies had uniformly achieved high living standards by the usual measures. Right in the midst of reasonable prosperity and ascendance he was speaking of a desolation in thought that had nothing to do with the efficacy of thinking or the success of its translation into action. To understand Nietzsche, we have to make a special effort to distinguish between an insight into the structure of thinking, and sociopolitical criticism of the action of thought available in a bewildering variety of social chatter.

And what is of great concern is that the most thoughtful of thoughts is easily reduced to "platitudes," and spread and circulated as platitudes. "Script easily smothers the scream…The burden of thought is swallowed up in the written script, unless the writing is capable of remaining, even in the script itself, a progress of thinking, a way."[43] Writing redeems itself only if it is underway, in the discovery of what it means to think. Nietzsche, it seems, succeeded in writing such a piece of text:

> That written scream of Nietzsche's thought is the book which he entitled *Thus Spoke Zarathustra*. That work thinks this thinker's one and only thought: the thought of the eternal recurrence of the same. Every thinker thinks one only thought…The thinker needs one thought only. And for

[42] Friedrich Nietzsche, *Thus Spoke Zarathustra* (London: Penguin Classics, 1973), p. 33.

[43] Heidegger, *What Is Called Thinking*, p. 49.

> the thinker the difficulty is to hold fast to this one only thought as the one and only thing that he must think; to think this One as the Same; and to tell of this Same in a fitting manner. The limitlessness of the Same is the sharpest limit set to thinking. The thinker Nietzsche hints at this hidden fittingness of thought by giving his *Thus Spoke Zarathustra* a subtitle which runs: *A Book for Everyone and No One*. "For Everyone" means for each man each time his essential nature becomes for him an object worthy of his thought. "And No One"—that means: for none who merely intoxicate themselves with isolated fragments and passages from the book instead of getting underway on its way of thinking, and thus becoming first of all questionable to themselves.[44]

To each great thinker, may be attributed a single thought, as, for example, in *The Book of Kohelet* or Ecclesiastes: "Then I looked on all the works that my hands had wrought, and on the labour that I had laboured to do: and behold, all was vanity and vexation of spirit, and there was no profit under the sun."[45] Such is the singularity of the single thought that all phenomena unite under it for the thinker, and the thinker intuits each thing through this one and only thought. Again, from Ecclesiastes: "The thing that hath been, it is that which shall be; and that which is done is that which shall be done: and there is no new thing under the sun."[46] It is the Same. But this Same-ness is infinitude. We return again and again to the inner core of that single thought which is the Same, but that is also immeasurable sameness. Thinking opens out to its internal infinitude that has nothing to do with the multiplicity or homogeneity of content. The singularity of the single thought, its effulgence radiates limitlessly. What does this mean, is it not a hyperbolic claim? Singularities contain essence; the collapse of thought as representation gives rise to singularity. The power of thought becomes concentrated in the singularity. But the meaning of this will become clearer when we discuss Heraclitus.

In Nietzsche that single thought occurs in his notion of the Eternal Return or the eternal recurrence of the same.[47] Thought might leave its

[44] Ibid., p. 50.

[45] Ecclesiastes 2:11.

[46] Ecclesiastes 1:9.

[47] Nietzsche writes: "What, if some day or night a demon were to steal after you into your loneliest loneliness and say to you: 'This life as you now live it and have lived it, you will have to live once more and innumerable times more; and there will be nothing new in it, but every pain and every joy and every thought and sigh and everything

moorings, its inner self-nature momentarily in order to accomplish something but must return to its ontological core, which is ever the same. The limitlessness of the same is the sharpest challenge to thinking as also the harshest reminder of its limits. It demonstrates to thought the philosophical futility of constantly seeking new inspirations; all of existence, despite the apparent newness and variety under the sun, is always the same. This sameness is not the staleness of death but the endless creation of the living present that lies hidden in the innermost core of thought. But as the representational content muddles along seeking newness and novelty, thinking cannot turn to its own core, its own essential nature that remains the Same, thus remaining oblivious of it.

No philosophical formula or principle can capture this strange *noesis* of the Same. Thus when Nietzsche speaks, lodged in the within-of-thought, the writing appears full of ambiguities and confounding turns. And that is because we are still trying to understand the content of his thought and not really thinking with thought, as Heidegger puts it.

> Did Nietzsche know that through him something was put into words that can never be lost again? Something that cannot be lost again to thinking, something to which thinking must forever come back again and again the more thoughtful it becomes? He knew it...Let us not be deluded into the view that Nietzsche's thought has been found, just because there exists a Nietzsche literature that has been proliferating. It is as though Nietzsche had foreseen this; it is not for nothing he has Zarathustra say: "They all talk about me...but nobody gives me a thought." Thought can be given only where there is thinking...And Nietzsche's thought? Part of what is thought-provoking is that Nietzsche's thought has still not been found.[48]

Nietzsche's thought marks a transition in Western metaphysical thinking. It appears almost as though all of metaphysics until that point was bunched

unutterably small or great in your life will have to return to you, all in the same succession and sequence - even this spider and this moonlight between the trees, and even this moment and I myself. The eternal hourglass of existence is turned upside down again and again, and you with it, speck of dust!' Would you not throw yourself down and gnash your teeth and curse the demon who spoke thus?... Or how well disposed would you have to become to yourself and to life than this ultimate eternal confirmation and seal?" Friedrich Nietzsche, *The Gay Science*, trans. Walter Kaufmann (New York: Vintage, 1974), s. 341.

[48] Heidegger, *What Is Called Thinking*, pp. 53–54.

up at one end, and Nietzsche's thought was at the opposite end. Until that point traditional metaphysics had speculated on the nature of action, cognition, the foundations of moral judgment, and so on. Nietzsche, on the other hand, turns to the essence of idea forming, that is, to the very basis of our thinking itself and shows it to be uncomprehending of itself. That is to say, thinking, even at the highest level, was blind to its self-nature. Further, we must not be deluded by the fact that there is a mountain of Nietzsche literature today; it does not mean Nietzsche's thought has been found. For to find Nietzsche's thought also means knowing how to lose it again.[49] Nietzsche's thought, or rather, the real essence of his observations attempt to throw us back on the very conditions of the arising of thinking in each. But when we think we have found Nietzsche, we have merely succeeded in making his thought into another icon in memory, and not in churning our lives with the active philosophy therein. Hence the need to "lose" Nietzsche the moment we have "found" him. For otherwise we are no longer thinking. The very knowledge becomes an obstruction to self-observation. Each moment we have to be prepared to give up or lose what was found in the previous moment and return to the origin. Redemptive thinking must learn to lose what it has found and return to the essence.

Thus we come to the necessity of a human nature that can look beyond itself. Conventional man adheres with great obstinacy to the trivial surface of thinking and consequently to his own superficial nature. This would not matter so much if man had remained primitive in terms of the powers he wields. But his powers have grown enormously in terms of what thought can do and achieve outwardly. Man has begun to dominate the earth in an unprecedented manner. It is clear from Nietzsche's writing that he does not think that man is in any way ready to "assume dominion of the earth as a whole."

> Man so far is incapable of it, because he has not yet come into his own full nature. Nietzsche declares that man's essential nature is not yet determined—it has neither been found nor been secured. That is why Nietzsche says: "Man is the as yet undetermined animal." For Nietzsche neither man's physical, sensual side, nor man's non-sensual side—his reason, have been adequately conceived in their essential nature…In order to determine the nature of man so far, man as he has been must first of all be carried

[49] To his friend Georg Brandes, Nietzsche had written: "After you had discovered me… the difficulty is now to lose me." Cited in Heidegger, *What Is Called Thinking*, p. 53.

> beyond himself. Man so far has been not able or unwilling to subject himself to himself, and to despise what is despicable in his kind as it is so far. This is why a passage beyond himself must be sought for man as he is so far, why the bridge must be found to that nature by which man can overcome his former nature, his last nature. Nietzsche envisaged this nature and kind of self-overcoming man…[50]

Nietzsche calls such a figure the "*Ubermensch*." The translation of the term *Ubermensch* in *Zarathustra* is widely and often given in the English literature as "superman." However, such a translation is not only literally inaccurate but easily misconstrued. Superman seems to indicate a larger-than-life, super-dimensional will and power of action, something that is very far from what Nietzsche had intended. Instead, the key idea of self-overcoming contained in *Zarathustra* is better carried by the term 'overman,' which is literally more accurate. It refers to the man who passes over his former state into a completely new state of being. The overman is "qualitatively, not quantitatively, different from existing man," points out Heidegger.[51] Moreover, the overman is no specific person, but a trans-individual tendency-toward-emancipation that can manifest in anyone, at any time.

But what does the overman pass over and how did Nietzsche indicate the site of that passage? Nietzsche speaks of the "last man" or the man who lives in amnesia concerned only with what is immediately available and seizes upon what manifests itself easily in front of him.

> And thus spoke Zarathustra to the people: Alas, the time is coming when man will no longer shoot the arrow of his longing beyond man…Alas, the time of the most despicable man is coming, he that is no longer able to despise himself. Behold, I show you the last man. 'What is love? What is creation? What is longing? What is a star?—thus asks the last man, and he blinks. The earth has become smaller, and on it hops the last man who makes everything small. His race is as ineradicable as the flea-beetle, the last man lives longest. 'We have invented happiness'—say the last men, and they blink.[52]

[50] Ibid., p. 59.

[51] Ibid., p. 69. Further, Heidegger adds, "The thing that the [overman] discards is precisely our boundless, purely quantitative, nonstop progress. The overman is poorer, simpler, tenderer and tougher, quieter and more self-sacrificing and slower of decision, and more economical of speech." And "The [overman] constitutes a transformation and thus a rejection of man so far."

[52] Nietzsche cited in Heidegger, *What Is Called Thinking*, p. 64.

The site of passage is the 'last man.' The last man has no longing for anything beyond his own creations. He has forgotten to subject himself to himself, the sign of true rationality. Instead of being the rational animal that he was supposed to be he has become a rational vegetable. He no longer knows what love is, what creation is, or the true meaning of desire. He has made survival his main goal and so lasts the longest, that is, until this hour. The last men believe they have invented happiness by surrounding themselves with things and concepts of thought, even as "the wasteland grows" and the world slips out of grasp. Each of the above is an unexaggerated description of the state of modern man. He truly believes he has invented happiness. He believes he controls planetary technicity and it will ultimately contribute to the destiny he seeks. All problems are seen as procedural and circumstantial, more due to implementational issues than anything fundamental. Modern man believes that there is nothing fundamentally problematic about him that cannot be ironed out with a dose of psychoanalysis, economic upturn, a crash course in stress reduction, or even a visit to the spa. His real problem is death; for he does not believe in dying, and he does everything possible not to die. But that is not the reason why he lasts longest. He lasts because his is a deferred existence; he must continue till the overman can make its appearance among him and in him.

What lies behind this state of affairs? For a long time now, and ever since the Enlightenment, the belief has turned to particulars. A synthesis is attempted at various levels of diverse particulars that have presented and continue to present themselves to consciousness.

> [But] that which really is, Being, which from the start calls and determines all beings, can never be made out, however, by ascertaining facts, by appealing to particulars. That sound common sense which is so often "cited" in such attempts is not as sound and natural as it pretends. It is not above all as absolute as it acts, but rather the shallow product of that manner of forming ideas which is the final fruit of the Enlightenment in the eighteenth century. Sound common sense is always trimmed to fit a certain conception of what is and ought to be. The power of this curious understanding extends into our own age…the organizations of social life, the rearmament in moral matters, the grease paint of the cultural enterprise—none of them reach the *what is*. With all the good intentions and all the ceaseless effort, these attempts are no more than makeshift

> patchwork, expedients of the moment. And why? Because the ideas of aims, purposes, and means, of effects and causes, from which all those attempts arise are from the start incapable of holding themselves open to what is.[53]

The synthesis of particulars, attempted conceptually and heroically by Kant in his *Critiques*, and culturally by our social, economic, and political leaders fail precisely because *what is* is not to be reached empirically or synthetically.[54] We call ourselves human *beings*, but the being is not the patchwork of the contingent and the accidental; it *is* from the beginning and still *is*, and will be, after we are gone. Somewhere along the way thought entered into amnesia with regard to this basic fact. In its place it creates what is called common sense—a curious blend of power and prejudice mixed with certain practical realizations. This amalgam produces social realizations within particular forms of collective living that is largely its own product and which it considers as absolute. For all who grow up surrounded by this conventional absolutism, they no longer have the space to realize that *thinking is not responding to what is* but to its own selections and formulations which it has exteriorized and projected. The power of this absolutism has been able to make even philosophy renounce its true vocation which is the search for living wisdom.

A corollary is that the institutions with which we have surrounded ourselves, and in which we have invested great faith, also fail to respond to the Real. This has great implications for redemptive thinking. Heidegger quotes Nietzsche:

> Our institutions are good for nothing any more. However it is not their fault but *ours*. Now that we have mislaid all the instincts from which institutions grow, we lose institutions altogether because *we* are no longer good for them…The whole West no longer possesses those instincts out of which institutions grow, out of which a future grows: nothing else,

[53] Ibid., p. 66.

[54] For Kant, the question of Being had to be left out of the consideration as it was outside the domain of the sensibilities, that is, not realizable. But for Nietzsche "Caesar with the soul of Christ" [in a note to Zarathustra] was a human possibility and a distinct imagery of the overman. The crucial difference is that Kant was working within the image of thought available to him whereas Nietzsche rejected the limits posed by the existing beliefs of thinking about itself.

> perhaps, goes so much against the grain of its 'modern spirit.' Men live for the day, men live very fast—men live very irresponsibly: precisely this is called 'freedom.'[55]

The "instincts" from which reliable institutions grow, which link generations forward and backward, are the dialectical spillovers from a certain will-to-tradition in which traditions are confronted by change. These instincts are not playthings but underlying deep continuities that have power of endurance. It is a slow turning over of life that is involved in the contemplation of these instincts. But modern man is impatient; his obsession is with velocity and the speed of turnover. Instincts do not survive this obsession with speed. Therefore modern man finds himself constantly taking decisions about the unfamiliar often with disastrous consequences that come to be realized later. Thought has no patience to let instinct catch up. Thought goes ahead without the restraint of instinct, which is the background sense of origin. Modern man is in a hurry to get to "erehwon," and in his panicked urgency he has no time for developing the ability to respond to what is. Unfortunately, this unmooring, or dis-anchoring from deeper instinct, has come to be mistaken for freedom. But the overman is not dead; it is eternally hidden within thought, waiting to be realized. The seed of the overman does not appear all of a sudden in consciousness, but is present as potentiality at the very origin, and remains as a possibility each moment. This possibility of turning to the seed or essence again and again is part of the hermeneutics necessary for development of philosophical bilingualism.

Summary

Thinking, because we are born into it, does not appear as anything out of the ordinary. But when we pay attention to it, the possibility and phenomenon of thought appears stranger and stranger. That which is most familiar now looks inexplicable. And when we directly begin to contemplate this strange thing called thinking, by means of which each one unreflectively achieves their daily ends, a new dimension opens up before us which has no proper language in thought. In meditating on thinking, we can only be underway, as Heidegger puts it, and not arrive at quick or facile conclusions. Thought has inquired into phenomena, but has rarely

[55] Ibid., pp. 67–68.

inquired into itself. There is no ready path of inquiry to be followed but that of careful questioning and observing.

Keeping Heidegger's reflections as the key contemplative, we have looked into the reasons why it becomes necessary, and the conditions under which it becomes possible, for thinking to contemplate its self-nature. We began with the question: 'How does thinking even begin to suspect the possibility of inquiring into itself?' Of course, thinking does no such thing. What thrusts itself upon thought instead is pain and suffering born of mento-emotive activity: suffering due to the conflict and contradiction between the sensual on one part and rationality on the other, the two apparent halves of the human. Man remains caught between these two parts of his being that are neither fully realized nor brought together on one plane. To turn and face the origin therefore, we have to first understand and become aware of the volume of inner verbal and representational traffic that also tends to reduce language to its lowest form. The resultant slowing down is key to the mysterious process related to the development of proper reference points and angle of viewing for self-inquiry. Careful use of language contributes to this inner slowing down. For instance, we realize with a shock that thinking is closely related to thanking, and that memory did not originally mean recollection or remembrance. So turning to the origin also enjoins upon us the need to examine words carefully to see what they reveal about the beginnings of thought. We also realize that thought or the capacity to think is a gift, an unrealized gift since it is unable to turn to the inmost source where it is realizable.

As we gradually, and with care, become distanced from the stream of content, we begin to participate in ancient thought, that is, in a certain movement that is not so caught up in time. As we recoil still further, we become Janus-headed, looking inward and outward at the same time. This is called philosophical bilingualism in these pages. There is the slow development of an "enigmatic solitude" within thinking that allows us to view thinking as something quite different from the logistics of modernity. We phenomenologically come upon that unbridgeable gap between all that humans consider as thinking and what is being considered here as the essence of thinking—the looking-toward-origin. Therefore one of the critical things we must do is to "radically unlearn" what we have become habituated to consider as thinking. There is no "bridge" to redemptive thinking, but one must "leap" into it. We come to realize that there is no pre-existent way to discovering redemptive thinking, but the attention to the task itself opens the way. Attentive questioning keeps us on the move and it is only when we are on the move that the way comes forward to meet us. The emergent path before us reveals a triple necessity—the necessity of traversing a *choiceless* path, of considering the path itself as the destination, and the presence of the ontological limits of thought that cannot be pulled into the domain of habitual thinking. As we move forward in our inquiry, each of these elements will be explored further. When our instincts are sufficiently developed we begin to intuit the infinite solitude at the core of that indeterminate transfinitude that can never be experienced as knowledge but only as phenomenological intensity.

References

Browning, Robert. *The Collected Poems of Robert Browning*. New York: A&L Books, 2011.

Ecclesiastes. *The Book of Koheleth*.

Heidegger, Martin. *Being and Time*. Translated by Joan Stambaugh. New York: SUNY Press, 1996.

Heidegger, Martin. *What Is Called Thinking*. Translated by Fred D. Wieck and J. Glenn Gray. New York: Harper and Row, 1968.

Nietzsche, Friedrich. *Thus Spoke Zarathustra*. London: Penguin Classics, 1973.

Nietzsche, Friedrich. *The Gay Science*. Translated by Walter Kaufmann. New York: Vintage, 1974.

Plato. *The Collected Dialogues of Plato*. Bollingen Series. Princeton: Princeton University Press, 2005.

Roubach, Michael. "Heidegger's Primordial Temporality and Other Notions of Time." In *Cosmological and Psychological Time*, edited by Yuval Dolev and Michael Roubach, 165–176. New York: Springer, Cham, 2016.

Thomson, Iain. *Heidegger on Ontotheology: Technology and the Politics of Education*. Cambridge, UK: Cambridge University Press, 2005.

CHAPTER 3

Schelling's Great Leap

If philosophy is to go beyond interpretation as well as its own history, and engage directly with the world as Marx had suggested, then it has to arouse consciousness "from its dream of itself," as Marx again put it in a letter to Arnold Ruge in 1843 to which I refer later in the book. What is this "dream" from which philosophy must arouse us? Philosophy cannot let us forget that a specific configuration of the world including the reflecting consciousness is not something in itself but a concatenation of effects retained as cultural sediment, and solidified over time, with its own peculiar understandings, categories, judgments, and oppositions. Rather than something sovereign or integral, thought-bred reality is a particular kind of limitation imposed upon the indeterminate Open or anarchic continuum in order to make things passable. Philosophy's task is to remind us again and again of this negation that lies within every situation, and help us shake out of cultural habits of thought and reality making. We cannot entrust this to some temporal progression or self-realized historical process. Rather, such a praxis must be prepared to "philosophize with a hammer" as Nietzsche put it, in order to try and free each lived instant from the tyranny of encrusted patterns of thinking. No true solution can be available within the existing frameworks of thinking—social, political, cultural—since the problem lies with the framework itself.

Philosophical bilingualism, or the radical rethinking of thought is more than a conceptual activity. It requires a phenomenological meltdown of the hard cultural separations such as subject/object, thinker/thought, experiencer/experience, and at the same time it requires

K. Roy, *The Power of Philosophy*,
https://doi.org/10.1007/978-3-319-96911-4_3

the hospitability to a new intuition of strangeness. We are pitched onto a ground of unfamiliarity in which we have to learn to perform self-consciousness differently. This requires a sublime mix of poesy and philosophy, and there is no thinker, to my mind, better placed than Friedrich Wilhelm Joseph von Schelling who can help us remain underway in this task. A contemporary of Fichte and Hegel, Schelling's main problem was the relation between mind and nature, or subject and object, and in response to this he offered a metaphysic of nature that was by far the boldest of philosophical statements of his time. From the point of view of the present exercise, Schelling's early work helps us understand self-consciousness, and glimpse beyond the usual opposition between thinker and thinking, an enigma closely bound with the problem of freedom with which we have to deal. Thought, it may verily be said, can only turn toward the origin once it overcomes the peculiar opposition within itself.

> Self-consciousness is the act whereby the thinker immediately becomes an object to himself....The ability to intuit oneself therein, to discriminate oneself as thinker and as thought, and in so discriminating, again to acknowledge oneself as identical [is necessary to understand transcendental Idealism]....Thus we have here that original identity of thought and object, appearance and reality, which is nowhere else to be found. The self simply *has no existence, prior* to that act whereby thinking becomes its own object, and is thus itself nothing other than thinking becoming its own object, and hence absolutely nothing apart from the thought.—That this identity remains hidden from so many, is due solely to the fact that they neither perform the act of self-consciousness in freedom, nor are able to reflect in so doing upon what arises therein.[1]

Schelling insists that "The *I* think, *I* am, is, since, Descartes, the basic mistake of all knowledge; thinking is not my thinking, and being is not my being..."[2] Well before Nietzsche, Schelling throws down the central

[1] F.W.J. Schelling, *System of Transcendental Idealism* (Charlottesville: University of Virginia Press, 1978/1800), p. 25.

[2] Schelling writes: "If all *knowing* has, as it were, two poles, which mutually presuppose and demand one another, they must seek each other in all the sciences; hence there must necessarily be *two* basic sciences, and it must be impossible to set out from the one pole without being driven toward the other. The necessary tendency of all *natural science* is thus to move from nature to intelligence. This and nothing else is at the bottom of the urge to bring *theory* into the phenomena of nature. – The highest consummation of natural science would be the complete spiritualising of all natural laws into laws of intuition and thought.

challenge to philosophy of determining the nature of the thinker by showing the untenable supposition implicit in the Cartesian position. But if the Cartesian position on the *cogito* is a philosophical error of great magnitude, what might be an adequate understanding of the relation between thinker and thinking? This question is addressed in the above quote, which offers the understanding that the self or thinker is nothing other than an action in thought. From an original unity, which must be presupposed, and which is unthinkable, there is a split between thinking and thinker in which thinking becomes its own object. In other words, the thinker or experiencer is nothing other than thinking objectified.

Why don't we perceive this fact directly as such? To this, Schelling answers that we do not "perform the act of self-consciousness in freedom." First, what does it mean to *perform* self-consciousness? The thinker or self is nothing other than a performance of thought, a reflexive act of presentation by itself, of itself, to itself. As the unknown substance pulses, it encounters some "other" (obstruction) and splits into thinker and thought rather in the manner of a bamboo that meets a splitter to split in two. But this performance is rarely, if ever, free. Thought is immediately bound by intentionality and direction that do not allow thinking to observe clearly what is going on. The content of thought imposes conditions and directionality nullifying the original freedom

The phenomena (the matter) must wholly disappear, and only the laws (the form) remain. Hence it is, that the more lawfulness emerges in nature itself, the more the husk disappears, the phenomena themselves become more mental, and at length vanish entirely. The phenomena of optics are nothing but a geometry whose lines are drawn by light, and this light itself is already of doubtful materiality. In the phenomena of magnetism all material traces are already disappearing, and in those of gravitation, which even scientists have thought it possible to conceive of merely as an immediate spiritual influence, nothing remains but its law, whose largescale execution is the mechanism of the heavenly motions. – The completed theory of nature would be that whereby the whole of nature was resolved into an intelligence. – The dead and unconscious products of nature are merely abortive attempts that she makes to reflect herself; inanimate nature so-called is actually as such an immature intelligence, so that in her phenomena the still unwitting character of intelligence is already peeping through. – Nature's highest goal, to become wholly an object to herself, is achieved only through the last and highest order of reflection, which is none other than man; or, more generally, it is what we call reason, whereby nature first completely returns into herself, and by which it becomes apparent that nature is identical from the first with what we recognise in ourselves as the intelligent and the conscious." Ibid., p. 6.

of the impulse; miracle is not in what we can think, but *that* we can think. But thought is quickly captured by the social element, and from that moment, the channels of the *socius* drives thinking. Consider these lines in Heidegger: "Everybody understands, "The sky is blue," "I am happy," and similar statements. But this average comprehensibility only demonstrates the incomprehensibility. It shows that an enigma lies *a priori* in every relation…"[3] Such commonplaces as in Heidegger's example above are widely shared, and we assume we know their meaning whenever we encounter them, which is perhaps many times each day. But on closer analysis of each such commonplace statement, there arises a wonder and a deeper incomprehensibility, as, for example, with regard to the location of the object (is the object inside the perceiving consciousness or outside?), with regard to the arising of response in the perceiver (in response to what trigger?), with regard to the possibility of naming and classifying, and so on. All of these questions cannot be answered without a careful analysis of the relation of the inside and the outside, or between subject and object (mind and nature) which Schelling helps us to do.

Heidegger has impressive words for Schelling: "Schelling is the truly creative and boldest thinker of this whole age of German philosophy. He is that to such an extent that he drives German Idealism from within right past its own fundamental position."[4] Moving backwards for us, thus, has its own advantage in the sense that it reveals the 'cave behind the cave' using Plato's metaphor. The enigma of thought has been from the beginning, and it is not as if the moderns know more about thinking itself than those before them did. Thought has gathered much, say, since the classical period, but it has become more impervious to itself during that time. However, the real forward-looking connections as we move backward in time will become apparent as we get deeper into the discussion.

In order to appreciate Schelling's theory of reflexivity and its central relation to our problem, we must acquire a rudimentary understanding

[3] Martin Heidegger, *Being and Time*, p. 13.

[4] Martin Heidegger, *Schelling's Treatise on the Essence of Human Freedom*, trans. Joan Stambaugh (Athens: Ohio University Press, 1985), p. 4. Even as we note Heidegger's appreciation of Schelling, it must be acknowledged at the same time that Heidegger was quite skeptical of Schelling's system building efforts in the manner of traditional philosophers. For the purposes of the present work, however, we can safely ignore those parts of Schelling's oeuvre that have those ambitions, and limit ourselves to the early insights to which continental philosophy owes so much.

of his metaphysical theory of nature and mind. For only then shall we be able to surmise the basis of his comprehensive rejection of Cartesianism together with the notion of pure subjectivity, and begin to appreciate the essentially non-dual cognitive world he inaugurates instead. But, before that, we must also take into account Schelling's exasperation with famous thinkers apart from Descartes and the reasons for it. Let us begin by looking at certain intriguing comments he makes against scientists such as Newton, Boyle, and others.

> After the blind and mindless type of natural research, which has generally established itself since the corruption of philosophy by Bacon and of physics by Boyle and Newton with the Philosophy of Nature, a higher knowledge of Nature begins...What distinguishes the Philosophy of Nature is that the latter concluded to the grounds from the phenomena, arranged causes according to effects, in order subsequently to derive the latter from the former. Apart from the everlasting circle in which those fruitless endeavors revolve, theories of this sort could still, even on reaching their peak, establish only a possibility that such is the case, but never the necessity.[5]

First, only a mind such as that of Schelling's could have dared to come out so strongly against some of the greatest thinkers in natural science without fearing for or jeopardizing his own reputation. But what precisely is his objection to raw empirical science? Schelling's objection, not surprisingly, is of a fundamental kind. When we examine the history of development of Western science we detect a gradual slide from natural philosophy to involvement only with phenomena that present themselves directly to consciousness. There is no longer any question about the ground in which phenomena arise, or their necessity, all of which begin to be regarded as speculative philosophy, and are shunted aside from the doing of "pure science." We are thus released into a world of phenomena without the noumenal consideration of the Being of beings.[6] In other words, there is a hiving off of the world of Being from the world of Action. The latter world is an unrestrained one because it is available to anyone without the necessary meditation on what phenomena ultimately mean in terms of *necessity*. Schelling objects

[5] F.W.J. von Schelling, *Ideas for a Philosophy of Nature* (Cambridge, UK: Cambridge University Press, 1988), pp. 52–53.

[6] Kant merely formalizes a viewpoint that has been in the making for a long time.

to this disregard of necessity and the consequent bestowing of all attention on contingency (empirical arising). He calls it "dissection" without the spiritual element.[7] The focus on contingent phenomena ultimately makes the "separation between man and the world *permanent*, because it treats the latter as a thing-in-itself, which neither intuition nor imagination, neither understanding nor reason, can reach."[8] Realizing the danger, Schelling's work attempts to bring together necessity and contingency on a unified plane. In order to do this Schelling clearly distinguishes ordinary cognition, and transcendental cognition or the plane of integration:

> Transcendental cognition would thus differ from ordinary cognition on two counts. *First*, that the certainty that external things exist is for it a mere prejudice, which it goes beyond, in order to discover the grounds thereof. (It can never be the transcendental philosopher's business to demonstrate the existence of things-in-themselves, but merely that it is a natural and necessary prejudice to assume that external objects are real.) *Second*, that it separates the two propositions, 'I exist,' and 'There are things outside me,' which in ordinary consciousness are fused together; setting the one before the other, precisely in order to prove their identity, and so that it can really exhibit the immediate connection which is otherwise merely felt. By this very act of separation, if complete, it shifts into the transcendental mode of apprehension, which is in no way natural, but artificial.[9]

There is no way to theoretically prove or disprove that there is a material reality outside of us. Such avowal can only be treated as a deep-seated prejudice (the commonsense one of immediate certainty), possibly a useful one, and one that we cannot perhaps do without. Taking up that prejudice as a starting point, Schelling attempts to sort the mixed bag of preconceptions that constitute 'common sense' by splitting it into

[7] Schelling, *Ideas for a Philosophy of Nature*, p. 11. Further, in a later page, Schelling notes: "I maintain, however, that we as little understand empirically a life *outside* us as we do a consciousness *inside* us, that neither the one nor the other is explicable from physical causes, that in this respect it is completely indifferent whether the body is regarded as an accidental aggregate of organized particles, or as a hydraulic machine, or as a chemical laboratory," ibid., p. 37.

[8] Ibid., p. 11.

[9] Schelling, *Transcendental Idealism*, pp. 8–9.

two artificial propositions above. Such analysis is attempted in order to prepare to ultimately transcend the preconceptions. For to comprehend truth, one must closely study falsehood; the search for redemption is really the nailing of untruth within the everyday habits of thought. The "transcendental mode of apprehension," a useful artifice, is introduced in the important step of sorting out thinking as it moves in the entrenched ways of habit. In being underway, we also learn about the phenomenological effort that must be directed at locating false composites, and the method of their separation, that may be ***negatively experienced*** as redemptive thinking.

Let us be underway in that direction and try to uncover for ourselves the manner in which the "artificial" effort of separation mentioned above can be properly utilized through philosophical exertion. How can we do this? Separation—of existence and existents, or, of being and phenomena—evokes a time when it might have been otherwise, or a time when separation might have been unnecessary. This presumably lies at the source or origin. Subsequently, to develop organic intuition of such a state, human existential potential must be traced to source events of cultures. Redemptive thinking requires such an expansion of intuition in the direction of the original separation (of inner and outer), in order to grasp the system of differentiation set in motion by the original parting. Just as we know that we cannot do anything about the original separation (appearance of subject/object duality in consciousness), we should be in no doubt as to the possibility of developing intuition in unexpected directions once philosophy gets underway and is put to proper use. In other words, redemption in thought is always potentially available once we begin to seriously demand it of ourselves-in-dialogue, when we make it our central goal. All psychic substance (like all substance) must logically be *sub specie aeternitatis*, and hence must carry somewhere within itself the stamp of its primordiality (origin) and the potential seed of its own liberation, even as it remains bound to and trapped within conditions.[10] The task of thinking is to intuit past the content of thought, which is society, which is habit, which is conditioning, and keep the possibility of retrieval constantly in view.

[10]The difference between psychic matter and ordinary (unorganized) matter is that the former is able to exert toward origin again as a self-conscious project.

> As soon as man sets himself in opposition to the external world, the first step to philosophy has been taken. With that separation, reflection first begins; he separates from now on what Nature had always united, separates the object from the intuition, the concept from the image, finally (in that he becomes his own *object*) himself from himself. The greatest philosophers were always the first to return to it, and Socrates (as Plato relates), after he had stood throughout the night sunk in contemplation, prayed in the early morning to the rising sun. [Thus] philosophy must presuppose that original divorce, because without it we should have no need to philosophize. Therefore it assigns to reflection only *negative* value. It proceeds from that original divorce to unite once more, through freedom, what was originally and necessarily united in the human mind, i.e., forever to cancel out that separation. And so far as philosophy itself was made necessary only by that separation—was itself a necessary evil, a discipline of errant reason—so it works in this respect for its own destruction.[11]

There is an original unity in which beings are not separated from Being. Schelling mentions that the recollection of such a state or condition is present in the cultural-archetypal memory of most thinkers. We know that it is also present in ancient myth, in poetry, in folk narrative, and in scriptural texts.[12] But as soon as this initial condition is ruptured—philosophy has necessarily got to presuppose that "original divorce" otherwise there would be no need for philosophy in the first place. And thereby reflection begins. It is not necessary, or perhaps impossible, to grasp the "reason" for the original rupture for it may not be given to reason; it is enough to acknowledge it. And this is where we come upon one of those bold insights characteristic of Schelling: *philosophical reflection has only negative value.* Of course we must be careful here. The word negative does not carry in this case the common connotation of being undesirable, adverse, or harmful. It simply indicates that philosophical reflection does not add anything; in and of itself it is not an end but a pointer toward what has been forgotten. It is a return path to our original home (*oikos*) from which we have been, for whatever reason, displaced. Therefore it has value *only* in relation to that which is lost or absent, and must not be regarded as something independent and

[11] Schelling, *Ideas for a Philosophy of Nature*, p. 10.

[12] See C.G. Jung, *Collected Works, Vols. 8, 9, & 11*, trans. R.F.C. Hull (Princeton: Princeton University Press, 1975).

valuable in itself. The task of philosophy is to help take us beyond the separation since it was made necessary only because of the separation. Thus philosophy has its end built into it, which resides in the possibility of being underway toward realignment with the origin.[13]

Let us then turn to the original philosophical question of the relation between the finitude of particulars and the Undifferentiated, or between determinate substance and the matrix of representation. How is it possible for things external to me, for example, to affect me cognitively? Or to put it the other way around, how can the mind form ideas about things 'outside' of itself?[14] Such a question absolutely presses itself upon us in our pursuit of redemptive thinking as it takes aim at the ontology and ground of that which we call thinking. Schelling's inquiry into the problem of origin commences with such questions. But in order to inquire into such questions as the relation between things and the matrix of their representation,[15] we have first to formulate a basic understanding of what determinate things are. Schelling gives us a theory of matter that is at sharp variance with the mechanistic worldview of conventional scientific thinking of his time, which objectified the world and failed to tell us anything about why or how phenomena appear for us.[16] To Schelling on the other hand, a credible philosophy of nature begins with such questions.

[13]We might say that the Nietzschean Overman is a man returned-to-origin and therefore signaling the death of metaphysics.

[14]Schelling writes: "Our present concern is not how we might present such a system, once it exists, but how in general such a system could exist. The question is not whether and how that assemblage of phenomena and the series of causes and effects, which we call the course of Nature, has become actual ***outside us***, but how they have become actual ***for us***, how that system and that assemblage of phenomena have found their way to our minds, and how they have attained the necessity in our conception with which we are absolutely compelled to think of them. For it is presupposed, as undeniable fact, that the representation of a succession of causes and effects external to us is as necessary for our mind as if they belonged to its very being and essence. To explain this necessity is a major problem of all philosophy." Schelling, *Ideas for a Philosophy of Nature*, p. 23.

[15]In Indian *advaita* philosophy of the *Upanishads*, there is the discussion of *vikara* (form) and *nirvikara* (formless), and their relation.

[16]Schelling rejects the Kantian picture of the arising of matter on the ground that it rests on a false "form-matter distinction," and requires the assumption of the "nonsensical things-in themselves (Kant's *ding-an-sich*), and further, that the Kantian schema fails to explain how the things come to have representations in the mind.

> [F]orce as such can affect us only insofar as it has a particular degree. But so long as we think of these dynamical forces quite generally—in a wholly indeterminate relationship—neither one of them has a particular degree. We can picture this relationship as an absolute *equilibrium* of these forces, in which the one always cancels out the other, and neither allows the other to grow up to a particular degree. So if *matter* as such is to acquire *qualitative* properties, its forces will have to have a particular degree, i.e., they will have to depart from the generality of the relationship in which the mere understanding thinks of them—or more plainly—they will have to deviate from the equilibrium in which they are originally and necessarily conceived.[17]

The material basis or the quality of phenomena, as outlined by Schelling, is *disequilibrium*. Thought cannot speculate on the original disequilibrium that set "forces" in motion in which there is an unfolding of difference from an original Unity. But once in motion, Schelling admits of only two opposing potencies, those of attraction and repulsion through which spatial concentrations are formed. In some respects, this polarity theory of matter is similar to the idea of basic matter-interactions as consisting of opposed electrical charges. But what is "force?" We get no clear picture from Schelling—in the same way as no adequate mental idea exists of a (electrical) charge or of gravity—for these are not things but expression of primary agitations that make up (secondary) sensible things of the world. Thus, we can say that, at base, elements are nothing other than spatial concentrations, and these 'elements' combine with other elements to form determinate appearances through attraction and repulsion. Therefore, matter is not something to be taken as existing by itself but as the result of a primary *activity*. At least four key points may be extracted from Schelling's analysis of matter:

> [1]. Schelling concludes that matter is not something that exists in itself, but as a solution to the metaphysical problem of the construction of the spatial dimensions. And the same holds for authentic science: matter is not a reality in itself, but a solution to the mathematical problem of the relation between the two forces. [2]. Since matter and space are coincident, there is no space without matter, and matter-space is singular, not plural. The operational or dynamic homogeneity of nature suggests the same thing: there is only one entity and in it there occurs only one operation: *ontological deflation*. [3]. Being nothing in itself, matter is but a mirror

[17] Schelling, *Ideas for a Philosophy of Nature*, p. 216.

> of the cosmos, hence a quantum of affirmation or activity allied to one of being-affirmed or passivity. As part of the affirmed, it is body and appears in space, the form of mere externality; as ensouled or part of the affirming, it is in time. The very forms of appearance express the non-being of things. [4]. Pure space combined with the point yields the line of time. The dimensions of space contracted to a point yield impermeability. The apparent materiality of the finite item of appearance is therefore a product of a process of expansion and contraction—the process that in the development of the plant Goethe termed *metamorphosis.*[18]

If the finitude of particulars (matter) does not exist by and of itself then it must exist in relation to something else that provokes or brings forth finitude as such. In other words, matter must exist in a mirror relation to something akin to consciousness given birth out of the same "ontological deflation." Schelling calls this primal cognitional activity "intellectual intuition." Intuition arises in reciprocal relation to matter, and vice versa; both of these unities are reciprocally the product of original ontological deflation from a higher absoluteness. Inert matter is thus a kind of lazy superstition viewed from one side of a reciprocal relation, just as is the self-contained concept of Mind. All conventional knowledge is but a failure to understand reality from the perspective of this basic mirror relation. To something that turns out to be no other than a passage, a transition between various disequilibria, commonsense thinking grants independent status.

> All thinking and presentation in us is therefore necessarily preceded by an original activity, which, *because it precedes* all thinking, is to that extent absolutely *undetermined* and *unconfined.* Only once an opposing element is present does it become restricted, and for that very reason a determinate (thinking) activity. If this activity of our mind were originally restricted (as is imagined by the philosophers who reduce everything to thinking and presentation), the mind could never feel itself to be confined. It feels its confinement only insofar as it feels at the same time its original lack of confinement. Now upon this original activity there works (or so at least it seems to us, from the standpoint we here occupy), an activity opposed to it, which has hitherto been no less completely undetermined, and thus we have two mutually contradictory activities, as necessary conditions for the possibility of an intuition.[19]

[18]Michael Vater, "Bringing Nature to Light: Schelling's *Naturphilosophie* in the Early System of Identity," *Analecta Hermeneutica*, 5, 2013.

[19]Ibid., p. 174.

First, no cognition can arise until or unless there arises an opposition or restriction by an opposing condition. Thinking is preceded by a primal activity upon the restriction of which there is the phenomenon of thought. It is a grave philosophical error to accept thought as original or foundational. Hence we can admit of a transcendental dimension as a necessary condition of all perception. Second, a transcendental deduction of the opposition of basic forces in the object can serve to explain its intuition in consciousness. Both object and intuition arise in a symmetrical manner through limits and restrictions imposed by opposing forces (attraction and repulsion), and it is only due to the identical processes that objects can be mirrored in intuition. This reciprocal action, which, makes experience of the object possible is however not itself available in experience but grounded at the transcendental level. Here we see the need, philosophically established, for thinking to turn to face the origin.

But we must go further, and use the above understanding to interrogate apparent composites such as the idea of the isolated perceiver or the thinking subject. Conventionally, as soon as the question of thinking, intuition, or representation arises, there is a tendency to associate it with, or see it in terms of, the function or predicate of a fully formed nucleus or entity such as the *cogitus*. In other words, whether at the intuitive level or at the formal level, the existing habits of thinking jump to a Cartesian assumption of a sovereign presence behind intuition or thinking. The important question is how, and wherefrom, does this belief or assumption arise in the first place of a sovereign element, and what is its validity?

> One who for himself is nothing other than what things and circumstances have made him, who, without dominion over his own ideas, is seized by, and dragged along with, the stream of causes and effects—how will he wish to know whence he comes, or whither he goes, or how he has become what he is? Does the wave know this, that drives hence in the stream? He has not even the right to say that he is a result of the collective effect of external things; for in order to be able to say this, he must presuppose that he knows *himself*, that he is therefore also something *for himself*. But this he is not.[20]

[20] Schelling, *Ideas for a Philosophy of Nature*, p. 14.

There is little reason or justification to assume the mental picture of the enduring nucleus, or even the question itself as a query arising from within a fully formed state; in fact, such an assumption contradicts the fundamentals of the model under discussion. If we resist this tendency, a more useful picture makes its appearance before us. What we understand as cognition, or intuition, or consciousness etcetera, cannot be assumed to emerge simply at an arbitrary level of composite such as, for example, that which is called the human, or even the animal, or the plant. To be consistent with the idea of reciprocity between mind and matter, we have to admit that each determinate particle carries in it its corresponding element of sentience or "mind." The qualitative difference between a self-animated body and an inert body thus only lies in the *extent* of the build-up of the respective orientations, or in the distribution of their tensions or forms of excitation.[21] Consciousness does not arise separately or uniquely, and neither is it the attribute or quality of any specific body or amalgamate.[22] Such preferentiality does not make sense within the present model. Schelling's model remains consistent if we indeed assume that there is consciousness or sentience at all levels, its particular quality and intensity dependent upon the level of complexity of the amalgamate or compound in question.[23] At each level the "fit" between the object world and sensory world is perfect since they reciprocally determine each other. The central problem of philosophy, namely, the relation between subject and object, is thus resolved. In the case of human subjects, the

[21]To give an ordinary analogy, two iron bars may contain the same number of magnetized particles and yet only one of them might exhibit magnetic properties such as polarity due to the manner of alignment of the elements within it. To keep the discussion at a simple level, we are only considering the difference between two groups namely "sentient" bodies and inert ones, without getting into the problem of differences within each group.

[22]"This philosophy must accept that there is a hierarchy of life in Nature. Even in mere organized matter there is life, but the life of a more restricted kind. This idea is so old, and has hitherto persisted so constantly in the most varied forms, right up to the present day—(that the whole world was pervaded by an animating principle)—that one may very well surmise from the beginning that there must be some reason latent in the human for this natural belief. And so it is. The sheer wonder which surrounds the problem of the origin of organic bodies, therefore, is due to the fact that in these things necessity and contingency are most intimately united. Necessity, because their very existence is purposive; contingency, because this purposiveness is nevertheless actual for an intuiting and reflecting being." Schelling, *Ideas for a Philosophy of Nature*, p. 35.

[23]This is no different than, say, the phenomenon of gravity; the relative mass determines the intensity.

object appears as given to consciousness in a routine or fixed manner only because we see it from one side of the relation, and also because we remain unaware of the sentience of sub-aggregates.[24]

> In the object, however, those opposing activities, from which it emerged in intuition, have at the same time become permanent. The mental origin of the object lies beyond consciousness. For with it consciousness first arose. It therefore appears as something that exists quite independently of our freedom. So those opposing activities, which intuition has united in it, appear as forces attaching to the object in itself, without any reference to a possible cognition. For the *understanding*, they are something merely *excogitated* and found by inference.[25]

The 'we' or the 'I' who perceives is only a special case in the sense of a particular arrangement or distribution of mind/matter. To put it differently, the "mind" which "cognizes" is itself a build-up of the tension of opposites that also produces the object of understanding at the elemental level. Ordinary consciousness of course cannot grasp this because this process is prior to experience and can only be transcendentally established. The object therefore appears as existing independently of "us." The "object" is an object and is not "us" only because the amalgamate that is the "object" has lesser degree of concentration of elementary sentience and therefore is less oriented toward consciousness, just as an average iron rod has polarized particles in it that are randomly distributed without exhibiting obvious magnetic properties or polarity on the whole. It is obvious that although the above might be a reasonably accurate description, it would take considerable phenomenological and hermeneutic effort to set our sights straight opening the door to insight. This book can only lay waypoints in the direction of such a meditation.

But philosophically, the biggest error of judgment we make is when we think of the mind/matter or object/consciousness relation as an ontological division, treating (often unconsciously) the outward cohesion or unity of the observer as inward fact. That is to say, we fail to take into account the fact that consciousness at any level, including the plane of the so-called human, is an aggregate unity of finite particulars, a

[24] This insensitivity eventually brings about ecological ruin.

[25] Schelling, *Ideas for a Philosophy of Nature*, p. 182.

composite of sub-aggregates. In other words, what appears to the human as an integral self-presence is in actuality a construct of many layers of subordinate consciousness, which is turn, have their own subordinates, and so on. The commonsense perspective confounds us here, and a certain phenomenological effort is essential to bracket it out. Little by little one has to break out of the habit of consciousness that sees the aggregate consciousness as the unified 'mind' that 'belongs' to someone. It is suggested that a *phenomenological disaggregation* is essential by learning to pay more careful attention to each thing and everyday objects, each movement and everyday thoughts, so that we develop an intuition of these sub-aggregates. The center of attention, which is normally the nucleus or the 'I,' must be made to shift to a new point between the observer and observed (object) not unlike the center of mass between two bodies. The phenomenological disaggregation leads to a new center of attention that is neither the observer nor the observed but which indicates strictly an *inter-aggregate interaction*. Thus we get past habit and enable the arising within us of a new sensibility, an intellectual intuition, or a new organ of perception that is necessary for being underway. This perception is not personal but lies in an inter-relational space that is neither within us nor without.

In the final analysis, cognition is not an act between an active mind (within) and passive matter (without) but an interaction between two levels of matter/mind combination. However, it takes a certain "critical aggregation" of mind-like tensions in matter-like formations for the particular sensibilities to bind together in self-consciousness or to cognize the presence of an 'other.' We are unable to intuit below the (largely accidental) anthropic threshold due to our limitations as sentient beings.[26] This is not surprising. Everyday consciousness tends to find its own reflection mirrored in the particular construction of reality of which it is a part, and builds its sense of operational hierarchies and habits of performance from the normalization of those levels and differences; our general taken-for-grantedness comes from the corresponding psychological adjustments that follow from it. Moreover, it is not unreasonable to say that humans have directed their efforts mostly at consolidating false positions (in the interests of power, accumulation, and domination),

[26]For example, we are not able to discern the mind-like properties of, say, water, which we treat as inert.

rather than continually deconstructing the accretions of inaccurate ontological understanding. True philosophical effort is always negative; it consists in removing the outgrowths of long-settled culture to disclose once again the pathways to being.

As a corollary, it is also therefore not inaccurate to say that the civilizational process strengthens and hardens the divide between the 'sentient' and the 'inert.' Anthropologically, the so-called 'primitive' peoples, whose perceptions had not become so stabilized by civilizational processes, were far more receptive to the animated 'spirit' like qualities of what appears to moderns as inert. The formers' beliefs, seen by the civilized as primitive superstition, turn out to be subjectively more accurate in the evaluation of relative object-ness and sentience. When man is new to the consciousness of his particular aggregate level, and it has not yet become a habit for him, the aggregate is yet to petrify and become impermeable. It retains the memory of a prior and less aggregated state, retaining as well the capacity to intuit the primary movements in other lower placed aggregates.

As we saw earlier, phenomenological disaggregation, or careful and minutely attentive watchfulness of the sensibilities, sensations, thoughts, memories, movements, and object relations, is thus key to the recovery of some elements that momentarily shake cognitive habits out of the aggregate template called the human and give us a new perspective. In learning to think, this recognition and perspective is absolutely essential: the composites must be analyzed and not be allowed to remain uncritically as part of the primary assumptions of thought. This helps thinking to enter into a more fluid state away from the habitual or commonsense state.

While we have attempted to draw out some implications of Schelling's formulation for our project that were presented by the great thinker across the two editions (1797 and 1803) of *Ideas*, we must also take into account his later work on what is known as Identity Philosophy. From the perspective of finite particulars and their aggregates, we now reverse the perspective and look from the perspective of undivided Absoluteness, or the nature of the movement of "indifference" into determinate form. If the former is a bottom-upward approach, the latter bespeaks of a movement from top downwards. These are two vital parts of Schelling's work and each has unique implications for the project of redemptive thinking that we are embarked upon here.

> The absolute is an eternal act of cognition, which is itself matter and form, a producing in which, in eternal fashion, it converts itself in its totality as Idea, as sheer identity, into the real, into the form, and conversely, in equally eternal fashion, resolves itself as form, and to that extent as object, into the essence or subject. Simply in order to make this relationship clear to oneself, let the absolute be thought of, to start with, purely as matter, as pure identity, as sheer absoluteness; now since its essence is a producing and it can take the form only out of itself, yet is itself pure identity, so the form too must be *this identity*, and thus essence and form in it must be *one and the same*, namely, the equal pure absoluteness.[27]

We have encountered the term "Absolute" earlier, in a passing manner, at the very beginning of the chapter as something that spontaneously differentiates and from which proceeds the initial disequilibrium toward finite matter. The absolute identity is the unconditional identity of the subjective and the objective, matter and form both at once, immediately posited. When the essence turns to form, the whole subjectivity turns to objectivity, and in the reverse, as form moves back into essence the entire objectivity becomes subjectivity, enclosed in itself. This continuous transformation, that gives rise to the sensible world, is not in time, meaning there is no history, no progression, or "transition to action." It is *itself* this eternal activity. In other words, while time might be an effect of this activity, the activity is not in time.

> Since it is not subject, not object, but only the identical essence of both, it cannot, as absolute act of cognition, be here the pure subject or there the pure object, and as subject where it resolves the form into essence, and as object where it molds the essence into form, it is always the pure absoluteness, the whole identity. Any difference which can take place here is not the absoluteness itself, which remains the same, but only the fact that in the one act, as essence, it is changed undivided into form, and in the other, as form, is changed undivided into essence, and so fashions itself eternally into unity with itself.[28]

It is not a question of unity: it is not that the subjective and the objective essences unite in the Absolute; rather, it is the case that these are two sides of the *same* activity. Form and essence, Idea and the Real

[27] Schelling, *Ideas for a Philosophy of Nature*, p. 47.

[28] Ibid.

resolve eternally into each other as absolute acts. And further, "The absolute produces nothing out of itself except itself, thus again an absolute."[29] The Absolute cannot be broken down into parts but is reproduced or embodied in each difference. However each production-pulse is qualitatively unique (free) and combines uniquely with the conditions, or what has gone before it, in transformation. Thus "each of the unities is the whole absolute act of cognition, and, as essence or identity, itself becomes form again, just as does the absolute itself."[30] The elemental transformation, or the slowing down of essence into form, results in cognition, which returns it to essence. Thus there is no fixed perceiver, observer, or cognizer. From the point of view of the Absolute, the observer is a moving, transforming unity, each constitutive elementality eventually finding passage back into essence (eternal return). Thus there is nothing but performativity on all sides of the equation.

> In each of the unities, seen from its formal side, there is a special feature, for example, that in it the infinite is embodied in the finite, or vice versa, but this special character does not remove the absoluteness, nor is it removed by itself, although in the absoluteness where the form is fashioned in complete equality to the essence, and is itself essence, this special character is not distinguished.[31]

Although undergoing transformation (acquiring finitude, etc.), each finitely determined object or unity in cognition contains the original pulse of totality or infinite essence (*sub specie aeternitatis*). Thus form maintains its equality to essence at all times.

But then how are we to account for individual differences? Individual differences are due to differing concentrates that arise as ideas. At any moment, the sum total of differences is always zero. To give a very commonplace analogy, when we rip apart a smooth piece of paper, there appears numerous jagged edges (differences), but each jagged edge has left a negative counter-edge that nullify each other if the torn pieces are brought together again. Schelling responds: "The ideas are nothing

[29] Ibid.

[30] Ibid.

[31] Ibid., p. 48.

other than syntheses, in which the absolute identity of universal and particular (of essence and form), so far as this identity is itself again universal, is combined with the particular form; and precisely because this particular form is again equated to the absolute form or essence, there can be no individual thing in these Ideas."[32] The key word is synthesis, or cognitive synthesis. There is no sovereign thing in cognition. There are only syntheses, or what Spinoza called composites, whose local concentrations and representations we can refer to as mind for want of a better word.

> Only insofar as one of the unities, which again in the absolute itself are as one, conceives itself, its essence, its identity, as mere form, and accordingly as relative difference, does it symbolize itself through individual actual things. The individualized thing is only one moment of the eternal act of transformation of the essence into the form; for this reason the form is distinguished as particular, for example as the embodiment of the infinite into the finite; but that which becomes objective through this form is still only the absolute unity itself.[33]

We must not be misled by our particular sense of time and extensionality. The individualized object or form is merely a passage, a moment in the ceaseless transition of essence into form and return. The transition of form into essence and essence into form is played out at all levels of creation. For reasons of habit and inattention human cognition gets stuck on one side of the relation and has to make a special effort to regain fluidity of perception.[34] Each aspect of a finite or determinate being is constantly going through ceaseless transformation. Our attention has strayed from the *in-forming* and become culturally trapped in the forms, which is why we become entombed in the past and history becomes more important than the living present. It is also the reason why the present discussion might appear excessively abstract, because the necessary refocusing is resisted by the nucleus of apparent continuities.

But, at the same time, it is important to raise the question: What maintains in cognition the apparent continuity of determinate bodies? The eternal act of phase change in the infinite subdivisions in each

[32] Ibid.

[33] Ibid.

[34] This is possibly what Buddhist doctrine calls "*avijnya*" or ignorance.

finite aggregate (determinate object) and sub-aggregate do not coincide or is not coordinated in time since the history of each pulse is obviously different. Thus each determinate body is in reality a statistical or stochastic body which gives rise to the impression of stability in space and continuity in time (neither of which have independent ontological existence as we have seen earlier). The corollary of this principle is that if all the infinite subdivisions of a determinate thing were to go through phase change simultaneously then there would arise no perceptible determinate body in cognition. Therefore, in a word, accumulated phase differences give rise to finite bodies in cognition, the latter itself being not something independent but one side of the eternal act.[35]

> The real side of the eternal act is revealed in Nature; Nature in itself, or eternal Nature, is just Mind born into objectivity, the essence of god introduced into form, save only that in Him this introducing immediately grasps the other unity. Phenomenal nature, on the other hand, is the embodiment of essence in form appearing as such or in particularity, and hence is eternal Nature, so far as it takes on itself for a body, and so presents itself through itself as particular form. Nature, so far as it appears as Nature, that is, as this *particular* unity, is accordingly as such already external to the absolute, not Nature as the absolute act of cognition itself (*Natura naturans*), but Nature as the mere body or symbol thereof (*Natura naturata*). In the absolute, it exists with the opposed unity, which is that of the ideal world, as one unity, but just for that reason the absolute contains neither Nature as Nature nor ideal world as ideal world, but both are as one world.[36]

All subsequent differences are subordinate ones that must be traced to the original caesura. It is perhaps the strangest assertion, but nevertheless true, that nature appears to *itself* as Nature (cognition) and not to something else. This "Nature" does not exist as Nature or a particular unity in the Absolute but as a moment of alternation in the essence. Thus the commonsense Us/Nature binary, on which so many civilizational ideas are founded, falls apart as a kind of immature and incomplete

[35]The *Karma* theory of the Hindu *Advaita* or non-dual Philosophy carries similar notions.

[36]Schelling, *Ideas for a Philosophy of Nature*, p. 51.

perception.[37] The collection of symbols that human cognition designates as Nature faces continuous extinction at infinite levels of disaggregation, due again to which it makes its reappearance as other aggregates. Thus the ideal world and the material world mirror each other and neither exists independently of the other.

> Where the embodiment of the infinite into the finite reaches the point of absolute indifferencing, it immediately resolves itself again into its opposite and therewith into the aether of absolute ideality, so that with the perfectly real image of the absolute in the real world, the most perfect organism, the completely *ideal* image, also immediately enters, as reason, although even this again only for the *real* world; and here, in the real world, the two sides of the absolute act of cognition show themselves as archetype and ectype of each other, just as the absolute act of cognition does in eternal Nature; and the organism transfigured into absolute ideality in reason, just as Nature is transfigured in the eternal resumption of the finite into the infinite.[38]

From absolute indifference there is an ontological deflation or a coming away leading to the *immediate entrance* or production of a cognitive pulse, and the corresponding appearance of the "real" world. When the totality goes through the "phase change" from essence to form it does so in a trans-temporal manner. But the pulse so released manifests itself in time, *is*, in fact, time. The pulse degenerates or breaks down into conditioned concentrations as it meets and interacts with the past. Matter or objectivity thus manifests out of various disequilibria as we have seen before.

What we learn from the above analysis is that finite objects are in part being and in part *non-ens. Inter alia* they are "real" or finite, that is, determinate bodies, only by the fact that the ground of their existence does not lie within themselves but in that absolute identity of form and essence. Therefore, the finitude of particulars which commonsense understanding calls reality must not be regarded as a process of emergence or discharge from the absolute identity, but as a negativity (holding back of essence) that constitutes all finite things. This negativity, however, must be understood in the correct perspective as a process of creative or generative inflorescence and not as lack. Each particular

[37] It is also the reason why all decisions taken on this basis lead nowhere, and ecological debates have floundered in contradiction.

[38] Schelling, *Ideas for a Philosophy of Nature*, p. 51.

finitude relies regressively on prior elemental engagements ad infinitum leading to no ultimate positivity. Further, since these finite "objects," including sentient aggregates, cannot have positivity of being within themselves, they must therefore have their being *only in relation* to other finite things; that is to say, all sensuous cognition of them can only be a relative and non-positive act.

In other words, all "presence" is always a relative and qualified presence, necessarily dependent on other contingent particularities, and in turn on the collectivity or totality. Hence a transcendental totality must be posited as the necessary condition of possibility for any sentience-cognition to arise. Schelling here profoundly departs from the Kantian schema, foregrounding the transcendental or the Absolute as the sole measure of the reality of existents. For Kant all cognition is cognition of the sensible and validated within its epistemic boundaries by means of the categories. In other words, Kant regards cognition as a positive act of knowledge. By contrast Schelling argues that all of our sensory knowledge is only a privation, arising out of the withholding of essence. As for the production of particular meanings, these are generated in the clash of different phenomenal drifts, the resultant restriction of flow along infinitesimal pathways (deprivation) spawning a resonance-cusp called meaning. Redemptive self-consciousness (reflexivity) within this process might imply the operation of a mature intuition with regard to the essence, and a consequent facing-toward the essence, even as thinking (a specific concentrate) is borne along by the confused tumult of the phenomenal drift controlled by culture.

Why is the difference between Kant and Schelling significant in the way we might regard phenomenological actuality? The Kantian schema faces in the direction of knowledge-cognition for judgement about itself by means of the conceptual categories. Whereas for Schelling all judgment is in the tension between being and non-being. For the latter, knowledge cannot come to any truthful conclusion about itself, by and of itself. All such cognition really amount to illusion or non-cognition. The personal or private intelligence is philosophically thus superseded in favor of an immanent terrain of pure tensionality. The reality aperture developed by a transcendent cognitive wrinkle in the mindstuff—viz. category—is seen as inadequate and discarded in favor of the immanent ontological tension within the mindstuff itself. That is to say, isolated persistence or discrete cognition (including notions of self) in terms of in-advance mental categories is given up in the realization of matter-mind concentrates that 'judge' in terms of being and non-being, or essence and phenomena.[39]

Let us, at this juncture, collect the thoughts developed so far in this analysis in order to turn back to our central question. What philosophical disclosures present in the above analysis are useful for thinking to be underway in the direction of redemption? In other words, what do we learn here about the ontological process of thought that orients us toward a new kind of thinking that needs to be thought? Let us summarize some key points here for the sake of clarity.

- First, thought is born in the pulse between pure subjectivity (essence) and pure objectivity (form).
- Second, thinking is therefore ontologically an inter-state or in-between state; it is neither form nor essence, or rather, it has characteristics of both (representationally form, ontologically essence).
- Third, thinking is thus necessarily transitory and unstable. It needs to be Janus-faced, looking simultaneously toward the empirical and origin in order to apprehend itself correctly.
- Fourth, it can neither grasp form nor essence directly, both of which are prior to the thought impulse.
- Fifth, thinking can only form a mental representation of the Real which is always incomplete.
- Sixth, thinking as content (representation) only eternally misses the point (in its effort to grasp reality) and goes around in circles, for all conclusion lies in essence.
- Seventh, thinking as ontological movement carries the imprint of its nascence.
- Eighth, it is profitable for thinking to therefore dwell on its ontological structure rather than on the differentiation in its representational or semantic content.
- Ninth, the recollection of its ontological essence re-turns thinking toward its source.
- Finally, to be true to itself, thinking must always be in relation to the origin, as we saw in the previous chapter.

[39]This is not to say that perceptional categories are irrelevant, but that they are incomplete or insufficient for apprehending the totality of the existential plane. Ordinary, or commonsense perception cannot be given up, instead, a new organ of perception must be generated through facing-toward-being. Both levels must operate together in the act of redemptive thinking.

Next, let us examine each point in turn. First, thought as a pulse of difference has no being-in-itself. It exists only in relation to other thoughts, and especially in relation to the thought of the "they" or the generalized other. It is the generalized other (including things-at-hand) that animates thought; otherwise, in terms of substance, all thoughts are the same. In other words, there is no ontological difference between the most pious thought and the most devious one. Both are empty agitations in an unknown medium, although they may lead progressively to different deployments and promulgations (in combination with other conditions and aggregates). The ontological emptiness or non-being of thought, which, as we have seen, appears in the form-essence transition, must ever be reflexively kept in sight as it works itself incessantly into new networks and combinations, thus propagating itself, acquiring a pseudo-independence and reality as it moves forward. The recognition of the non-sovereignty of thought, although conceptual and not the actual stuff of intimate consciousness at this stage, is of significant import in the process that leads to the uncovering of the nature of thinking, or thought's self-understanding.

Second, thought is neither form nor essence but an inter-being that *represents* other beings/things in consciousness. Therefore there is a second level of complexity associated with thinking involved here that is to be noted: it is the complex problem of self-referentiality, as we use thinking to reflect on thinking. In other words, unlike other representations, thinking represents itself in consciousness. One standard difficulty with self-referentiality is that there are always questions or propositions raised within a closed system that are unanswerable or whose truth value cannot be ascertained within that system. Thought as an ontologically closed system cannot escape this difficulty. An obvious question that faces this uncertainty regarding thinking is: Who or what observes thinking? Thought cannot observe itself: that would be like the proverbial cat trying to catch its own tail. The answer to that question is at once obscure and staring at us in the face (like so many other things with thinking). As we saw earlier, the truth of thought is its non-being or negativity. But this negativity is not a thing or a lack of matter that can be imagined by the mind. It is negative such that each finite contortion or kink momentarily leaves its trace like an evanescent vapor trail. Hence it is the *emptiness that receives* (traces) without judgement. It is the truth-about-thought that is imprinted by the movement of thinking. This is what I have called intelligencing. Negativity here is not indicative of a quality; it is not the mere absence of anything, for then there must have been a prior presence. It is absence ab initio. But is this not counter-intuitive? How can negativity or emptiness observe? We must not confuse observation here with optical sensibility; there is no observation in the sense of organization of visual sensation, but a moment to moment inner change of state in the psycho-matter or mind-stuff. Again, this is not to be seen as a process of recording but an immanent sensation. Therefore, when we use the term observation, we mean a trackless trace is produced immanently. Hence phenomenological observation and a developing intuition remain the major tools of disclosure rather than conceptual ones in the case of thinking. One does not arrive at such perception, or perception of perception, merely by thinking about it. The maturing of intuition may be said to be underway once thinking is oriented not just toward phenomena but simultaneously toward essence, that is, toward ontology. Otherwise, the image or self-enclosure of itself as independent something develops into an intractable problem for thinking.

Third, thinking must be Janus-headed, looking simultaneously toward substance and origin. In *Being and Time*, Heidegger writes of the various activities of thought, and notes that in its daily "Falling," thinking meanders through several states among which are: "Tempting," "Tranquilizing," "Alienating," "Entanglement," "Turbulence," and "Anxiety." Each of these states is a divorce from Being, each suffers from amnesia to the extent that thought can no longer even raise the question of Being. For Schelling, even the best scientific thinking suffers from the incapacity to raise the question of consciousness or the ground of phenomena. Instead, the states of thought are made up of various projections and introjections, of calculations and comparisons, of reverie and phantasy, of memory and recall, and of intent and futurism, in short, of the phenomenal chatter that occupies thinking and the inner mapping of objects which constitutes average reality. The internal 'kaleidoscope' imposes its transient schema on 'what is' thereby to construct individual reality. Meditative thinking must study this kaleidoscope with great care without interference in order to fully reveal its arbitrariness and conflictual characteristics. Thus is a deep recoil produced within thinking itself—a thoughtful desire for flight from contradiction and the sorrow that is born of it. And thus it becomes possible for thinking to turn toward the origin from which it had turned away. Thought can never 'drag' the origin into itself, nor can it give a description of it, but can only find it in intellectual intuition (which is a process of tending toward or being underway).

This silent facing-toward-origin disciplines thought and brings about the quality of Reason—not logistical reason but holistic one. The genesis of Reason is in loss of contradiction. From here on, thought's activity is no longer random or arbitrary. It has learnt its main lesson toward redemptive thinking: to be Janus-headed as well as recognize the principle of eternal return. This bridge in intuition is key to being underway to that which may be called redemptive thinking; it enables thought to be able to respond to phenomena and be free of it at the same time.

Fourth, the limitations of thinking must become apparent to thought. Thinking appears to itself as limitless. But this is an illusion, a hallucination that is the product of its incessant uncritical and circular activity. Careful consideration shows thinking to be anchored in the past, and nothing else. The most sophisticated outgrowths of thought can be nothing else but the modified projections of the past. The pulse between form and essence is already in the past when a thought is fully developed. In other words, the genesis of thought is always in the past. No matter what it claims, thinking can never enter into the present, into the now of *Kairos*. As civilization is carried forward by the thought impulse, it is ever in anticipation of a superior present, which never arrives. In other words, we reach a 'future' without ever tasting the present. But that 'future' is always the past in a new form. That is why Schelling says that all of life is covered by a "melancholy." This melancholy is not because eventually we will be returned to the dust organically, nor is it because the limited or calculable present has little to offer. Rather, it is because we do not arrive at our present, which alone has Presence, containing therefore the possibility of redemption. The arrival into the present is concomitant with the loss of that very certainty sought by thought. The past is that certainty; only that which has *happened* can have certainty. But in the absolute present anything can happen, due to the fact that memory, the repository of the past, is not involved. Memory as recall remains one of the greatest stumbling blocks to creative apprehension. When memory as recall is set aside, that is, not associated with emergent thought forms (mental chatter), the breakdown of the thought forms release unencumbered space that might phenomenologically be experienced as expansive ecstasy or as elation. Melancholy, or the psychic biliousness, is overcome and the inner fragmentation of thought and the corresponding conflict turns into libation. From psychic bile to libation, the turn is one of correct orientation: the former aggrandizes epistemic content, the latter anticipates luminous spatiality.

Fifth, thought must acknowledge that thinking cannot apprehend the transcendental or the ground of cognition. This Kant knew, but his solution to the problem was the positing of opposition between mental categories and the thing-in-itself (*ding-an-sich*), which Schelling correctly rejects as a false and misleading binary. Nevertheless, the very working of thinking is through binaries and oppositions which is its primary mode of apprehension and detection. The binary is a useful device in dealing with first-order realizations such as wet/dry, or up/down, that is, with regard to the sensible. The difficulty arises with second-order realizations such as beautiful/ugly or lovable/hostile, and so on. These synthetic judgments exceed the brief of thought as these are immanent in the corresponding intelligibilities (mind-matter agglomerates) the understanding of which requires the phenomenological journey we are attempting to make here. In the "preparation for a readiness" toward redemption we must simultaneously accept and deny the sublime possibilities of thought. This means, in the ordinary progression of thought, we must deny that thinking can exceed the sensible, and yet, at the same time, in thinking itself there must be the recognition of, and the effort to be open to, the transcendental, to the possibility of being transformed by it. In a poetic sense, thought must continually bring itself to the edge of Grace, to its ontological boundary. For Kant, the ontological domain was not thinkable or approachable. Whereas for Schelling, it becomes an open question due to the mind-matter equation, and its logical corollary being that the human is not a necessarily privileged site. With the image of the human as a special agglomerate out of the way, the transcendental becomes so much more of an obvious reality, a necessity for the arising of phenomena. Hence thinking has a double, and apparently contradictory, task before it: it must acknowledge its incapacity to approach the *noumenal* or pretend to know anything about it, and simultaneously orient itself toward it. Attending to this antinomian double task keeps thinking on its way and the preparation toward a readiness.

Sixth, thinking as content always remains turned away from its source because it is mesmerized by its own activities, projections, and powers of action. Thinking regards its effects on the world as *independent* of itself and hence having sovereign value. Considering technologization as an example, thinking sees its experiments and the discovery of new *techne* as something quite independent of itself and not as its own imprint on matter or the projection of its own innate structure on the world. This propensity to separate itself from the world and then consider its effects on the world is philosophically damaging and phenomenologically distorted because it necessarily involves objectification of that which in actuality is a continuum. The objectified world mistakenly becomes fodder for thought which then starts to devour what it objectifies, not unlike the horror of an organism devouring its own entrails. What commonsense perspective holds as development and progress, on ontological analysis, turns out to be nothing other than a dangerous descent into uncomprehending materiality and commodification. This stance might appear strange given modernity's celebration of indiscriminate technologization and belief in material salvation. Nevertheless the foregoing analysis presses upon us the realization that representational or calculative thinking will ultimately act upon the world in a predatory manner against its own interest. But such admission and consequent disciplining of thinking is not easy given the incredible success thought has had in modeling reality and choosing pathways of action in the world toward goal attainment. To concede all of the reality-management as one-sided requires a measured dose of philosophical humility and insight. But it also requires a firm resolve toward truth, meaning an extraordinary steadfastness in the desire to break through the curtain of mental modifications or thought-products. While it is not being suggested that we can get by without thought-products, it is conceivable that we can consciously use them in a manner so as to essentially remain free of them, retaining the capacity to "let go of them at any time" or engage them in a manner that "does not affect our inner and real core" and "lay waste our nature."[40] It is clear from Schelling and Heidegger that our "nature" is not determined by thought but by what is beyond and primal to the thought form, or that which is the condition of possibility for thinking. A daring and deep consideration of the ground of thought brings about what Heidegger has called "Releasement," referring to an openness that is not dominated by the calculations of thought, representation, or material products of thinking. Releasement does not objectify the things of experience, letting them remain at the level of sensation and collective regions of sensibility.

Next, thinking as ontological movement has no development as it has no content, but remains identical to its source impulse. Meditative thought must remain focused on this point of no evolution as it is in stark contrast to the received notion that thinking evolves in time.

[40] Martin Heidegger, "Memorial Address," in *Discourse on Thinking*, trans. John Anderson and E. Hans Freund (New York: Harper & Row, 1966), p. 54.

To be sure there is differentiation and elaboration but metaphysically thought remains the same. Ontological thought merely "regions" as Heidegger would put it, implying that it covers cosmic ground without doing anything or changing anything. It ranges without intent or direction. It is always the Same and is oriented toward itself, its death. It returns to the origin as essence—it has nowhere else to go—even as the theatre of (mental) modifications continue within it. From that perspective, it cannot be caught in the net of artifice produced by incessantly differentiating content. To put it differently, ontologically, the compression-modification or spatial concentration that is the thought impulse cannot be anything other than itself, something that it has always been from the beginning. Lightning is lightning, whether in antiquity or modernity. The intuitive development of this perspective is important. Meditative thinking comes upon the realization that the domination of content in representational thinking must be counter-balanced or delimited by this structural understanding or tempered by the understanding of the Origin. This keeps us underway toward redemptive thinking. It is to be conceded that we are embarked upon a difficult journey—the simultaneous grasp of the internal and external view of thought. The realization that thought is the Same from antiquity releases us from the various fevers of technological modernity at the core of which is the mistaken belief in psychological evolution that putatively accompanies *techne*. Further, if thought is the same, then our image of the thinker must be a shallow and superficial thing, not unlike a reflection on the surface of the water that disappears once we penetrate the surface. However, the understanding of the observer or thinker cannot merely be an intellectual effort; it has necessarily got to rely on an awakened intuition that has no stake in the maintenance of the status quo.

And finally, meditative thinking arises in intuition, as ontological pulse (contraction and expansion), in an act of fullness and elegance almost akin to a religious act. Here I turn to Schelling for one more time: "After all *finite* forms have been struck down, and there is nothing more in the wide world to unite mankind but collective intuition, it can only be the contemplation of absolute identity in the fullest objective totality that afresh, and in the final development to religion, unites them."[41] What are the finite forms? These are all things and their inter-relations that, for unregenerate thought, constitute reality. These finite forms are always

[41] Schelling, *Ideas for a Philosophy of Nature*, p. 55.

on the verge of breakdown, *enroute* to other forms. Thought might build colonies in outer space or do other equally wondrous things. But in the end, all its constructions including itself face the same conclusion, and none bring emancipation or true relief. To be struck down in Mars or Jupiter is presumably no different than being struck down on earth: change of form (death) amounts to the same thing, whether here or elsewhere. Thought attempts to escape the finality of death by escaping the immediate with studied fanfare, but to state the obvious, the systematic planning fails, only causing more despair, and in turn, a more desperate effort. The Heideggerian "being-towards-death" of the human remains ill-understood. The only thing that can unite thought is the proper understanding of phenomena and the contemplation of the changeless background. Meditative insight is able to gather the essential nature of morphology or the endless progression in right perspective. It grasps the non-identity in the ceaseless change and by means of negation arrives at its own true self-nature. This becomes thinkable once meditative thought grasps the central point made by Schelling that "Nature is Mind made visible," and at the same time, Mind is invisible Nature. Only in this absolute identity of Mind and Nature and its fullest contemplation can thinking be led to the ending of metaphysical contradiction within itself, and consequently to the possibility of resolving conflict in the temporal world.

Summary and Transition

Schelling's "great leap" begins by cutting adrift of two of the foundational concepts of modern metaphysics—Descartes' *I think—I am,* and Kant's *thing-in-itself.* The former establishes the pre-critical 'I' as the sovereign experiencer and consequently anoints the duality of the experiencer and experience, and the latter introduces the second key binary of modern thinking: that of the "thing-in-itself" versus "appearance." Schelling negates both and reaches beyond to look for a way of establishing the source of our reality in "unities" rather than in binaries. Going beyond Descartes and Kant, Schelling offers two perspectives: one from the phenomena upwards to the Absolute, and the other, from the Absolute down to the particulars. Together these two perspectives show conventional thinking to be foundering in misapprehensions regarding the world of finite particulars as well as its own nature. This includes the haloed world of empirical science. Heidegger's statement that thought has not learned to think even in the scientific world is borne out by Schelling's analysis that shows the apprehensions of all thinking to be one-sided: from a taken-for-granted consciousness, phenomena are studied without regard to the necessities that are involved in the very arising of the finitude of particulars. In this regard, Schelling helps us to take Nietzsche beyond himself. The powerful but enigmatic idea of the Eternal Return is much better understood when we apply Schelling's construction of the phenomena/essence relation. Eternal Return is not to be thought of in terms of a perpetual return to accidental composites of external conditions, that is, in terms of recuperating contingent social formations or personal circumstances indefinitely (the latter is both improbable and a misapprehension). Rather it is to be thought of in terms of things returning to their essence as an underlying principle of ontological necessity. This necessity, once understood, helps thinking to be underway—facing object and essence at the same time. But a phenomenological effort toward the development of intellectual intuition is *sine qua non* for such understanding. It is suggested that an attitude that could help us to be underway in the path to an adequate subject/object relation is Goethe's idea of delicate empiricism which we discuss in the following chapter. The nature of empathic understanding deliberated upon by Goethe is invaluable in the maturation of the instincts that is necessary to go beyond the one-sidedness of the intellect as it operates habitually and conventionally.

References

Heidegger, Martin. "Memorial Address." In *Discourse on Thinking*, translated by John Anderson and E. Hans Freund. New York: Harper & Row, 1966.

Heidegger, Martin. *Being and Time*. Translated by Joan Stambaugh. New York: SUNY Press, 1996.

Heidegger, Martin. *Schelling's Treatise on the Essence of Human Freedom*. Translated by Joan Stambaugh. Athens: Ohio University Press, 1989.

Jung, Carl Gustav. *Collected Works, Vols. 8, 9, & 11*. Translated by R.F.C. Hull. Princeton: Princeton University Press, 1975.

Vater, Michael. "Bringing Nature to Light: Schelling's *Naturphilosophie* in the Early System of Identity." *Analecta Hermeneutica* 5 (2013). http://epublications.marquette.edu/cgi/viewcontent.cgi?article=1507&context=phil_fac.

von Schelling, F.W.J. *Ideas for a Philosophy of Nature*. Translated by Errol E. Harris and Peter Heath. Cambridge, UK: Cambridge University Press, 1988.

von Schelling, F.W.J. *System of Transcendental Idealism*. Translated by Peter Heath. Charlottesville: University of Virginia Press, 1978/1800.

CHAPTER 4

Goethe and Delicate Empiricism

If the task of philosophical praxis is to move between two levels of thinking—content and structure—as is the suggestion here, then engagement with gross representation must make room for attention to the subtle sensations (of differentiated centers of consciousness within sub-aggregates) already present but unnoticed under the press of settled realities. The philosopher must take seriously the hint of the possibility of a new dawn in consciousness, and not be seduced by the smoothness of the existing order or its reward system or even be intimidated by the pain of sacrificing the picture of a settled reality. The shift from obsession with thought content to the ontological background—facing toward origin—demanded by redemptive thinking cannot be accomplished without a corresponding shift in the focus of attention. The human agglomerate must learn to reinvent itself as a disaggregated laboratory for its own investigation. The taken-for-granted form with its taken-for-granted reactions and responses must undergo a loosening or phenomenological disaggregation helping us to move away from the customary habits of thought. In *Culture and Value*, Wittgenstein writes:

> What makes a subject hard to understand is not that before you can understand it you need to be specially trained in abstruse matters, but the contrast between understanding the subject and what most people *want* to see. Because of this the very things which are most obvious may become

K. Roy, *The Power of Philosophy*,
https://doi.org/10.1007/978-3-319-96911-4_4

> the hard-est of all to understand. What has to be overcome is a difficulty having to do with the will, rather than with the intellect.[1]

Often, to make the obvious visible is a formidable task. The difficulty presented by a matter under scrutiny arises not from the fact that one must be an expert in specialized knowledge or possess great intellectual capacity, but that an accurate grasp of it is against the grain of commonsense expectations, and calls for a resolve toward truth about the phenomenon. It is the embedded cultural expectation that often makes what is palpable and in front of us the most difficult to understand when confronted directly. Everyday things become blindingly familiar; due to the over-familiarity we lose their profound otherness and true significance. Cognitive habits that enframe or circumscribe our realities, once established are difficult to shake off. Their overcoming requires a deliberate exercise of the will rather than that of the intellect. But perhaps we might have to go further than 'will' in the present case. How might 'will' come to be exercised in this case? Why would anyone wish, for example, to exercise their will to overcome hardened commonsense or cognitive habits? Rather, it is suggested, that a wide-ranging phenomenological inquiry must be initiated in social thought as part of securing a more adequate pedagogy of existence. Within a larger pedagogical effort to rethink the mento-corporeal human composite, or what has been referred to here as the task of phenomenological disaggregation, small but careful observations may succeed in displacing entrenched cognitive habits. Such is the effort of hermeneutic phenomenology and the labor before us in these pages.

Looking into thought in a systematic manner is prevented by the glare of familiarity. Everyone is born into thinking, *but no one is thinking*, meaning, no one is thinking from the realization of what thinking is, as Heidegger continually reminds us. Each waking minute we are placed squarely in the drift of thought but we rarely stop to examine thinking itself. Therefore the proposition 'thought never thinks,' seems very puzzling. For it is always thinking, but in the direction of *things*; it is taken up with representing the object. Why is thinking thus pressed to be relentlessly pointed toward the object? That is the question with which we shall be concerned next. For to understand thinking we must inquire

[1] Ludwig Wittgenstein, *Culture and Value*, ed. George Henrik von Wright (London: Wiley-Blackwell, 1998), p. 17.

into its characteristic shaping, and routine en-formations. In other words, we need to grasp the "morphology" of thought, and fittingly for this we turn to the very thinker who coined the term morphology, namely Johann Wolfgang von Goethe.[2] This great poet-philosopher-scientist, who lit up the intellectual firmament of the late-eighteenth/early nineteenth centuries, challenged some of the root metaphors by which thinking, especially Western scientific thinking had proceeded since the Enlightenment. The Enlightenment attitude enshrined within thought an epistemic understanding of reality rather than the ontological, privileging appearance over essence. To put it differently, representation rather than direct contact with reality increasingly became the legitimate form of grasping the world. But Goethe was one important thinker who departed from the epistemic culture and remained grounded in the possibility of awaking to essence.

For instance, it would not be inaccurate to say that isolation and atomization were fundamental to the advancement of science whereby the clinical separation of the phenomena under study from the phenomenological was considered basic to scientific reliability and rigor. The fact that this was a choice has disappeared from the daily deliberations of thought since then. In contrast to this, Goethe seems to take a very different viewpoint, underlining the possibility of alternate pathways:

> There is a delicate empiricism which makes itself utterly identical with the object, thereby becoming true theory... The ultimate goal would be to grasp that everything in the realm of fact is already theory... Let us not seek for something beyond the phenomena – they themselves are the theory.[3]

[2]Johann Wolfgang von Goethe, *Scientific Studies*, trans. Douglas Miller (Princeton: Princeton University Press, 2005), p. 57. Further, Ernst Cassirer writes: "It was Goethe who first coined the word 'morphology'... With Goethe's idea of 'morphology,' with his conception of the 'formation and transformation of organic natures,' a new ideal of knowledge was created... To put it briefly, Goethe completed the transition from the previously generic view to the modern genetic view of organic na-ture... According to him, what we grasp in the [generic view] are only the products, not the process of life. And into this life process he wanted, not only as a poet but also as a scientist, to win an insight..." Ernst Cassirer cited in John Shotter, "Goethe and the Refiguring of Intellectual Inquiry: From 'Aboutness'-Thinking to 'Withness'-Thinking in Everyday Life," *Janus Head* 8 (1), 2005, p. 135.

[3]Goethe, op. cit., p. 307.

The tender or delicate, as opposed to gross, empiricism was a sound self-description of Goethe's own methodology. Our entrenched cognitive habits continue into formal thinking such as science which ends up sanctifying, among other things, the naïve and pre-critical division between the observer and the observed.

But there is also an observer/observed duality within thought itself which manifests itself as the (false) internal distinction between thinker and thought to which we desperately cling, as we have seen in the previous chapters. The "thinker" seems able to control, direct, and manage thought toward its intentions. Both these dichotomies, the outward-facing and the inward-facing, already naïvely entrenched in thought through forms of non-observation or non-awareness, became formally enshrined in the epistemic culture and empirical ethos of the Enlightenment. First, it assumed that reality could only be apprehended by a sovereign mind through the mental categories, and while the categories themselves were transcendental, no direct or intuitive knowledge of the world was possible. Second, it formalized the idea that separation between experiencer and experience was key to dependable knowledge. But for Goethe, on the other hand, a deep empathic observation held the possibility of slipping past conventional and commonsense habits of perception and emerge onto a different topology of sensibilities. For Goethe, within such a process, the sensible merges with the intelligible to produce a perceptual holism. What science garners as cold datum, having isolated observation from lived resonances, reappears as *theoria* in its pristine sense in delicate empiricism. The organic presentation of the "fact" in consciousness is always already this *theoria* or a way of looking. Thus there is no longer any gap between a way of looking that is intensely empathic and the datum itself. The internal "thinker" disappears under the relentless glare of mindful observation, just as the monadic observer now appears as a form of perceptual laziness and inattention introduced into the process of observation. In negating this double inattention we have the phenomena themselves as theory: their self-presence as equivalent to their re-presentation in thought.

> Goethe's empiricism provided an alternative and complementary epistemology to conventional scientific practice and its underlying dualis-tic and rationalistic epistemology that categorically separates the observer and the observed. Goethe employed an epistemology that could be called conscious-process-participation. This epistemology focuses on process

> and relationship and allows for intuitive perception of direct knowledge of the world. It focuses attention on the phenomena themselves and on the dynamic relationships they form in space and time and between the observer and the observed. Goethe rec-ognized the observer as a participant.[4]

When we leave behind the core superstition consisting of the observer/observed duality, we find ourselves in the world of *participation*. A philological or etymological inquiry throws interesting light on the word. The word 'participation' is made up of two parts: Latin *parti* 'division,' and *capere* 'to grasp.' A little creative philology leads us to the phrase: *to grasp the division*. When we grasp the division we are no longer caught in it and hence *we are participating*. That is to say, when our attention is located or focused on the commonsense division (between observer and observed), the cognitive function is freed of it in the very act of comprehending. This is not to ignore or substitute the everyday meaning of the word 'participation' but to deepen its significance by taking into account the source meanings. The drift of language is caught and turned back upon itself to reveal something more than that to which contingent usage has brought the word.

Implicit in *participation* is a directness or im-mediacy that is distinct from the epistemic lens through which rationalism organizes its relations with the world. The empathy in participation can also be understood as a certain raised level of being different from the blandness of the ordinary level of reality with its binaries and oppositions that can establish direct or intuitive connect with phenomena. Recoiling from the ordinary fixation of thought with measurement, meditative thought, by means of in-gathering or in-dwelling, prevents loss of existential intensity thereby providing a corporeal basis for embodied participation.

> Barfield proposed that Goethe tried to understand process by perceiv-ing the phenomena and potential phenomena directly "as such" and not as "hypotheses inferred from actual phenomena" (Barfield 1988, p. 138). The Goethean epistemology is to be understood as complementary to but incom-mensurable with the Cartesian epistemology. It may help us in achieving a more holistic understanding of the processes in which we

[4] Daniel C. Wahl, "Zarte Empirie: Goethean Science as a Way of Knowing," *Janus Head*, 8 (1), 2005, pp. 58–76.

> participate... Goethe engaged with science out of the same deep empathy for and curiosity in nature that drove him to express nature's creativity as a writer and an artist. He was doubtful as to whether conventional scientific meth-odology should be accepted as the only and exclusive approach to gaining meaningful knowledge and insights about nature. While recognizing the importance and power of the measuring, quantifying, analytical and purely rational focus of his contemporaries in their scientific studies, Goethe fol-lowed his intuition and relied on his own, direct experience of the natural world as a source for his scientific insights.[5]

Conventional approach to empirical science is through the formulation of hypotheses and their testing in the light of observed behavior. Goethe endeavored to do away with formal hypothesizing and instead attempted to immerse himself directly into the flow of things themselves. In traditional science, when we hypothesize about a flower, we attempt to leave out all intuitive impressions and phenomenological sensations save what the object presents to us in measurement. But for Goethe, such isolation of the object was not possible or desirable; the esthetic dimension necessarily entered the observation (at the very least in the precise act of objectification). The esthetics apparent in Schelling's discussion of ontological necessity—the totality of the phenomenal world (its presence in cognition) being a continuous reciprocal passage between form and essence—would seem to lend substance to Goethe's position.

To Goethe, the esthetic dimension was not whimsical distortion but equally objective, arrived at through careful dismantling of the traditional barrier between experiencer and experienced. At the same time, this perspective was not meant to replace conventional empirical methodology but was offered as a complementary viewpoint that gave insights into nature from other equally important perspectives. As Schelling had noted, conventional science tells us about the 'what' of things but not the 'why' of things. To understand the necessity of things one must listen to nature very carefully in all its splendor and not expect to receive quick answers by breaking her up into parts. In *Conversations*, Goethe remarks:

> Aristotle observed nature better than any modern, but he was too hasty with his opinions. We must go slowly and gently to work with nature, if we would get anything out of her. If, on investigating natural objects,

[5] Ibid., pp. 59–60. Text rearranged.

> I formed an opinion, I did not expect nature to concede the point at once, but I pursued her with observations and experiments, and was satisfied if she were kind enough to confirm my opinion when occasion offered. If she did not do this, she at any rate brought me to some other view, which I followed out, and which I perhaps found her more willing to confirm.[6]

Notice that it is against the background of the "her" (not 'it') or the totality of creation alone, that each part-phenomenon makes sense. In other words, things have meaning only in relation to the whole and not in themselves. And yet, the whole may not reveal its connection to the part easily. One cannot be too hasty in arriving at this understanding. Great patience is necessary for the part to intuit its connection to the whole as well as to other parts.

Further, it is amply clear from the language above that Goethe perceives nature as unity and proceeds to listen from that holism, persevering in a different kind of sensorial alignment. This is not an additive from the outside or something extra over the usual, but the unique development of an ***instinct-toward-totality*** from which perspective the sensible is organized. This latter perspective is outside the epistemic bounds of natural science which has no concept of nature or totality as such. This is the key difference between the two approaches. While Goethe proceeds through intuition into necessary unity, empirical science constructs reality from the finitude of particulars. Thus it is that Goethe says: "In living nature nothing happens that is not in connection with a whole. When experiences appear to us in isolation or when we look at experiments as presenting only isolated facts, that is not to say that the facts are indeed isolated. The question is: how do we find the connections between phenomena or [events] within a given situation?"[7] Merely because phenomena present themselves to consciousness in an isolated fashion does not imply that at their source these are unconnected or isolated. Our task is rather to discover the intrinsic relations between phenomena (including ourselves) and not merely study them as isolated objects.

[6]J.W. von Goethe, *Conversations of Goethe with Eckermann and Soret, Vol. II*, trans. John Oxenford (London: Smith, Elder, 1850), p. 71.

[7]J.W. von Goethe, "The Experiment as Mediator of Object and Subject," trans. Craig Holdrege, *In Context*, No. 24, Fall 2010, p. 17. Source: "*Der Versuch als Vermittler von Objekt und Subjekt*," in Goethe's *Werke*, Hamburger Ausgabe, Bd. 13 (Munich: Verlag C. H. Beck, 2002, pp. 10–20).

But such discovery cannot be accomplished without a proper examination of the existing nature of thinking which objectifies and projects. That is to say, in order to understand thinking, which is our present project, we have to grasp the manner in which thought objectifies and then expends itself on the object in turn.[8]

The morphology of thought must be uncovered delicately as it reveals itself in its various preoccupations and engagements. In order to change the habits of thought and direct it toward itself, a hermeneutic phenomenology of thinking must be developed toward which lessons can be drawn from Goethe's attempt to discover a new consciousness of matter and to inhabit it through loss of fragmentation. In other words, Goethe's inquiry into science can be seen at the same time as an inquiry into the habits of thought, for science, or the systematic inquiry into causes and effects, cannot but be in reciprocal relation with the cognitive matrix which organizes it. Therefore it is true to say that it is only when thought engages directly with itself, voluntarily sacrificing the built-up image of itself, that a new intuition can arise about phenomenal relations, and an ontologically participatory world visualized.

> Goethe...directed his conscious awareness toward the process of engagement itself. He developed a methodology for a participa-tory, phenomenon-focused science which allows anybody who engages in its sustained

[8]Goethe observes: "We can never be too careful in our efforts to avoid drawing hasty conclusions from experiments or using them directly as proof to bear out some theory. For here at this pass, this transition from empirical evidence to judgment, cognition to application, all the inner enemies of man lie in wait: imagination, which sweeps him away on his wings before he knows his feet have left the ground; impatience; haste; self-satisfaction; rigidity; formalistic thought; prejudice; ease; frivolity; fickleness—this whole throng and its retinue. Here they lie in ambush and surprise not only the active observer but also the contemplative one who appears safe from all passion. I would venture to say we cannot prove anything by one experiment or even several experiments together, that nothing is more dangerous than the desire to prove some thesis directly through experiments. ... Every piece of empirical evidence we find, every experiment in which this evidence is repeated, really represents just one part of what we know. ... Every piece of empirical evidence, every experiment, must be viewed as isolated, yet the human faculty of thought forcibly strives to unite all external objects known to it. ... We often find that the more limited the data, the more artful a gifted thinker will become. As though to assert his sovereignty he chooses a few agreeable favorites from the limited number of facts and skillfully marshals the rest so they never contradict him directly. Finally he is able to confuse, entangle, or push aside the opposing facts and reduce the whole to something more like the court of a despot than a freely constituted republic." Ibid., p. 21.

> practice to access an experience of reality as process, interac-tion and relationship. Moreover, the resulting experiences are not arbitrary projections by individuals but can be verified by others.[9]

Rather than look for quick scientific results, that is, be guided by the pressures of establishing conventional cause-effect relations, the Goethean approach focuses on "the process of engagement itself," or a participatory mode of being-with-all-that-is. Rather than a cold appraisal of objects and forces, the approach calls for an intense engagement with phenomena that promotes conditions leading to the intuition for assessing immanent connections. An investigation into a flower might involve the gradual opening of a plane of intuition in which all naming is set aside; with the arrest of the usual movement of thought-naming, a different upsurge of concentrated attention overwhelms the situation. One can see that reality as "process, interaction and relationship" above leads toward de-subjectification, or the displacement of the experiencer as the collater of things. Opticality as principal cognitive habit is supplanted by corporeal and tactile sensibilities. This constitutes steps for psychic development toward parallel realities. Once beyond the optical habit, or the privileging of the visual apperception that sees reality in terms of discrete objects in space, the subject is placed within the draft of the phenomena and their continuities beyond discreteness. Here, the privileging of the observer ends, and along with that ends the deadly intentionality of the human.

The implications for thinking now become clear. Across dominant cultures, thought has become used to segregating, naming, framing, postulating, shaping, and commandeering the "outer." The Will-to-action in thought as legitimate pragmatics has been historically enshrined as an unquestionable formal doctrine. That is to say, thought will translate into action whatever it is capable of doing, and hence whatever is thinkable in thought as possible action and intervention in the outer is carried out or attempted as legitimate modification of the real. In contrast, here, thinking is required to engage not in further will-to-action or modification, but to awaken to its own *in-tuition*, which means 'to watch over.' This is true *phronesis* or practical wisdom coming from meta-knowledge of thought. A persistent existential vigilance is demanded in Goethean empiricism that leads not to the representation of isolated forms and

[9] Wahl, op. cit., p. 61.

deductions about those forms, but to the *en-formations*, that is, the fluid coming-to-be and ceasing-to-be of those forms. In short, the ceaseless transformations in reality are the only true "things" in nature. Goethe notes: "Form is a moving, a becoming, a passing away. The study of form is the study of transformation. The study of meta-morphosis is the key to all the signs of nature,"[10] and again, of the fundamental connection between things, "Let me say only so much here: since everything in nature, especially the more common forces and elements, is in eternal action and reaction, we can say of every phenomenon that it is connected to countless others, just as a radiant point of light sends out its rays in all directions."[11] Forms continually morph into other forms, and ultimately, we can think of a specific form as nothing other than an effect on its way to another effect ad infinitum. Only habit of thought makes us break up the world into the constancy of discrete objects.

> Employing a conscious-process-participation epistemology in the study of the natural world results in a new way of perceiving the spatial-temporal dimensions and relationships of form. Form becomes an expression of the process of its continuous transformation, which in turn is linked to a larger process that unites the form with its environment and its observer.[12]

The gentle disclosure of the continual transformation is the task of intuition, which moves outward and inward simultaneously to overcome the naturalized division in thought. As our view of the object changes, so does our perception of the viewer.

But at the same time, Goethe warns against the caprice of imagination in thought; one must not get carried away by resourceful imaginings:

> For at this pass—the transition from experience to judgment, from knowledge to application—lie in wait all our inner enemies: imaginative powers that lift us on their wings into heights while letting us believe we have our feet firmly on the ground, impatience, haste, self-satisfaction, rigidity, thought forms, preconceived opinions, lassitude, frivolity, and fickleness. This horde and all its followers lie in ambush and suddenly attack both the active observer and the quiet one who seems so well secured against all passions.[13]

[10] Wahl, op. cit., p. 66.

[11] Goethe, "The Experiment," p. 19.

[12] Ibid.

[13] Goethe, "The Experiment," p. 20.

When imagination "creatively" rearranges what is perceptible then that can hardly lead to useful intuition or insight. We must be very careful when we use the word imagination with respect to thinking. Intuition and insight is to be sharply distinguished from imagination. Goethe writes, "...my thinking is not separate from the objects; that the elements of the object, the perceptions of the object, flow into my thinking and are fully permeated by it; that my perception itself is a way of thinking, and my thinking a perception."[14] There is a difference between thinking *about* objects and thinking *with* objects. The subject facing the world presents a psychological "skin" from within which there is a looking out on reality. This psychological skin is the subjective filter that in part determines object relations. Intuition in this instance is a negative capacity that restrains the operation of the filter. Only when the filter is restrained can the "object" be truly revealed as a process, and even a psychic process. The imagination, which is otherwise seen as an active process, has no useful role here, as imaginative thinking can only interfere with disclosure. When we have gotten so far in our understanding of thought, we have realized something quite vital: without the resistance of the "skin" of thought, the highly acute apperceptions have a different flow within the psyche. These are no longer determined and disciplined by the specific cultural forms of knowledge and recollection. Rather we experience a situation where there is a breakdown of the inner/outer barrier. It is no longer easy to determine where the object ends and the observation begins. In conventional science, the termination of the object is crucial in order to define its causal limits, and the cloistering of the observation process is equally important to establish the clinicality of the procedure. Whereas in Goethean manner of looking what are mainly visible are changes and entanglements (joint flows) that nevertheless produce wholesome being-in-knowledge. There is a gradual overlap here between epistemology and ontology.[15] The singularities—conglomerates of form

[14]Goethe, *Scientific Studies*, p. 39.

[15]Noted thinker Rudolf Steiner observes: "This view is in a position to unite two things that are regarded today as completely incompatible: the empirical method, and idealism as a scientific world view. It is believed that to accept the former means necessarily to reject the latter. This is absolutely not true. To be sure, if one considers the senses to be the only organs of apprehension for objective reality, then one must arrive at the above view. For, the senses offer us only such relationships of things as can be traced back to mechanical laws. And the mechanistic world view would thus be given as the only true form of any such world view. In this, one is making the mistake of simply overlooking the other

and essence—cannot be separated in the old manner. The old signposts are thus withdrawn and thought is thrown into a quandary. The shock in thought is essential for habit to be broken and for a new space and topology to make its appearance which is not a mere adjustment in the old. But at the same time we know that Goethe was not sacrificing any rigor of the old, nor are we, in our study of thinking, attempting to reduce thought to a mangled heap at the altar of experience.

> Nothing was farther from Goethe's nature than taking one's start in a conscious way from general concepts. He always takes his start from *concrete facts*, compares and orders them. During this activity, the ideas underlying the facts occur to him. It is a great mistake to assert that, because of that familiar enough remark he made about the idea of Faust, it is not ideas that are the driving principle in Goethe's creative work. In his contemplation of things, after he has stripped away everything incidental, everything unessential, there remains something for him that is *idea* in his sense. The *method* Goethe employs remains—even there where he lifts himself to the *idea*—one that is founded upon pure experience. For, nowhere does he allow a subjective ingredient to slip into his research. He only frees the phenomena from what is incidental in order to penetrate into their deeper foundations. His subject has no other task than that of arranging the object in such a way that it discloses its innermost nature. "The true is Godlike; it does not appear directly; we must divine it from its manifestations." The point is to bring these manifestations into such a relationship that the "true" appears. The true, the *idea*, already lies within the fact which we confront in observation; we must only remove the covering that conceals it from us. The true scientific method consists in the removing of this covering. Goethe took this path.[16]

component parts of reality which are just as objective but which *cannot* be traced back to mechanical laws... By approaching Goethe with these views, we believe we are entering into his essential nature. We hold fast to idealism and develop it, not on the basis of Hegel's dialectic method, but rather upon a clarified higher empiricism. This kind of empiricism also underlies the philosophy of Eduard v. Hartmann. Eduard v. Hartmann seeks the ideal unity in nature, as this does positively yield itself to a thinking that has *real content.* He rejects the merely mechanistic view of nature and the hyper-Darwinism that is stuck on externals. In science, he is the founder of a concrete monism. In history and aesthetics, he seeks concrete ideas, and does all this according to empirical inductive methods." Rudolf Steiner, *Goethean Science*, trans. William Lindemann (e.text edition: The Mercury Press, 1988), pp. 58–59.

[16] Rudolf Steiner, *Goethean Science*, trans. William Lindemann (e.text edition: The Mercury Press, 1988), pp. 58–59.

When thinking sticks to concrete facts (without the distraction of the thinker), and learns to move from fact to fact, rather than from some general idea, one may anticipate a revolution in thought. The truth, unfortunately, remains that thinking engages most often in reverie, expectation, or phantasy as psychologists well know, and does not remain anchored to facts, which is not to say that it does not refer to facts. But, if movement is to uncover or disclose truth about the manifest, then it is incumbent upon thought to move with precision, and simultaneously remain conscious of the geography of thinking that is free of expectation and the psychological. The movement from fact to fact, or truth to truth, reveals the underlying pattern which is the *idea*. It is this organic movement itself, and not something isolated or abstracted from it, which is the idea, and which in turn is not a mere construct but already lies hidden within experience. The true is God-like because it discloses a necessity and not something unessential or anthropocentric. And the method of apprehension is to lift one's being to the level of the underlying relationships between the manifestations by bracketing expectations along with the background psychological chatter of the observer.

In learning how to think, another superstition in thinking that must needs to be discarded is the conventional idea that the esthetic needs to be set aside from all serious (objective) consideration of what is. The esthetic domain is supposed to be something in the imagination and left to the private domain. It took the genius of Goethe to bring the esthetic and the scientific on the same plane of authentic observation. In learning how to think again, and toward the task of being underway, this is a stupendous realization.

> Our age believes itself correct in keeping art and science as far apart as possible. They are supposed to be two completely opposing poles in the cultural evolution of mankind. Science, one thinks, is supposed to sketch for us the most objective picture of the world possible; it is supposed to show us reality in a mirror; or, in other words, it is supposed to hold fast purely to the given, renouncing all subjective arbitrariness. The objective world determines the laws of science; science must subject itself to this world. Science should take the yardstick for what is true and false entirely from the objects of experience. The situation is supposedly quite different in the case of artistic creations. Their law is given them by the self-creative power of the human spirit. For science, any interference of human subjectivity would be a falsifying of reality, a going beyond experience; art,

> on the other hand, grows upon the field of the subjectivity of a genius. Its creations are the productions of human imagination, not mirror images of the outer world. Outside of us, in objective existence, lies the source of scientific laws; within us, in our individuality, lies the source of esthetic laws. The latter, therefore, have not the slightest value for knowledge; they create illusions without the slightest element of reality. Whoever grasps the matter in this way will never become clear about the relationship of Goethean poetry to Goethean science. He will only misunderstand both. Goethe's world historic significance lies, indeed, precisely in the fact that his art flows directly from the *primal source of all existence*, that there is nothing illusory or subjective about it, that, on the contrary, his art appears as the herald of that lawfulness that the poet has grasped by listening to the world spirit within the depths of nature's working. At this level, art becomes the interpreter of the mysteries of the world just as science is also, in a different sense.[17]

One of the biggest errors embedded in thinking is the assumption that art is subjective and idiosyncratic, the product of inward virtuosity, having therefore no value for reflecting on what is. In this view, there is no realization of objective reality in art. But authentic art is not subjective creation, nor is it the capricious outgrowth of some feverish imagination. The root of all authentic art is the primal source of existence whereby the psychic-existential flow re-turns to essence and essence back into form. Art merely captures that moment of transformation in multiple and various ways. If disclosure about the nature of the world is knowledge then art reveals through the intuition of the artist the deepest mysteries about the world, albeit in a different metaphor. In the writings of Goethe, for example, the exchanges between Faust and Mephistopheles, if followed carefully, take us to a plane wherein an insight into evil as ontology becomes possible.[18] In other words, a truth about the nature of the world is revealed in art. This is achieved not through propositional logic, nor through some pious discourse, but by taking the reader little by little into a space where the dark passages of the soul are exposed, and the normal defenses of the ego have already been left behind. Whereas science attempts to find causal connections between discrete facts, bracketing the phenomenological side of the scientist, art tries to disclose the

[17] Ibid., p. 60.

[18] J.W. von Goethe, *Faust*, trans. Bayard Taylor (University Park: Pennsylvania State University Press, 2005).

immanent connections and relationships without denying the psychic consciousness of the artist. The two are complementary to each other and are not to be ranked as more true or less true to reality. Those who set these in hierarchical terms neither understand art nor science or the proper relationship between them.

Goethe himself goes deep into the relationship between art and science in a manner that is highly interesting and useful for our reflections on thinking. "I think that one could call science the knowledge of the general, abstracted knowing; art, on the other hand, would be science turned into action; science would be reason, and art its mechanism; therefore one could also call art practical science. And finally then science could be called the theorem and art the problem."[19] One way of articulating the relation between art and science is to consider the latter as a mode of abstract apprehension and the former as a vehicle of insight into the sensible domain of the being. Equally, art could be thought of as intuition of the central existential problematic, and science, the formal theorizing of the same in its concreteness. From either end, the abstract necessity takes psychic form relevant to the human in its growth toward the idea. What science states as theorem therefore is what art might realize in nature. Further, Goethe notes: "In the works of man, as in those of nature, it is the intentions that are primarily worthy of note."[20] Intention must not be understood as private objectives but the deeper alignments within the organism that get revealed in works. So in nature, the specific form is a particular culmination of broader tendencies that maybe called intention. Goethe seeks out these "intentions" underlying the immense diversity of forms. He is not merely trying to piece together what is given to the senses, but attempting to uncover the tendency through which the manifest comes into being. Science for Goethe is the comprehension of these tendencies, and his artistic endeavor is to hold it up to consciousness in terms of form. Transposing this to thinking: on the one hand, thinking is an *organ of apprehension* not unlike the other senses that must be open to the affinities in the real.[21] On the other hand, thinking must carry out activities in alignment with these affinities. The action without the realization of the affinity is misconceived and empty.

[19] Goethe, *Science Studies*, cited in Steiner, op. cit., p. 42.

[20] Ibid.

[21] In Buddhist philosophy, thought is taken to be another (sixth) sense.

From each specific object or thing in nature one must go back to the tendencies that those formations are a culmination of, or that which they represent. For thinking as such, it means turning back always to the source of each thought.

> The point is not *what* nature has created but rather the principle by which nature has created it. Then this principle is to be developed in the way that accords with its own nature, and not in the way this has occurred in each particular entity of nature in accordance with thousands of chance factors. The artist has to evolve the noble out of the common and the beautiful out of the unformed.[22]

In the same manner, thinking assumes multiple and diverse forms each instant, but the task is to draw out each tendency and study it thoroughly and not be taken in by the specific form it has assumed in thought. The noble in thought arises when it realizes and admits for the first time that it has to learn to think. For the first time there is the glimpse of necessity rather than the accidental. Goethe writes that the esthetic is thus "a manifestation of secret laws of nature, that, except for the phenomenon of the beautiful, would have remained forever hidden to us. The great works of art have at the same time been brought forth by human beings according to *true* and *natural* laws, just as are the greatest works of nature. Everything that is arbitrary, thought-up, falls away; there is necessity, there is God."[23] We must realize this necessity in thought; such is called being underway toward redemptive thinking. Then there is no longer a difference between the ground of being and thinking. The esthetic is realized in thought when thinking fuses with necessity and becomes one with objective reality.

Obviously this requires phenomenological labor, for we are used to the operation of thinking as personal whim mixed with socially anointed "purpose," and conclusions from datum. To consider different aspects of thinking, their unconscious assumptions, the schisms and fractures brought about through and because of these assumptions, as well as the consequences of these divisions in social reality demand that we patiently and critically look at these determinations from multiple angles.

[22] Steiner, op. cit., p. 43.

[23] Goethe, cited in Steiner, op. cit., p. 53.

We have chosen the art/science opposition in thought as one such crucial division through which social reality is constructed—a potent lens through which we can examine the inner workings of thought. If we take away the signifiers 'art' and 'science,' that is, attempt to look without these labels, what we are left with are certain contents of consciousness distinguished by well-established norms of thought *validated in thought*. Occasionally a mind like Goethe's comes along, upsets all the divisions and imposed categories, and forces us to look at everything anew. For such a mind, the categories are merely pragmatic ones and not born of necessity.

> [To] Goethe, art seems to be just as objective as science. Only the form of each is different. Each appears to flow forth from *one* being, to be the necessary stages of one evolution. Any view was antithetical to him that relegates art or what is beautiful to an isolated position *outside* of the total picture of human evolution. Thus he says: "In the aesthetic realm, it is not good to speak of the idea of the beautiful; in doing so, one isolates the beautiful, which after all cannot be thought of as separate." Or: "Style rests upon the deepest foundations of *knowledge*, upon the being of things, insofar as we are allowed to *know* this being in visible and tangible forms." *Art rests therefore upon our activity of knowing*. The latter has the task of recreating in thought the order according to which the world is put together; art has the task of developing in detail the idea of this order that the world-all has. The artist incorporates into his work everything about the lawfulness of the world that is attainable to him. His work thus appears as a world in miniature. Herein lies the reason why the Goethean direction in art must supplement itself with science. As art, it is already an activity of knowing. Goethe, in fact, wanted neither science nor art: *he wanted the idea*. And he expresses or represents the idea in the direction from which the idea happens to present itself to him. Goethe sought to ally himself with the world spirit, and to reveal to us how it holds sway; he did this through the medium of art or of science as required. What lay in Goethe was not any one-sided artistic or scientific striving, but rather the indefatigable urge to behold "all working forces and seeds."[24]

In the consideration of art, thought often speaks of the "beautiful," mixing it up with the idea of the esthetic. Authentic or good art is not beautiful but profound in its disclosure. Beauty has a diminutive root in PIE *deu*, "to do" or "perform." Beauty is not a characteristic fixed in

[24]Ibid., p. 65.

time but a certain kind of performance. Beauty cannot be isolated from action and be regarded as an attribute or quality of a thing but instead is a certain active performance in thought. Beauty is that performance by the artist, and by extension, of the sensitive viewer, which holds the object under consideration for the purpose of recreating in thought the otherwise invisible relationships. The work that comes out of such beholding is the world of relationships in "miniature." This is another reason why science cannot be separated from art, and is in fact necessary for art. A good artist must have profound knowledge of science, just as a good scientist must deeply acknowledge esthetics. But, Goethe was not interested in science or art for their own sakes. Instead he was after the "idea," or that which is immanent within each leaf and every raindrop. In learning to think, thinking must proscribe one-sided pursuit of science or art, for all such one-sided pursuits lead to illusion (partiality masquerading as objectivity) even though they might result in some kind of knowledge. Recall, this is why Heidegger says that "science does not think." It merely uses the outer movement of thought to piece together description from facts, but the outer description from isolated facts is only one side of things which the habitual preoccupation with representation make us believe is the whole. It makes us believe that thought is the mirror of reality which is of course a dangerous deception.

The reversal of this deception demands the understanding that redemptive thinking is not born of truncated or one-sided descriptions of reality. Rather, as we have seen earlier, it is born of Janus-headedness—of facing simultaneously toward origin or essence. And where thinking is whole, it is radically different from thinking as we know it. In speaking of Goethe, Steiner remarks that the school of J.S. Mill and others assume that all we can do with experience is merely bring particular things together into constellations of intelligibility that we then hold as abstract concepts, which is not true knowing. "For, those abstract concepts of Mill have no other task than that of bringing together what is presented to the senses with all the qualities of direct experience. A true knowing must acknowledge that the direct form of the world given to sense perception is not yet its essential one, but rather that this essential form first reveals itself to us in the process of knowing."[25] Grouping phenomena or forming constellations does not lead us to true knowledge

[25] Steiner, op. cit., p. 69.

although it might lead us to useful worldly strategy. Instead, knowledge must deliberately move inward from phenomena to *noumenon* or essence. Knowing must provide us with that which sense experience cannot directly offer us, but work toward the uncovering of the essence within sense experience which is the door to the Real. Mill's will-to-knowledge does not therefore lead to true knowing, because it is merely an elaboration of sense experience itself. "It is not that we should leave the realm of the experienceable and lose ourselves in a construct of fantasy, but rather, we should advance from the form of the experienceable as it presents itself to us in what is given to the senses, to a form of it that satisfies our reason."[26] In taking forward the project of thinking therefore the question that we must address is: How does what is directly (sensorially) experienced relate to *what is*? For the sensible meets us in a form that we cannot directly regard as true to *what is*. Hence, if phenomena facing our sense perceptions, or any constellation of them, is not the true disclosure of what is, what then is true disclosure? We first taste its true form when we release our thinking into a previously unknown fluid state. That means allowing the movement of thought without technical manipulation involving the conventional separation of controller and controlled. Thus we arrive at the realm of holistic thinking in the present context. Authentic disclosure means: to add the perception of *this* thinking to the half reality of sense experience so that this picture of half reality becomes complete. Here then is the key to the mystery.

We taste true disclosure when we bring our *thinking into flux*, or into discord with its own linear, categorical functioning, as well as its typical pious scheming. Disclosure occurs naturally when thought melts down, as it were. Thought is resistance working in recognition. It habitually operates as a reaction to appearances and occurrences, to needs and challenges. That is the conventional working of thought. But redemptive thinking must attempt to do what thought has never done before—flow immanently without directionality. The separation between itself and phenomena is operationally dropped because it is no longer separating, measuring, calculating, resisting, etc. Now there is flux, meaning fluidity, without a flight from essence. The corpus of thought arises and then breaks down without registration (eternal return), and is thus able to merge with the arising of the phenomena in thought without

[26]Ibid.

preconceptions or formulations. It must be admitted that even a minimal grasp of this requires substantial phenomenological effort and sacrifice.

It is certainly not being suggested that there is nothing to know objectively but to flow with experience, but rather to realize the place of the immanent alongside the transcendental character of thought-experience. Recall the Mind/Nature equation in Schelling. Now the cognition comes not from mental picture alone but from *ontological correspondence* of mind and nature. The rhythm within phenomena that had remained undetected is now found in the ontological correspondence, which is far from the unity of the Kantian synthesis. There is no invention of, and intervention by, epistemic categories. This is not to belittle the scientific viewpoint which arrives at synthetic judgements after carefully examining facts and their causal relations. Rather, this is to recast *our relations* with those facts. As Steiner puts it, "Truth is not the coinciding of a mental picture with its object [of reference], but rather the expression of a relationship between two observed facts."[27] The correspondence theory of truth is misleading; what we can truly know are relationships and our meaningful place within those relations. We are in need of a poesy and a holistic pedagogy of meaning that goes far deeper than the conventional subject/object duality and its cognitive resolution. The subtle poesy of nature then re-establishes itself in perception, and thinking operates according to necessity. Thus, a poesy toward establishing ontological correspondence in thought becomes the key philosophical praxis in our investigation regarding learning how to think, and understand the meaning and process of being underway toward redemption in thought.

The question of poesy of nature manifesting in philosophical poesy needs further explanation, from which arises a pressing need to illustrate the last point regarding ontological correspondence. Let us look for this intuition directly in the work of the poet-philosopher. I quote from no other source than Goethe's *Faust*:

> Go, find yourself a more obedient slave!
> What! shall the Poet that which Nature gave,
> The highest right, supreme Humanity,
> Forfeit so wantonly, to swell your treasure?
> Whence o'er the heart his empire free?
> The elements of Life how conquers he?

[27] Ibid., p. 70.

Is't not his heart's accord, urged outward far and dim,
To wind the world in unison with him?
When on the spindle, spun to endless distance,
By Nature's listless hand the thread is twirled,
And the discordant tones of all existence
In sullen jangle are together hurled,
Who, then, the changeless orders of creation
Divides, and kindles into rhythmic dance?
Who brings the One to join the general ordination,
Where it may throb in grandest consonance?
Who bids the storm to passion stir the bosom?
In brooding souls the sunset burn above?
Who scatters every fairest April blossom
Along the shining path of Love?
Who braids the noteless leaves to crowns, requiting
Desert with fame, in Action's every field?
Who makes Olympus sure, the Gods uniting?
The might of Man, as in the Bard revealed.[28]

The Poet rejects worldly prize and glory for that which Nature has entrusted to him. Reading ontologically, what is this nature's treasure? Is it not a particular manifestation of essence, a specifically bounded expression of the Principle? What would tempt the Poet to forfeit the intuition of essence with which Nature had entrusted him and instead give into the fruits of glib expression? His heart's empire is boundless in the glory of essence. What, after all, can exceed this supreme quality? It is not to be exchanged for the dependence on the phenomenal, which is but an instant in the movement between form and essence. Nature has given the Poet the "highest right" to manifest that which is supremely human: the possibility of tracing phenomena back to their essence. It is thus that the Poet conquers the "elements of life." The Poet has been en-tasked with producing unity between the phenomenal world and himself. In other words, he seeks ontological correspondence between the rhythm that is himself and the rhythm that is the objective world. He seeks to disclose this correspondence as the true poetic activity. The restless activity of Nature spins and casts its thread widely and outwards in befuddling ways, meaning that phenomena arise and subside in Nature

[28] J.W. von Goethe, "Prelude at the Theatre," in *Faust*, trans. Bayard Taylor (Pennsylvania: Pennsylvania State University Press, 2005), p. 16.

in myriad ways. Within the welling up of this "sullen jangle" or aggressive simulacra, the Poet must find the "rhythm" that is hidden in their midst. Who but the Poet can, by means of his deepest intuition, crown these anarchies, and call upon the divine to preside over the coronation. In the Poet's receptive bosom does the storm as phenomenon take the shape of an organic stirring that is pure activity, and through his breast does the sunset's splendor reach each "brooding soul." It is the poetic sensibility that brings fully to us Spring's renewal, and takes us beyond the melancholic turn of life, toward Love. It is the poet's ability to get to the essence that makes barren lands also appear full of promise and bring reconciliation among quarreling gods. With the help of poesy, we now begin to understand ontological correspondence also as a form of transcendental Love.

Compare this sensibility with Faust's bitterness about his empty existence that, in his own words, was an existence full of barren knowledge that does not bring him the insight or power he seeks:

> I've studied now Philosophy
> And Jurisprudence, Medicine,—
> And even, alas! Theology,—
> From end to end, with labor keen;
> And here, poor fool! with all my lore
> I stand, no wiser than before:
> I'm Magister—yea, Doctor—hight,
> And straight or cross-wise, wrong or right,
> These ten years long, with many woes,
> I've led my scholars by the nose,—
> And see, that nothing can be known!
> *That* knowledge cuts me to the bone.
> I'm cleverer, true, than those fops of teachers,
> Doctors and Magisters, Scribes and Preachers;
> Neither scruples nor doubts come now to smite me,
> Nor Hell nor Devil can longer affright me.
> For this, all pleasure am I foregoing;
> I do not pretend to aught worth knowing,
> I do not pretend I could be a teacher
> To help or convert a fellow-creature.
> Then, too, I've neither lands nor gold,
> Nor the world's least pomp or honor hold—
> No dog would endure such a curst existence!

Wherefore, from Magic I seek assistance,
That many a secret perchance I reach
Through spirit-power and spirit-speech,
And thus the bitter task forego
Of saying the things I do not know,—
That I may detect the inmost force
Which binds the world, and guides its course;
Its germs, productive powers explore,
And rummage in empty words no more![29]

Faust has learned everything from Jurisprudence to theology, from Philosophy to Medicine, and yet he stands "no wiser than before." Why? Faust has discovered that "nothing can be [truly] known" and it is *this* knowledge that is destroying him. But why is it that nothing can be known despite the labored acquisition of tomes of esoteric doctrine? No doubt Faust is a clever man through all his learning, but he does not have the wisdom and the truly productive powers that he seeks. All his learning has not endowed him with insight into the world. In this epic verse, Goethe is obviously alluding to the human condition: Faust is an allegory of Man. We have amassed formidable knowledge and yet humanity is fundamentally forlorn, perpetually in a fallen state. Knowledge has not delivered us from suffering, which was its early promise.

A basic error of thinking-as-knowing is the implicit faith in *expansionism*. Thought believes in the expansion of knowledge with a religious fervor. It believes that by expanding its knowledge base systematically it is edging closer to the real secret of the world and of life. A related and equally important error is the belief that thinking realizes *independent* knowledge. Both these beliefs are closely related, and together produce the grand illusion of a rationally progressive humanity.[30] However, a dispassionate and careful analysis shows that what thinking recovers in reality is not something independent but largely its own footprint and its own imprint in matter. It can hardly be otherwise, for the concept through which it manages the form in cognition is its own constellations

[29] Goethe, *Faust*, p. 23.

[30] To discover, say, six new varieties of frogs or two more "fundamental particles" no doubt expands the store of knowledge but does nothing to tell us about the meaning or import of these phenomena in the larger scheme of things. This is true even when such finds have "practical" use because these remain external to us and do not alter the fundamental status of the human being as a fragmented and alienated self.

of intelligibility. This is not to say that we must disregard outer knowledge but to recognize that for that very reason, increasing the quantum of knowledge at our disposal does nothing to bring about wisdom or freedom. Faust's pain and predicament comes from this realization and its frank admission. The wisdom that Faust seeks consciously, and humanity unconsciously, is not available in the proliferation of thinking-as-knowing precisely because each piece of knowledge has meaning only in relationship to the living whole which is not available in thought. In the absence of insight into the whole (wisdom), knowledge of the fragment remains dead knowledge without emancipatory value.

Learning to think must learn to jettison the glorification of the fragment, refraining from increasing worldly and mental clutter, without disrespecting existing formal knowledge. This *parsimony* of thought is a major lesson we learn here. Parsimony is not the poverty of thought but a sacrifice of needless proliferation. The "rummaging" throws up clouds of simulacrum obscuring the singularities within. Faust sets aside all his books, rejects all the dead knowledge within, and concentrates on the sign of the Earth-Spirit. Thinking turns to face what it had for so long turned away from. Then,

> Ha! what a sudden rapture leaps from this
> I view, through all my senses swiftly flowing!
> I feel a youthful, holy, vital bliss
> In every vein and fibre newly glowing.
> Was it a God, who traced this sign,
> With calm across my tumult stealing,
> My troubled heart to joy unsealing,
> With impulse, mystic and divine…[31]

A new vitality, unknown till then, rushes through the corpus sensorium. For the first time the essence at the core of the being is stirred. But alas, as we see later, the essence turns away from Faust, leaving him bereft once more. For what he seeks is not essence but magical powers, that is, in other words, *techne* or control over phenomena. He is not the kindred-spirit, and so the Earth-Spirit quickly disappears. In due course, Mephistopheles will present himself and promise Faust what he seeks. The divine essence is not *techne*; it does not bestow anything but

[31] Goethe, *Faust*, p. 184.

'is-ness.' In one masterstroke, Goethe empties out the ethical discussions around technology that we hear today, and that were still in the making in a distant future, showing these to be basically a result of confusion of categories. The im-mediate present or Presence is always technologically empty. Only those who are prepared to be with this, and in this, space that is empty of *techne* can simply *be*, or grasp essence. But the 'sheerness' of the present that has no formal content is unthinkable and intolerable for many.

The past, on the other hand, accumulates as technological content, which is a substitute for Spirit. For those such as Faust, the preference must lie with technology which is the accumulated past: "Wherefore, from Magic I seek assistance/That many a secret perchance I reach ...." Faust seeks the will-to-power by which he could uncover or disclose for himself secret world relations and thereby exercise magical (technological) powers for self-optimization. He does not recognize any other onto-theology toward self-actualization. But as Heidegger has warned,

> What has long since been threatening man with death, and indeed the death of his own nature, is the unconditional character of mere willing in the sense of purposeful self-assertion in everything. What threatens man in his very nature is the willed view that man, by the peaceful release, transformation, storage, and channeling of the energies of physical nature could render the human condition, man's being, tolerable for everybody and happy in all respects.[32]

That is to say, the view that has increasingly taken hold, that has even attained virtual monopoly today, is that the only path to relevant world disclosure is by means of exercise of the will, and its concomitant technological expressions, such as the kind sought by Faust. The latter discovers a deep emptiness and want in himself which he wishes to overcome through will-to-knowledge.

This worldview, whose validity is unquestioned and unquestionable in the West, has succeeded in entrenching itself globally today. In comparison to this view that sees humans along with all other objects as intrinsically meaningless, as having no essence, and as mere resources at permanent standby for eventual optimization, all other viewpoints and

[32] Martin Heidegger, cited in Leslie Paul Thiele, *Timely Meditations: Martin Heidegger and Postmodern Politics* (Princeton, NJ: Princeton University Press, 1995), p. 211.

ways of being are vilified, trivialized, and even seen as downright treachery toward the modern way of thinking and being. "As this technological understanding of being takes hold and spreads, it dramatically transforms our relations to ourselves and our worlds, yet we tend not to notice these transformations, because their very pervasiveness helps render them invisible."[33] The "law of proximity" states that what is closest to us remains out of view. Thinking has brought us to the point where the historic reductionism escapes our ability to comprehend: "we late moderns come to treat even ourselves in the nihilistic terms that underlie our technological refashioning of the world."[34] It is important to recognize this as a certain kind of arrangement of thought: the use of pronouns such as "we" must not camouflage this fact. "We," in this case, are nothing but glorified thought, a particular arrangement or representation of a formal process. Hence it is inescapable that, while thinking has refashioned the world in technological terms, in this process it has refashioned our being itself in those very terms, all of us being arranged and ordered on a scale of efficiency and utility waiting for optimal utilization.

To counter this, the greatest need of the hour, Heidegger postulates, is the authentic need of "needlessness." Thinking must distance itself from the 'will-to-fill' and be prepared instead to question the epistemic narrative of need. In a world obsessed with the idea of scarcity and unlimited want, to talk about needlessness seems irrational and out of this world. The talismanic incantation of scarcity has made all modern humans bow instinctively and unquestioningly before the altar of need and want. But in learning how to think, we discover the historic discourse of scarcity as a particularly malignant concoction of thought. This invention of thought has underpinned and functioned as the justification for much of the economic activity of modern man, and the consequent ravaging of the planet. The invocation of need and the resultant perennial engagement with ontic clutter has not brought human beings an inch closer to the fullness of being. Hence the suggestion that it is actually needlessness that needs to be understood and embraced must be considered seriously as thinking enquires into redemption. That the *being* of the human has really no need of anything (other than basic organic ones), and is complete in itself, is the most counter-intuitive and

[33] Iain Thomson, *Heidegger on Ontotheology: Technology and the Politics of Education* (Cambridge, UK: Cambridge University Press, 2005), p. 56.

[34] Ibid.

radical notion that thinking must come to terms with. It challenges the expansionist core of thinking as it is practiced.

But to push that thinking further and make this discussion momentarily digress onto the social, can the argument about thinking afford to ignore the empirical fact of scarcity? Is there not food crisis, malnutrition, and the lack of proper health, housing, and education for a large portion of humanity? Are we attempting to philosophize away the shrill reality of want? It is doubtless true that there is great lack of the most basic kind across the world. Philosophy must acknowledge it, otherwise it fails in its most basic task of mitigating suffering. But it is nevertheless true that almost always this suffering is man-made or thought-made, this suffering is wantonly or callously visited upon peoples by the action of others.[35] In other words, thinking in its present mode lays the ground for systematic oppression calling it advancement. From our foregoing analysis, this oppression arises from a wrong understanding of the subject/object relation. Philosophical blindness has often led to the inability to free life and see it in correct perspective. Systematic deprivation has led to path dependencies that have stripped human collectivities of their native simplicities and equations with the land. Nation building pride has often led to the most hapless losing their small holdings and the disruption of their communities. Ideas of progress have destroyed sustainable and simple living. And so on. The point is that in each case, these are associated, directly or indirectly, with the philosophical thoughtlessness and psychological cravings (thinking habits) of certain groups who see themselves as integral subjects standing over and against an objective reality which is under their management. The truth is that almost all social ills are the consequence of a false manner of apprehending reality, and the problems are not to be mistaken as independent manifestations. Thinking must take the responsibility for all these ravages. But the unfortunate fact is that it does not deeply acknowledge this. Instead it proposes technological

[35]One objection often heard in this context is that the claim that all suffering is man-made is gross exaggeration, that nature compounds human woe through deluge, drought, disease, and so on. The simple answer to that objection is that we are not concerned here with natural disasters. We are, instead, concerned with the machinations of thought (that include war, exploitation, criminal deprivation, destruction of habitat, etc.) and those that are produced through direct human intentionality, or are the side effects and consequences of human action. The actions of Nature upon nature can only be understood in their proper perspective once humans cease to bring suffering upon planetary life. To speak of nature's contribution to misery is to avoid facing the issue.

solutions for the perceived problems seeing them somehow as independent of its own workings. This is the central deception. The problem is not with technology, which is but an offshoot of thinking, but with the problem creating mechanism itself, which is thought.

When thinking proposes a technological solution to a problem which is rooted in its own way of operation, then that solution cannot be an authentic one, since it is based on self-deception. Indeed, the deceptive solution breeds new problems in its very implementation, for both problem and solution essentially lie in the same activity of thought. That is why the technological solution is no true or lasting solution to human problems, and the effort leads to further degradation of an already precarious situation. And this is verified time and again in experience everywhere: thought has not found wholesome solution—a solution that does not set off a new chain of consequences—to anything.[36] For the "solution" comes from the same source as the problem itself. Thought agitates to create problems which it then tries to solve but cannot. Thus Faust is unable, in the end, to come to that absolute knowledge which he sought, by means of which he craved deliverance. Allegorically conveyed, Faust is nothing but a certain human temperament, a figment of thought—the persona is the mere outer cladding—that seeks the secrets of nature. But the secret comes to him as an illegitimate child forced to be destroyed. His "love" stays back in the prison unable to free herself or accompany him. Faust's last unfortunate words are "O had I ne'er been born!"[37] Faust had embarked on a mission of direct knowledge that would let him operate on the Real in an immediate way, but without developing the self-critical eye that questioned the nature of the division between object and subject. It is this latter task upon which we are embarked here throughout the present text.

[36] One argument heard time and again in defense of the technological concerns the domain of modern medicine. But one has only to read *Medical Nemesis* by Ivan Illich to get an exhaustive account and balance sheet of modern technological medicine. Modern pharmacology might allay much individual discomfort but cannot ensure health in general.

[37] "A shudder, long unfelt, comes o'er me;
Mankind's collected woe o'erwhelms me, here.
She dwells within the dark, damp walls before me,
And all her crime was a delusion dear!
What! I delay to free her?
I dread, once again to see her?
On! my shrinking but lingers Death more near." Goethe, *Faust*, p. 177.

Summary and Transition

Delicate empiricism of Goethe is not an esoteric doctrine. It is an approach that challenges the settled habits of thought as it has degenerated in the aeons through which thinking has moved away from what truly needs to be thought. In turning away from its source, thinking has invented empiricism as the sole way of arriving at objective truth. While this method does establish certain external results that are useful, it tells us nothing about why these results are there. As thought advances on the basis of the 'how' and without the 'why,' it invents a dangerously lop-sided reality in which each action results in multiple unforeseen consequences—the result of philosophical blindness. Delicate empiricism as distinct from gross empiricism opens up thought to the experienceable in a different manner. A deep esthetic intuition is called for, the gradual development of which has been the subject of the foregoing pages. The intuitive alignment of thinking-cognition with phenomena brings about participation (not mere knowledge), and a new organ of apprehension is born. This immanent process is further clarified by next looking into Heraclitus, the greatest of ontologists, who declared that all could be discovered by looking into one's being.

References

Shotter, John. "Goethe and the Refiguring of Intellectual Inquiry: From 'Aboutness'-Thinking to 'Withness'-Thinking in Everyday Life."*Janus Head* 8(1) (2005): 132–158.

Steiner, Rudolf. *Goethean Science*. Translated by William Lindemann. e.text edition: The Mercury Press, 1988. http://www.philosophyoffreedom.org/files/Goethean_Science.pdf.

Thiele, Leslie Paul. *Timely Meditations: Martin Heidegger and Postmodern Politics*. Princeton, NJ: Princeton University Press, 1995.

Thomson, Iain. *Heidegger on Ontotheology: Technology and the Politics of Education*. Cambridge, UK: Cambridge University Press, 2005.

von Goethe, J.W. *Conversations of Goethe with Eckermann and Soret, Vol. II*. Translated by John Oxenford. London: Smith, Elder, 1850.

von Goethe, J.W. *Scientific Studies*. Translated by Douglas Miller. Princeton: Princeton University Press, 2005.

von Goethe, J.W. *Faust*. Translated by Bayard Taylor. University Park: Pennsylvania State University Press, 2005.

von Goethe, J.W. "The Experiment as Mediator of Object and Subject." Translated by Craig Holdrege. *In Context*, No. 24 (Fall 2010): 17.

Wahl, Daniel C. "Zarte Empirie: Goethean Science as a Way of Knowing." *Janus Head* 8 (1) (2005): 58–76.
Wittgenstein, Ludwig. *Culture and Value*. Edited by George Henrik von Wright. London: Wiley-Blackwell, 1998.

CHAPTER 5

Among the "Presocratics": Heraclitus

Let us begin with a keen observation from Heidegger concerning the human penchant for easy labeling: "To present Parmenides as a Pre-Socratic is even more foolish than to call Kant a pre-Hegelian."[1] Without doubt this objection can be extended to apply to Heraclitus as well. As is obvious, the term "Pre-Socratic" has as its reference point Plato and Plato's Socrates, for in classical scholarship, Plato appears as a watershed. Anything prior to Plato is looked on differently, and often with a subtly inferior lens. But Heidegger's derision is well-founded: could Plato have come about without Parmenides or Heraclitus? Could Hegel's central problematic have surfaced clearly without Kant's analysis of the human project? Could Schelling's insights have arisen entirely independent of the work of Leibniz and Spinoza? Each aids the others succeeding them to remain underway while retaining the timeless luminosity of their principal insights. There is no finality. The error in thought consists of seeing each insight as a metaphysical conclusion instead of in terms of being underway that makes our approach more flexible and co-extensive with what is. The backward leap from Goethe to Heraclitus must be seen in this light, that is, be seen from the perspective of being underway to a greater plasticity of thought. Within the praxis of hermeneutically clarifying thinking, a most rewarding journey awaits us in the consideration of

[1] Heidegger, *What Is Called Thinking*, trans. Fred D. Wieck and J. Glenn Gray (New York: Harper and Row, 1968), p. 184.

K. Roy, *The Power of Philosophy*,
https://doi.org/10.1007/978-3-319-96911-4_5

the sages of ancient thought in the reverse sequence. Reversing the time sequence helps us to unfreeze thought systematically. From Goethe's empiricism, we can look back, say, at the Parmenidean assertion with astonishment and see how it has been presaged in an all-encompassing form: "The thing that can be thought and that for the sake of which the thought exists is the same...."[2] In this, we also see a very cryptic form of the Schelling equation between Mind and Nature which we have discussed at length, and which is seen in its experienceable form in Goethe. Thus there is a growing fullness of understanding in the bringing together of these philosophers, and a significant reward in stitching together a line of thinking that has lain at the margins of philosophy for a long time. In Parmenides and Heraclitus, we find a notable effort to shift the attention from phenomenal multiplicity to a singularity of consciousness in which the thing and the thought are ontologically one. Both see it as within the horizon of phenomenological possibility of the human to be attuned to this singularity not as experience (which reintroduces the problem of experiencer) but as introducing a different existential plane or intensity of being.

Therefore, let us return to the task of being underway to a certain freedom of observation, and remind ourselves that our task is to discover in our midst a thinking that is self-critical and free of deception (i.e., aware of its ontological limits). We turn to Heraclitus of Ephesus who had turned away from the conventional wisdom, rhetoric, and practices of his time to bring forth an ontological insight that astonished his listeners. Let us begin with, for reasons that will become clear, the issue of a certain well-known silence of Heraclitus, with which he is reputed to have often parried philosophical queries flung at him by his countrymen. We must hermeneutically return to the reasons for this silence of the philosopher who famously declared that he had learnt all that there was to learn by looking into himself.[3] There is a profound silence implicit in this manner of looking. But to understand it properly let us ask: what is this looking, what was there to learn, and what is the "himself" into which he looked?

[2] Parmenides, "On Nature," in *Early Greek Philosophy*, ed. John Burnet, 3rd ed. (London: A & C Black, 1920).

[3] Heraclitus, "Fragment" 101 (εδιςησαμην εμεωυτόν), in William Harris, *Heraclitus: The Complete Fragments* (Vermont: Middlebury College, 1987). This text follows the authoritative Diels Kranz listing.

Heraclitus writes: "A single thing is wisdom, to understand knowledge, that which guides everything everywhere."[4] A single thing is wisdom could mean that wisdom is a unitary thing or that a particular occurrence or phenomenon can lead to its disclosure, or both. Let us consider the first possibility. Wisdom is *one* thing, and that is "to understand knowledge." Significantly, Heraclitus does not speak of knowing or acquiring knowledge, but the *understanding* of knowledge, or the comprehension of the material process of knowing.

What, specifically, is the *understanding* of the material process of knowing? It is more than the *meta* level of knowledge, which is still an epistemic idea. Thinking strings together constellations of intelligibility which it calls knowledge about the world or even the world itself. Heraclitus appears to demand that we take hold of this arising process itself, and suggests that from the phenomenological grasp of the positivity (deployment) of thought arises wisdom or true disclosure. The movement of thought as phenomenal knowledge appropriates the world in a certain way, or represents it in specific ways. That, however, is not wisdom no matter how far reaching or powerful. Metaphysics is knowledge about the source of knowledge, or being, or ontology. This is direct knowledge, or, in terms of our analysis, aligning with essence. Intuition of the latter gives us insight about the way in which knowledge about the world is cogitatively produced, thereby opening up a psychic distance from the representational form of knowing. This distancing, in turn, opens up a space of composure and silence.

Next let us consider the second possibility of the above utterance: a single piece of knowledge is adequate to bring about disclosure about all. Investigation into the core of any representation can reveal its true nature which is at the same the true nature of everything. The ultimate essence of light is not different from the essence of water or the essence of air, as we have seen in Schelling—all are transitions consisting of phase differences; phenomena are different expressions or forms (finitude of particulars) in passage to other forms. To uncover the essence of anything is to uncover the essence of everything.[5] In other words, one does not need great accumulations of knowledge to understand the world. The underlying essence of each thing is the same, although the form of

[4] Ibid., Fragment 41.

[5] Cell differentiation, for example, begins from a single cell. Thus the complex organism arises from the same basic essence.

expression or phase of agitation in the matrix of determination may be different. This realization again brings about a certain shocked stillness in the consciousness that is conventionally busy, in a Faustian manner, gathering more and more information about the world in the hope of revealing the ultimate secrets of nature. In recognizing the futility, there comes about a certain stasis in thought which might explain the strange silences of Heraclitus.

Next, what might be the exact significance of Heraclitus's claim regarding looking into himself? Let us recall Kant's significant statement in *Critique of Judgment*: "It is quite certain that we can never get a sufficient knowledge of organized beings, and their inner possibility, much less an explanation of them, by looking merely to mechanical principles of nature. Indeed, so certain is it, that we may confidently assert that it is absurd from men even to entertain any thought of so doing… Such insight we must deny mankind."[6] On the basis of a very accurate judgment on the empirical plane Kant unfortunately shuts the door on the possibility of insight or immediate knowledge on a different plane. Goethe realizes the truth of the former but does not accept the latter closure, offering instead the possibility of a tender empiricism that puts the observer on the same level as the phenomena under observation. "Truth is Godlike," we hear him say, it does not present itself directly, but must be gathered or intuited from various manifestations. Heraclitus goes even further. For him truth existed within himself; he only had to look inward to find the source of all knowledge. This might be taken to indicate a phenomenological contact with the agitation of mindstuff or endopsychic matrix whose direction and resolution produce the finitude of particulars, or the range of phenomenal certitude on the cognitive horizon.

True knowledge of the principles that guide the body—micro or macro—is wisdom, but this wisdom does not lie in acquiring more and more knowledge about the manifested body. Rather it lies in grasping or entering into the nature and substratum of knowing itself as a material movement. This understanding is not substantial (i.e., does not constitute epistemic content or symbolic substance) but consists in a leap into the movement of knowing itself. In other words, one must ride

[6] Immanuel Kant, *Critique of Judgment*, trans. J.C. Meredith (Oxford: Clarendon Press, 1952), p. 54.

knowledge, much in the manner in which Einstein, as a boy, wanted to ride a light beam (the light beam can reveal no information to the rider about the phenomenal world, but only about itself as revealer). To crack open the form of thought, and not be seduced by content, *that* is the "single thing" which discloses the truth about mental formations revealing its core beyond interminable contortions. Thinking thus comes to the edge of its own materialization and enters into a pure confrontation with itself making representational knowledge secondary.

In another fragment that throws further light on the nature of thought-knowledge, Heraclitus continues: "Of those whose discourse I have heard, none arrives at the realization that wisdom is set apart from all else."[7] Wisdom is the direct realization of *what is*, something that Kant, the master of modern metaphysics, had insisted was impossible: "From this deduction of our faculty of cognizing a priori…there emerges a very strange result, namely that with this faculty we can never get beyond the boundaries of possible experience, [and] that such cognition reaches appearances only, leaving the thing in itself as something actual for itself but uncognized by us."[8] A split is introduced between thing and cognitive possibility; the human entity apparently has access only to appearance. Further, below is Kant's strongest argument against the possibility of direct knowledge or wisdom in the formulation of what he called "transcendental idealism":

> We have therefore wanted to say that all our intuition is nothing but the representation of appearance; that the things that we intuit are not in themselves what we intuit them to be, nor are their relations so constituted in themselves as they appear to us; and that if we remove our own subject or even only the subjective constitution of the senses in general, then all constitution, all relations of objects in space and time, indeed space and time themselves would disappear, and as appearances they cannot exist in themselves, but only in us. What may be the case with objects in themselves and abstracted from all this receptivity of our sensibility remains entirely unknown to us. We are acquainted with nothing except our way of perceiving them, which is peculiar to us, and which therefore does not necessarily pertain to every being, though to be sure it pertains to every human being. We are concerned solely with this. Space and time are its

[7] Heraclitus, Fragment 108.

[8] Immanuel Kant, *Critique of Pure Reason*, eds. P. Guyer and A. Wood (Cambridge: Cambridge University Press, 1998), p. xix.

> pure forms, sensation in general its matter. We can cognize only the former a priori, i.e., prior to all actual perception, and they are therefore called pure intuition; the latter, however, is that in our cognition that is responsible for its being called a posteriori cognition, i.e., empirical intuition. The former adheres to our sensibility absolutely necessarily, whatever sort of sensations we may have; the latter can be very different.[9]

Thus the intelligible (*noumenal*) world cannot be approached or cognized by the sensible according to Kant. It did not occur to Kant to push this line of thinking even deeper and ask what would happen if indeed all sensible datum were to be voluntarily jettisoned or pushed out from the plane of cognition by some means. In other words, *Kenosis* or emptying of the consciousness of all datum, a distinct possibility held by several traditions, as a first step toward intuitive insight, is not considered as a possibility toward *what is*. Kant was too busy trying to bring moral philosophy in line with rationality. Although he was much concerned about limits, that the "intelligible" could possibly be approached from the other end, and not through the sensible end, seems not to have occurred to him.[10]

While breaking away from Kant, Hegel does not fare much better in respect of the possibility of phenomenological wisdom or ontological knowledge. We remain stuck within the dialectic and its ceaseless triadic mechanism. "Dialectic in Hegel is practical. Not only must an idea be faced with its contrary, but every person and situation must pass through a history that will be an experience of trial and rupture, in order to grow into something greater and more complete."[11] This is Hegel's *Aufhebung* or 'raising up.' It implies that all situations contain within themselves a potential contradiction which, in time, brings about a change in the existing relations. But wisdom in the sense of Heraclitean insight into essence is not contradiction or partial negation; rather, it is a complete cessation of all usual ways of thinking. It cannot be formulated or imagined within the dialectic. For, by definition, wisdom cannot be arrived at by any prefigured means or mechanism, and the Hegelian

[9] Ibid., p. 8.

[10] The ancient Indian thought in the name of *Advaita Vedanta* attempts this through the practice of '*neti, neti*' or negation of the sensible.

[11] Andrew Davidson, *The Love of Wisdom: An Introduction to Philosophy for Theologians* (New York: SCM Press, 2013), p. 213.

rupture remains bound to the limited finite character of each of the triadic elements. Even if one were to take the conception of the Hegelian 'World Spirit' at face value, no dialectic can get us there. We do not know where the dialectic is going in terms of world history, but wherever it is going, it is certainly not in the direction of redemptive thinking or getting us to think anew. It is unfortunately hide-bound by its own logic.

What then is wisdom in Heraclitus and what is its relevance for thinking? Heraclitus stresses the unique metaphysical realization of direct knowledge that is distinct from phenomenal knowledge and cultural construction, and in its wake makes the charge that few realize its distinctiveness, importance, or care about the radical nature of the singularity in question. One important philosopher, however, who did admit the possibility and importance of direct knowledge or wisdom was Benedict de Spinoza whose philosophical antecedents might indeed go back to Heraclitus and Parmenides. Therefore a brief excursus into Spinoza's thought will be useful here.

> After experience had taught me that all the things which regularly occur in ordinary life are empty and futile, and I saw that all the things which were the cause or object of my fear had nothing of good or bad in themselves, except insofar as [my] mind was moved by them, I resolved at last to try to find out whether there was anything which would be the true good, capable of communicating itself, and which alone would affect the mind, all others being rejected—whether there was something which, once found and acquired, would continuously give me the greatest joy, to eternity.[12]

Thus Spinoza set out on a daring philosophical venture to directly encounter truth. Is there an underlying substance or essence that morphs into various ephemeral arrangements through the day for humans? Can that underlying formless substance, if it exists, be known? What is the process of that knowing? Does its knowledge lead to permanent peace and goodness in the human being? How do we move from our inadequate ideas about existence to adequate ones? These and other questions concerned Spinoza. Friedrich Nietzsche wrote that he was amazed and

[12] Benedict de Spinoza, "Treatise on the Emendation of the Intellect," in *The Collected Works of Spinoza*, ed. and trans. Edwin Curley, vol. I (Princeton: Princeton University Press, 1985), para 1.

delighted when he first discovered Spinoza. Who was this philosopher and what did he discover that is relevant to the discussion on Heraclitus and thinking in general? [13]

> The fact is that consciousness is by nature the locus of an illusion. Its nature is such that it registers effects, but it knows nothing of causes. The order of causes is defined by this: each body in extension, each idea or each mind in thought are constituted by the characteristic relations that subsume the parts of that body, the parts of that idea. When a body "encounters" another body, or an idea another idea, it happens that the two relations sometimes combine to form a more powerful whole, and sometimes one decomposes the other, destroying the cohesion of its parts. And this is what is prodigious in the body and the mind alike, these sets of living parts that enter into composition with and decompose one another according to complex laws. The order of causes is therefore an order of composition and decomposition of relations, which infinitely affects all of nature. But as conscious beings, we never apprehend anything but the effects of these compositions and decompositions: we experience joy when a body encounters ours and enters into composition with it, and sadness when, on the contrary, a body or an idea threaten our own coherence. We are in a condition such that we only take in "what happens" to our body, "what happens" to our mind, that is, the effect of a body on our body, the effect of an idea on our idea. In short, the conditions under which we know things and are conscious of ourselves condemn us to have only inadequate ideas, ideas that are confused and mutilated, effects separated from their real causes.[14]

[13]The philosopher Gilles Deleuze introduces Spinoza the man in the following terms: "This frugal, propertyless life, undermined by illness, this thin, frail body, this brown, oval face with its sparkling black eyes how does one explain the impression they give of being suffused with Life itself, of having a power identical to Life? In his whole way of living and of thinking, Spinoza projects an image of the positive, affirmative life, which stands in opposition to the semblances that men are content with. Not only are they content with the latter, they feel a hatred of life, they are ashamed of it; a humanity bent on self-destruction, multiplying the cults of death, bringing about the union of the tyrant and the slave, the priest, the judge, and the soldier, always busy running life into the ground, mutilating it, killing it outright or by degrees, overlaying it or suffocating it with laws, properties, duties, empires-this is what Spinoza diagnoses in the world, this betrayal of the universe and of mankind." Gilles Deleuze, *Spinoza: Practical Philosophy*, trans. Robert Hurley (San Francisco: City Lights Books, 1988), p. 12.

[14]Ibid., p. 19.

Conventional thinking is obsessed with form, and the effects of forms on other forms. However, not unlike Goethe, Spinoza discovers that forms are basically transitional, and what really exists are sets of composition and decomposition, of tendencies in motion that come together and fall apart under the influence of still other tendencies, and so on. Thus in our reflections on redemptive thinking, or in encountering a pressing need in which thinking must turn to face itself, Spinoza's framework of cause and effect helps in deflating consciousness as a mere passage and not something that is true in itself. In this manner thinking is turned away from transcendental idealism and more and more toward immanent modes of existence which is crucial for its self-discovery.

Returning to Heraclitus, we encounter a warning against a common manifestation and consequence of inadequate ideas and the attachment to form: "Insolence, more than a fire, must be extinguished."[15] Insolence is concerned with effects and is more dangerous than fire that reduces things to ashes. Insolence is the result of petty egotism, and egotism, in turn, is the result of obsession with the form—usually, the form of oneself pitted over and against others. When thinking operates obsessively with the picture of the form and its assumed superiority to other forms, there is manifestation of the mental disposition called conceit. From conceit and self-importance arises insolence or disrespect. Thus "insolence" is worse than a fire as it destroys the truth of relationality, and of causes, hence must be put out with greater alacrity than even an actual blaze, since it ultimately misleads and misidentifies the very relation between the microcosm and the macrocosm.[16] Hence, more than anything else, insolence is thought's wrong or distorted relationship with being. Just as draught feeds fire, the amplification of a peculiarly obsessive inner representation of form feeds the "fire" of insolence. Further, fire also produces smoke, and insolence is a smokescreen that obscures the possibility of looking correctly or adequately; what requires careful

[15] Heraclitus, Fragment 103.

[16] "Every particular thing, like the human body, must be conditioned by another particular thing to exist and operate in a fixed and definite relation; this other particular thing must likewise be conditioned by a third, and so on to infinity (I. xxviii). As we have shown in the foregoing proposition, from this common property of particular things, we have only a very inadequate knowledge of the duration of our body; we must draw a similar conclusion with regard to the duration of particular things, namely, that we can only have a very inadequate knowledge of the duration thereof." Benedict de Spinoza, *The Ethics*, I. Prop. XXXI.

consideration is lost in miasma. The underlying continuities are obscured by the smokescreen, and events and objects are seen in isolation when viewed through it, reducing the vast interconnectedness of phenomenal life to a narrow corridor of self-exaggeration. And just as an unattended blaze spreads quickly, insolence feeds on the psychic energies rapidly in order to produce its halo, leaving "ashes" in its path. The revealed structure of the Fall of Man is one of the most dramatic instances of impertinence held in collective memory. But we read it wrongly when we understand it in moral terms rather than in ontological ones.

Insolence here is not mere moral turpitude; rather it must be read ontologically, as a failure in the understanding of forms and their composition/decomposition that give us the true nature of the Real. One of the most primal acts of ontological misunderstanding results in the original (Biblical) Fall, one that epitomizes the above, and which event may be more adequately understood in the following terms of analysis:

> "Thou shalt not eat of the fruit … ": the anxious, ignorant Adam understands these words as the expression of a prohibition. And yet, what do they refer to? To a fruit that, as such, will poison Adam if he eats it. This is an instance of an encounter between two bodies whose characteristic relations are not compatible: the fruit will act as a poison; that is, *it will determine the parts of Adam's body* (and paralleling this, the idea of the fruit will determine the parts of his mind) *to enter into new relations that no longer accord with his own essence*. But because Adam is ignorant of causes, he thinks that God morally forbids him something, whereas God only reveals the natural consequence of ingesting the fruit. Spinoza is categorical on this point: all the phenomena that we group under the heading of Evil, illness, and death, are of this type: bad encounters, poisoning, intoxication, relational decomposition.[17]

Insolence is thus ignorance of ontology, a confusion of categories. The original prohibition is understood as a moral injunction whereas it is about the production of bodies of affect and a problem of decomposition. The "fruit" would change the nature of Adam's mind and its substratum not morally but ontologically. Speaking of Spinoza, Deleuze continues, "a difference of nature is constantly manifested between knowledge and morality, between the relation of command and

[17] Deleuze, *Spinoza*, p. 22.

obedience [on the one hand] and the relation of the known and knowledge [on the other]."[18] The tragedy of thinking is that it takes the moral route because it wrongly identifies with the illusion of form; there is

> [a] practical confusion which theology instills in us between these two orders that differ in nature. In this, as we shall see, there is a confusion that compromises the whole of ontology; the history of a *long error* whereby the command is mistaken for something to be understood, obedience for knowledge itself, and Being for a *Fiat.* Law is always the transcendent instance that determines the opposition of values (Good-Evil), but knowledge is always the immanent power that determines the qualitative difference of modes of existence (good-bad).[19]

Thought's greatest error is to reduce ontology to morality. What thinking traditionally reads as an opposition of values between good and bad is in actuality a qualitative difference between worthy and non-worthy modes of composition or states of being. The so-called moral injunction is a warning against going into a lesser mode through decomposition. Composition and decomposition is thus a ceaseless occurrence in what we know as Nature.

And who better than Heraclitus to tell us of this ceaseless morphing of cause turning into effect and effect into cause. We are on to the fragment for which Heraclitus is both celebrated and disparaged, due more to intellectual confusion and popular misunderstanding than its possible merit: "It is impossible to step twice in the same river" (*ποταμωι γαρ ουκ εστιν εμβηναι δις τωι αυτωι*).[20] This is often taken to mean that the whole world is metaphysically in a state of flux, so much so that Heraclitus is often known as the philosopher of flux and change. Perhaps Plato among others, who exhibited a scornful attitude toward Heraclitean thought, might have been largely responsible for this reading. However, it is not difficult to show that this is a vulgar misreading of the proposition. For if everything was in a state of change, then we could not possibly identify a river even as a river, and such an obvious point could hardly have escaped an insightful philosopher such as Heraclitus. So there was both permanence and change built into that aphorism.

[18] Ibid.

[19] Ibid., pp. 24–25.

[20] Heraclitus, Fragment 91.

What is often missed, and from our point of view much more important, is the possibility of reading more into the pronoun "We." We do not step into the same river twice because *we* do not remain the Same. Irrespective of the state of the river, the actors have undergone a change between the two events. For deciding the relation between the river and myself at two points in time, it does not matter if we treat the river as in flux and myself as identity, or the river as identity and the 'myself' as in flux. This symmetry is beautiful and immediately sets up a reciprocal relation between myself and the river in an organic manner: the river cannot be defined without me, nor can myself be identified without the river. Each becomes the other's point of reference. Reality requires determination, and hence a point of reference, and this point of reference enjoys a basic symmetrical relation with any other point. Going beyond the metaphor of the river, this means 'I' determine 'you' experientially just as 'you' determine 'me,' and *I determine your determining me* and so on with no privileged or permanent observational perch. It is not so much about flux but about mutuality and reciprocal relation. This point is much more significant than the banal fact that things morph into one another which is one of the more usual interpretations of the citation above. The cognitive constants of determination are but mutually produced indefinitely throughout the horizon of experience, infinitely exchangeable, mutually upholding in reciprocal relation. This metaphysical truth is mistaken as incessant flux which is really the other side of the habit of seeking permanency. A more unbiased and careful reading of Heraclitus cuts the ground from underneath the permanence/impermanence or identity/flux opposition revealing the drawback of one-sided metaphysical determinations such as that envisioned in the Platonic *idea*.

But before we move on, let us ask to glimpse a mechanism for this reciprocal determination if possible, and for this I turn to Deleuze and Deleuze's Spinoza once again to help us acquire a probable key to the cryptic aphorisms of Heraclitus. That is to say, we wish to do more than leave the process of change as an outer idea and demand a basis for adopting it as a clear existential mode of being for ourselves. This, no doubt, helps us to be underway toward our project of redemptive thinking. It merits repeating that the task of phenomenological appropriation of a new direction is not an easy one, requiring many levels of effort and intuition to make it the stuff of consciousness.

> Thus, the kinetic proposition tells us that a body is defined by relations of motion and rest, of slowness and speed between particles. That is, it is not defined by a form or by functions. Global form, specific form, and organic functions depend on relations of speed and slowness. Even the development of a form, the course of development of a form, depends on these relations, and not the reverse. The important thing is to understand life, each living individuality, not as a form, or a development of form, but as a complex relation between differential velocities, between deceleration and acceleration of particles. A composition of speeds and slownesses on a plane of immanence. In the same way, a musical form will depend on a complex relation between speeds and slownesses of sound particles. It is not just a matter of music but of how to live: it is by speed and slowness that one slips in among things, that one connects with something else. One never commences; one never has a *tabula rasa*; one slips in, enters in the middle; one takes up or lays down rhythms. The second proposition concerning bodies refers us to the capacity for affecting and being affected.[21]

Our endeavor is toward thinking to develop within itself a new intuition through which it can learn to look differently. First to understand ourselves as a combination of sub-entities in motion, including thought in motion, frees us from the static conception of the form. Each living moment has to be reconceptualized as a relation between different velocities. The breath, sound, internal movements, affects, heart beats, contractions, all are different things in motion, but held in symphony. Starting from these elementary but concrete observations, thinking becomes alert to the subtle movements and velocities. One is never at a starting point, but always in the middle of a melody in which the composite is inserted or interpellated. At any moment we are inserted into an array of movements that may be thought of as the "river" of Heraclitus. Thus we never step into the same river twice because the symphony of movements and co-rhythms change and are never at one place. Different "forms" are therefore different moments of agglomeration of motions and rest, and appear as solid forms due to habit and untrained sensibility. Thinking must learn the art of disaggregation. A new form of learning is due and a new organ of perception has to be developed that can take us beyond the usual orientation of thought.

[21] Deleuze, *Spinoza*, p. 123.

Let us return hermeneutically to the initial avowal of Heraclitus that "I searched into myself" in order to discover what was there to be discovered. But who is this 'myself?' What was there to learn from 'myself?' Besides, is this the declaration of thought, or of a different element such as the corpus sensorium, or of a deeper intuition? And what is the process of the search, that is, how does the self-same element look into itself? All these questions and more arise from that incredibly compact fragment, and these need to be looked into carefully. From the previous postulate of impermanence it appears that all bodies are in flux and yet the claim that "I searched into myself" seems to be suggestive of a transcendental element that probed. From the ontological notion of the phenomenal world as one of eternal flux, there proceeds an important corollary: that there must exist correspondingly something that is immutable. The one requires the positing of the other. We cannot speak of change in a formally rigorous way if there is not at the same time an admission of the changeless. The very positing of change is predicated upon a point of stasis rather like the famous Brouwer's fixed point theorem in mathematics. From this perspective, the observation point of the inquirer becomes plausible, but in a very different sense. We turn to Spinoza, the most thoroughgoing ontologist, again for a possible key:

> [W]e have not assigned to the human mind any duration, definable by time, except in so far as it expresses the actual existence of the body, which is explained through duration, and may be defined by time—that is (II. viii. Coroll.), we do not assign to it duration, except while the body endures. Yet, as there is something, notwithstanding, which is conceived by a certain eternal necessity through the very essence of God (last Prop.); this something, which appertains to the essence of the mind, will necessarily be eternal. Note: This idea, which expresses the essence of the body under the form of eternity, is, as we have said, a certain mode of thinking, which belongs to the essence of the mind, and is necessarily eternal. Yet it is not possible that we should remember that we existed before our body, for our body can bear no trace of such existence, neither can eternity be defined in terms of time, or have any relation to time. But, notwithstanding, we feel and know that we are eternal. For the mind feels those things that it conceives by understanding, no less than those things that it remembers. For the eyes of the mind, whereby it sees and observes things, are none other than proofs. Thus, although we do not remember that we existed before the body, yet we feel that our mind, in so far as it involves the essence of the body, under the form of eternity, is eternal, and that

> thus its existence cannot be defined in terms of time, or explained through duration. Thus our mind can only be said to endure, and its existence can only be defined by a fixed time, in so far as it involves the actual existence of the body. Thus far only has it the power of determining the existence of things by time, and conceiving them under the category of duration.[22]

There is an "eternal necessity" that appertains to each manifest body during the time it endures. No bodies come about without this necessity. All bodies are therefore *sub specie aeternitatis*, or under the quality or principle of eternity. This principle does not belong to either the body or the mind both of which are of a limited duration. Yet both mind and body take effect under this ultimate cause. Eternity cannot be grasped by the mind, nor is it a temporal concept, yet it is posed synthetically as a matter of necessity by Spinoza after examining all possible causes by which bodies or agglomerates come about. If we accept this metaphysical necessity, as we must in terms of the present analysis, it is able to answer most of the questions raised earlier with respect to Heraclitus's fragment.

The central mystery of the 'I,' or the one who inquires, may be resolved by seeing the 'I' to be nothing other than the intuition of continuity, an indirect approximation of the principle of eternity, a shadow that extends throughout consciousness that may be used as a *starting point* of inquiry.[23] Therefore, with regard to the puzzling question 'who or what inquires' in a tumult of change and flux, one can advance the hypothesis that thinking carries with it an imprint of original essence, for it is *sub specie aeternitatis*, or under the principle of eternity, although it

[22] Spinoza, *Ethics Bk III*, ed. and trans. James Gutman (New York: Hafner Press, 1949), prop. XXIII.

[23] "It is true that Spinoza's method is synthetic, constructive, and progressive, and that it proceeds from causes to effects. But this does not mean that one can establish oneself in the cause as if by magic. The "proper order" does go from cause to effects, but one cannot follow the proper order immediately. Synthetically as well as analytically, obviously one starts with the knowledge of an effect, or at least of a "given." But while the analytic method seeks the cause simply as the condition of the thing, the synthetic method seeks, not a conditioning, but rather a genesis, that is, a sufficient reason that also enables us to know other things. In this sense, the knowledge of the cause is said to be perfect, and it proceeds as quickly as possible from the cause to the effects. At its beginning, synthesis does contain an accelerated analytic process, but one that it uses only for reaching the principle of the synthetic order. As Plato said, one starts from a "hypothesis" and goes, not towards consequences or conditions, but towards the "anhypothetical" principle from which all consequences and conditions follow." Deleuze, *Spinoza*, pp. 112–113.

is, in general, turned away from essence. This brings home the point that direct and intimate knowledge of reality is always latent in the human, accessible from within, and is not just the privilege of those culturally identified as the founders of knowledge. The task of philosophy or the philosopher is to generate this awareness rather than promote the offering of second-hand knowledge. This sense of the possibility of ontological transcendence emerges powerfully again in Nietzsche and Heidegger. "In Greek, *meta* is "beyond"; *meta ta physica* means beyond the physical, the sensual; the supra-sensual, in passing beyond the physical, is the metaphysical. Man conceived as the rational animal is the physical exceeding the physical; in short—in the nature of man as the rational animal, there is gathered the passing from the physical to the non-physical, the supra-physical: thus man himself is the metaphysical."[24] The human is defined by the innate possibility of transcending its present state, that is, to go beyond the human. But to realize this deeply, thinking must be carried, or be willing to go beyond, and "to despise what is despicable in [its] kind as it is so far."[25] It is by means of a profound negation of all that thinking has indulged in, up to this point, that a leap can occur to the ground of originary transcendence which is granted to the human as a possibility and by which thinking can go beyond itself.

Then the next question is, what is to be learnt from the looking or searching into oneself? What is the nature of such knowledge and how does it help thinking to think what needs to be thought?

> That which really is, Being, which from the start calls and determines all beings, can never be made out, however, by ascertaining facts, by appealing to particulars. That sound commonsense which is so often "cited" in such attempts is not as sound and natural as it pretends. It is above all not as absolute as it acts, but rather the shallow product of that manner of forming ideas which is the final fruit of the Enlightenment in the eighteenth century. Sound commonsense is always trimmed to fit a certain conception of what is and ought to be and may be. The power of this curious understanding extends into our own age, but it is no longer adequate. The organizations of social life, rearmament in moral matters, the grease paint of the culture enterprise none of them any longer reach what *is*.

[24] Martin Heidegger, *What Is Called Thinking*, trans. Fred Wieck and J. Glenn Gray (New York: Harper and Row, 1968), p. 58.

[25] Ibid.

> With all the good intentions and all the ceaseless effort, these attempts are no more than makeshift patchwork, expedients for the moment. And why? Because the ideas of aims, purposes, and means, of effects and causes, from which all those attempts arise—because these ideas are from the start incapable of holding themselves open to what is.[26]

Knowledge is reciprocally related with regard to "common sense." That is to say, commonsense or settled, habitual sensibility has long determined what can be considered knowledge, and knowledge in turn has modified common sense. But neither knowledge nor commonsense can any longer reach 'what is.' When knowledge offers solutions to social problems, these turn out at best to be simulated and "patchwork" solutions to intractable problems that keep cropping up in different guises. Further, a shallow rationality backed by technological capacity has created today what is generally known as "common sense." This commonsense is a cultural product that is typical of the age; it is cut and made to fit the existing prejudices and social fixations, helping in turn to make the latter seem natural. Despite the incessant exertions, all of human knowledge, and the existential attitudes aligned with these, have become incapable of being open to what is. All the developmental ideas, educational thoughts, moral visions, and reformatory ideals of the world are like so many ripples—the "grease paint of culture"—on the surface of water none of which can grasp the nature of 'water' itself. The concept is a precipitate on the surface of the non-conceptual substrate to which it has no access and without which it is mere flotsam. No matter how organized and well thought a system of ripples, it is nevertheless a reaction to other ripples, and cannot but share the ontological character of the ripple which is after all a transitory disturbance. If we take the ripple metaphorically as a cultural enterprise, it cannot reach the substrate no matter how high it rises or how low it dips, since it is but a surface agitation of the substrate itself. It is perhaps not an easy thing to acknowledge that no matter what we do, we are always getting away from the originary transcendence that alone is redemptive and all our effort is wasted in the final analysis. None of it reaches 'what is' because from the beginning the effort is not open to 'what is,' but a misunderstanding of what constitutes authentic action. The human condition arises precisely out of this non-reaching. This is the first knowledge, the negative knowledge that

[26]Ibid., pp. 65–66.

is required of thought. This knowledge makes thinking halt in its tracks and realize the futility of the incessant forward movement.[27]

The sense that all outer and progressive achievements of thought are ultimately meaningless are strengthened by another Heraclitean aphorism: "Time is a child playing dice; the kingdom is in the hands of a child" (*αιων παις εστι παιων, πεσσευων παιδος η βασιληιη*).[28] This is commonly understood in the English language scholarship as Heraclitus's indictment of the extant rulers of the State who are seen by Heraclitus to be infantile with the preoccupations of children. While such a political interpretation might be true at one level, nonetheless, as with the works of some philosophers of antiquity, there are different levels of meaning, sometimes even opposite meanings, hidden in the same text. Notice that Heraclitus uses the term *Aion* and not *Chronos* to indicate time. This gives us an important clue. Both *Aion* and *Chronos* are translated from the Greek into English as time, but they actually refer to very different conceptions of time. In Greek philosophy the latter is generally understood as the movement of time by the clock, or empirical time that structurally admits of a past, present, and future, that is, as march and progression of events. Whereas *aion* is eternity experienced as duration that has no beginning or end. Mythologically, *aion* envelops the whole of creation circling back onto itself sometimes pictured as a great snake eating its own tail. Seen from this perspective, any sequence of events will appear in experience as contingent or chance occurrence, and just as to the child, that is, to innocence, all outcomes of the dice are the same, to eternity all sequences or appearances have the same value. The "kingdom" or Creation is thus in the hands of Divine Innocence to which all ultimate distinctions between outcomes are pointless. All our, meaning thought's, great successes and failures have no ultimate significance to Innocence. The only thing of significance is the background Mystery in which phenomena appear and disappear. Thus it is evident that the usual political interpretation is an inadequate, even misleading, one; behind it lies a deeper metaphysical pointer showing the path that thinking must tread toward self-knowledge.

[27] This forward movement toward a future is what is usually extolled by thinking itself as progressive. What is fascinating is the self-congratulatory mode in which modern thought moves.

[28] Heraclitus, Fragment 52.

In the very next aphorism, Heraclitus goes on to say: "Children's playthings are men's conjectures."[29] Men try to decipher what "children" or Divine Innocence produces as play. That is to say, what Innocence produces randomly is taken seriously by men and foolishly conjectured about without understanding the *deep cause*; profound assertions are made about phenomena that are but cosmic games of Ludo whose ultimate significance cannot be known by the human mind.[30] Spinoza acknowledges something quite similar from a different angle:

> [...] there would be about as much correspondence between [Divine Will and human intellect] as there is between the Dog, the heavenly constellation, and a dog, an animal that barks. This I will prove as follows. If intellect belongs to the divine nature, it cannot be in nature, as ours is generally thought to be, posterior to, or simultaneous with the things understood, inasmuch as the Divine Essence is prior to all things by reason of its causality (Prop. xvi., Coroll. i.). On the contrary, the truth and formal essence of things is as it is, because it exists by representation as such in the intellect of the Essence. Wherefore the intellect of Essence, in so far as it is conceived to constitute Essence, is, in reality, the cause of things, both of their essence and of their existence. As, therefore, Divine Will is the sole cause of things, namely, both of their essence and existence, it must necessarily differ from them in respect to its essence, and in respect to its existence. For a cause differs from a thing it causes, precisely in the quality which the latter gains from the former.[31]

There is absolute discontinuity between Divine Will and human intellect due to which all conjectures about the phenomenal world essentially remain as speculations. But then this gives rise to a profound problem. If the human intellect cannot apprehend divine laws then how is any authentic knowledge possible? For both Heraclitus and Spinoza seem to indicate this impossibility. How then can thinking begin to think what needs to be thought?

Let us attempt to answer this question by listening carefully to another fragment that has confounded scholars: "The mixed drink

[29] Heraclitus, Fragment 70.

[30] Contrary to Heraclitus's image as an arrogant misanthrope built up by biographers, this points to a profound humility in his understanding of cosmic relations.

[31] Spinoza, *Ethics, Book I*, Note to prop. XVII.

separates, too, if not stirred."[32] The conventional explanation is as follows: "The 'mixed drink,' the *kykeon*, is an offering of wine, grated cheese, and barley. It separates into its component parts and loses its unity unless swirled or stirred together...This was to demonstrate to the other Ephesians both the need to put aside their desire for wealth and [instead attend to] the importance of unity of the city."[33] The importance of "stirring" may be seen at a mundane level as the need to maintain unity in times of crisis by setting aside wealth, rank and other markers of social privilege. But Heraclitus is a master of the cryptic art of *double entendre*, and we must read him against the grain. A very different interpretation of "stirring" emerges if we do not read the aphorism above as an advice to stir but as a subtle warning *against* stirring. Both understandings are possible from the fragment, as Heraclitus is merely making an observation and not suggesting any particular action. If we consider the human being itself as a "mixed drink," as a badly analyzed composite as Spinoza put it, then not stirring would sift the real from the unreal. In other words, letting mental accretions and habits settle would separate them from the intuition of essence.[34] The latter understanding is a metaphysical one: *Being discloses itself when we do not stir* memories, thoughts and other cognitive debris which cloud the horizon of mind-consciousness. The "mixed drink" or the human aggregate then decomposes into pure consciousness (noumenon) and precipitate (phenomena) if not stirred. Given the drift of the root assertion, that is, to find everything by looking into oneself, this interpretation seems quite plausible. In order to return to essence or source one must get past the cultural *maculi*. In an identical spirit, the *Bhagwad Gita* asks us to get past the smoke so that one can begin to intuit the eternal fire. Thinking needs not to ruminate upon and rearrange cultural debris, but to get past it.

This interpretation links up well with another puzzling fragment whose authenticity has sometimes been doubted: "May wealth not desert you,

[32] Fragment 125.

[33] G.T.W. Patrick, *Fragments Attributed to Heraclitus* (Baltimore: N. Murray, 1889), p. 26.

[34] In the *Yoga Sutras*, Patanjali, the ancient Indian sage suggests that the only thing for the mind to do is to let thoughts subside: y*ogaha chittavritti nirodhaha*, "yoga consists in the subsidence of mental formations." It is the subsidence that leads to correct perception.

men of Ephesus, that you be convicted of your wrongdoing."[35] Hence this fragment is shown by biographers of antiquity such as Plutarch, Diogenes Laertius, and others as a supplement to the previous.[36] But without being in a hurry to judge the authenticity of the fragment let us see what it could contribute to the total context of the foregoing discussion. "May wealth not desert you…" First, seen any which way, this is a sarcastic and mocking statement. The only question is what does "wealth" mean here? At the obvious level, it clearly is a reference to worldly wealth that insulates the rich from the consequences of their depredations. But seen from the metaphysical perspective, mental "wealth" or cognitive debris merely insulates us from essence or Being; the greater the amount of debris, the thicker the smokescreen. Accumulation of intellectual rubble does not bring about wisdom as we have already read in Heraclitus earlier. But when that debris melts away we are face-to-face with what is; we are naked and exposed. The activity of thought tries its best to avoid this eventuality and instead prefers to speak of the Day of Judgement etc. Thus, "may wealth not desert you" can be seen as a derisive "blessing" that consecrates the mental and spiritual blindness of the Ephesians and their preference for the *status quo* and the state of their ignorance. Worldly wealth and importance is the cataract that temporarily shields man from the consequences of his actions. To imagine that one can permanently elude the consequences is of course to be truly deluded. Continue as long as you can without atoning for your sins, Heraclitus seems to say, for if once the cataract falls from your eyes, you will realize your true situation and will have to atone for your wickedness, therefore let your illusions persist for as long as they might.

[35] Heraclitus, Fragment 125a.

[36] Ava Chitwood writes: "[This is] an addition that authors such as Kirk and Wilamovitz later questioned and rejected. Once we put the pieces of the mixed-drink anecdote together, two points emerge. First, by combining biographical elements of Heraclitus' work and character (such as reference to an authentic fragment, citation. Heraclitus' general contempt for his fellow citizens; and his refusal to speak generally or to those citizens specifically or to take their concerns seriously) with several biographical topoi ready to hand (such as the philosopher's disdain for wealth; the philosopher who aids the state in time of crisis; and a silent version of the philosopher's bon mot), we see how easily an illustrative anecdote is built upon a single fragment. Second, once the anecdote and its foundation fragment of the mixed drink were in place and accepted, an elaborated, second statement against wealth found its way into the text, winning at least limited acceptance." Ava Chitwood, *Death by Philosophy* (Ann Arbor: University of Michigan Press, 2004), p. 69.

All the acquisitions and accumulations of thought merely complicate the world in which we live without bringing true relief. Instead, thinking must practice the emptying of content if it is to turn to face its essence.

This leads us to yet another important fragment which reads as follows: "Having listened not to me but to the Logos, it is wise to agree that all are one."[37] With the characteristic negation of the self by the man of wisdom, Heraclitus speaks of listening to the Logos instead. But what is the Logos referred to here? What does it mean to listen to the Logos? How is it that "all are one"? Why do we need to agree on this proposition? And most importantly, what can thinking learn from this profound and mystical statement? Logos itself is not knowable as knowledge but is the origin and primal background of all knowledge. The path of awakening to the Logos is through searching into oneself as we saw earlier and not by gathering second-hand knowledge from whosoever or of whatsoever kind. Empirical knowledge is not an advantage and each one begins the search without any material advantage. In each is implicit the source of the mystery of consciousness (the mind-stuff in which phenomena take shape), and each one must solve the puzzle of their being immanently through direct contact with that mystery. The Logos is so intimate to the being that there is no intervening space for any direction as to its mode of attainment. In other words, no one can tell me what to do in order to attain to the Logos; at best one can repeatedly allude to its Presence attempting to turn or orient or deepen the attention. Intense personal search is incumbent upon each one. One cannot describe this search objectively, but it is possible to discuss the conditions of its possibility.

> Wisdom consists of knowledge not of the common or wide-ranging kind that Heraclitus condemns, but of a specific kind: understanding of the Logos. This knowledge comes only to an enlightened, wakened soul...Knowledge can come only from within. Second-hand knowledge, even if it were to come from Heraclitus and not from Pythagoras, Hesiod, Homer, or any other of the accepted teachers, would still be secondhand and therefore worthless. As philosopher and teacher, Heraclitus can only hint at or allude to the Logos and how one finds it; to explain the method is to destroy all chance of attaining its reward. The necessity of personal investigation is put forth...[38]

[37] Heraclitus, Fragment 50.

[38] Heidegger, *What Is Called Thinking*, p. 73.

Thinking must not speculate on the essence but begin by listening, and not by producing further differentiation in thought. It must profoundly and unreservedly acknowledge the necessity of unity (i.e., "all are one").

But what is the Logos-in-listening and how does one listen to it? Fragment 72 tells us: "From the Logos, which they associate most, and which governs all, they are apart and, even as those things they daily meet, seems to them most strange."[39] That which is most intimate to the human remains alienated from the very medium of its being. Its face is turned away from the very matrix on which its consciousness is afloat, by means of which it hears, speaks, and makes sense of things. To this Logos one must turn, and listen, which is simultaneously everywhere and nowhere. In that Logos all knowledge is one, meaning that, when one comes to be aware of, or develops adequate intuition of, the Logos there are no separate fragments of knowledge, and all merge into the One. But this medium of our very existence is alien to us; we have no intimation of it. Our attention is rather focused on what we are enabled to perceive in the outer. We are focused on the effects rather than the cause as Spinoza observed. Therefore the work of listening is of a slow and negative kind: one without preconceptions and the gradual making-strange of the familiar. It requires us to go beyond and behind the existing habits of thinking.

But "wisdom consists in speaking and acting the truth, giving heed to the nature of things (*...kai sophie alethia legein kai phroein kata phusin epaiontas*)."[40] Thus one must proceed from truth to truth letting the "nature of things" to lead one like Goethe suggested in delineating delicate empiricism. How shall we decode the hints given by nature? Heraclitus says: "The lord whose oracle is at Delphi neither speaks nor conceals, but gives signs."[41] 'What is' does not give information or direction, instead it intimates, it presents us with an emanation of sorts that must be absorbed by a correctly oriented being so that it appears in the corpus and is absorbed in it. "According to an ancient doctrine of metaphysics," writes Heidegger, "man is that 'rising presence' which can make appear what is present."[42] This is the task before us: to *make*

[39] Heraclitus, Fragment 72.

[40] Ibid., Fragment 112.

[41] Ibid., Fragment 93.

[42] Heidegger, *What Is Called Thinking*, p. 68.

appear what is present. To a query about the nature of what is, nature presents a vast interconnected riddle; but this riddle also is us, includes ourselves. The reason why it is so difficult to see this inter-corporeality is the conflict between so-called animality and so-called rationality in man. Post-antiquity, in the world of Western conceptions and ideas that was to follow, man became a peculiarly constructed combination of animality and rationality with neither of the two being determined, established or secured. Therefore, the two domains of being, animality and rationality, remain separate and perpetually clash. This rupture prevents the human from possessing unity of nature and thus being free to receive the real.

As concerns the animal nature, its present (contemporaneity) is a settled fact, a determinate occurrence. A lion is fully a lion in the present, nor can it transcend its givenness. But in the case of the human the present is in continuous formation, rising to meet him in unprecedented ways. That strange thing, time (rising to meet) itself is the essence of this becoming, which has compressed in it ontologically both the rational and the animal. Or better still, time's "decompression," or risenness, produces both animality as well as rationality as phenomena in the human. What cleaves the concurrent production (Eros) is the image of thought. Further, the cultural split between animality and rationality that is peculiar of the West turns this into a problem which it then attempts to solve in terms of available categories (cultural formations) but cannot. In other words, in its failure to understand the relation between animality-eros-corporeality on the one hand, and rationality-techne-sign on the other, thought creates an opposition, a fracture, which indefinitely produces newer and newer conditions and contradictions which typically go under the name of progress but never come to face what is. It produces endless knowledge without coming any closer to that which emancipates or frees the essence in each composite.

Therefore Heraclitus says, "the people should fight for their laws, as for their walls."[43] In other words, human composites must struggle to uncover the universal or cosmic laws that guide their existence with the same ferocity as they struggle to protect their material lives. That is to say, in other words, the need for this understanding should be treated with as much urgency and desperation as one employs to defend one's "walls," or means of material existence. Here we get a hint of the philosophical action that is incumbent on humans. One cannot expect the

[43] Heraclitus, Fragment 44.

ruling elite or the politician to provide us with those laws of existence. Ever suspicious of elite formations, the Indian thinker M. K. Gandhi understood this injunction very well—the absolute need for each of us to struggle for the metaphysical principles by which we live. He called this "*Swaraj*," or self-rule. The politico-esthetics of *Swaraj* demanded the awakening of a soul-force that was latent in the human, which alone, like Socrates's *daimon*, could give humans the necessary and true direction in their lives.

But what prevents men from coming to this realization directly, for is not the essence present in each being at all times? To that Heraclitus says: "What is divine escapes men's notice because of their incredulity (*apistiei diaphygganei me gignoskesthai*)," and "Human nature has no real understanding, only the divine nature has it (*Ethos gar anthropeion men oik ekhei gnomas, theion de ekhei*)."[44] The divine essence is present from the beginning since all are *sub specie aeternitatis*, or under the principle of eternity, but thought continually misses this since we have become *incredulous* of the divine, we have turned our face away from the essence. In other words, humans, devoid of the intuition of the essence, no longer believe that it is possible to approach the essence and nor are they willing to make the sacrifices necessary in order to be able to turn toward the essence. Heidegger says: "The one-sided view, which nowhere pays attention any longer to the essence of things, has puffed itself up into an all-sidedness which in turn is masked so as to look harmless and natural. But this all-sided view which deals in all and everything with equal uniformity and mindlessness, is only a preparation for what is really going on."[45] And what is going on for centuries now is the all-encompassing one-track thinking that masquerades as multi-sided vision, which continually takes us away from what needs attention most of all. Let us call this one-track thinking the technologization of being, after Heidegger, a major characteristic of which is the suppression or negation of true disclosure.

But Heraclitus says: "Unless you expect the unexpected you will never find truth, for it is hard to discover and hard to attain."[46] We have surrounded ourselves with the familiar and the expected, seeking security

[44] Heraclitus, Fragments 78 and 86 respectively.

[45] Heidegger, *What Is Called Thinking*, p. 34.

[46] Heraclitus, Fragment 18.

in the predictable. Like a fortress, the known and the expectable guard us against the unexpected. But truth always arrives unexpectedly, in a moment of surprise. "What is most thought-provoking is even closer to us than the most palpable closeness of our everyday handiwork,"[47] and yet it eludes us because we are too used to what we think of as 'ourselves.' The technological activities of thought harden the sensibilities closing us to the openness of the Real. This is a major reason why thinking is never ready to receive the truth because it is mired in expectations. Instead thinking must learn to expect the unexpected, and the latter must not be dismissed as subjective whimsicality. Disclosure or revelation about essence does not come through established, systematized, epistemic cultures, but arrives from an unforeseen direction, as a sudden unexpected whirlwind upsetting the known and the predictable. Thinking has invented innumerable apparatuses of capture—from language to particle accelerators, from jet engines to superconductors, and yet there is no true disclosure. The essence remains turned away from thought; there is no redemption.

Toward that, Heraclitus says, "Wisdom is one—to know the intelligence which steers all things through all things (*gar en to sophos, epistasthai gnomyn otey ekubernyse panta di panto*)."[48]

Thinking is invested in phenomena; its intentions are directed toward phenomenal disclosure in a bid to understand life instrumentally, that is, in parts. This compartmentalized grasp of life, while it might bring material benefits, is not wisdom. Rather, wisdom is unitary, the awareness of an intelligence that has no direction of its own and yet shepherds life force through all things which are inter-related in a complex web. This is beyond the rationalist worldview which sets up clear, linear lines of cause and effect, sifting and isolating matter. Wisdom is ontological correspondence with what is, being the intuition of the pulse of essence that is a singularity, and that weaves through everything, supporting everything immanently in an organic manner. Thus are all things led through all things, and thinking must learn this new way of thinking-thanking, withdrawing at least partially from its conventional stance of facing in only the direction of differentiation and fragmentation. "Whether, by way

[47] Heidegger, *What Is Called Thinking*, p. 34.

[48] Heraclitus, Fragment 41.

of this learning, though never by means of it, we shall attain relatedness to what is most thought-provoking, is something altogether out of the hands of those who practice the craft of thinking."[49] One can only listen very closely and observe the doings of thought against the background of all that we have learned from Heraclitus and others. But certainly we make close listening easier for ourselves if we rid ourselves of the habit of one-track thinking. "The dominion of this manner of perception is so vast today that our eyes can barely encompass it. The expression "one-track" has been chosen on purpose. Track has to do with rails, and rails with technology."[50] This technological thinking with its narrow compulsions and hegemonic drive assumes complete dominion today over human thinking in general and its directionality. Much redemptive labor is accomplished if thinking learns to walk away from the vicious intentionality of the present thought form, reeducating itself in serious play in keeping with the dice of Innocence.

Summary and Transition

With an astonishing economy of language, surrounded by a palpable silence, Heraclitus surgically cuts through the miasma of thought, guiding thinking past the quagmire of its own making. The vast empire of thought is brushed aside by a few sharp insights running like scalpel through tissue. It brings us to the point in our journey where we are enabled to make a few deductions that follow in the ensuing chapter. Pitting the intentionality of thought against an imperturbable Innocence Heraclitus brings thinking to its knees. Portraying Nature as "playing dice," Heraclitus makes nonsense of the idea of cultural progress. Observing that thought looks everywhere but into itself, Heraclitus opens the main ontological window away from cultural constructs and devious arguments. Demanding that we remain prepared and open to the unexpected, Heraclitus shows us the creative abyss that awaits the seeker of essence. And finally, denying that human nature can, by itself, ever apprehend truth, Heraclitus makes the all-important gesture toward a divine nature that encompasses all.

[49] Heidegger, *What Is Called Thinking*, p. 25.

[50] Ibid.

References

Chitwood, Ava. *Death by Philosophy*. Ann Arbor: University of Michigan Press, 2004.

Davidson, Andrew. *The Love of Wisdom: An Introduction to Philosophy for Theologians*. New York: SCM Press, 2013.

Deleuze, Gilles. *Spinoza: Practical Philosophy*. Translated by Robert Hurley. San Francisco: City Lights Books, 1988.

Harris, William. *Heraclitus: The Complete Fragments*. Vermont: Middlebury College, 1987.

Heidegger, Martin. *What Is Called Thinking*. Translated by Fred D. Wieck and J. Glenn Gray. New York: Harper and Row, 1968.

Kant, Immanuel. *Critique of Judgment*. Translated by J.C. Meredith. Oxford: Clarendon Press, 1952.

Kant, Immanuel. *Critique of Pure Reason*. Translated by Norman Kemp Smith, 2nd ed. New York: Palgrave Macmillan, 1929.

Parmenides. "On Nature." In *Early Greek Philosophy*, 3rd ed., edited by John Burnet. London: A & C Black, 1920.

Patrick, G.T.W. *Fragments Attributed to Heraclitus*. Baltimore: N. Murray, 1889.

Spinoza, Benedict de. *The Ethics*. Edited and translated by James Gutmann. New York: Hafner Press, 1949.

Spinoza, Benedict de. "Treatise on the Emendation of the Intellect." In *The Collected Works of Spinoza*, vol. I, edited and translated by Edwin Curley. Princeton: Princeton University Press, 1985.

CHAPTER 6

Philosophical Praxis

The present project is grounded in an unusual philosophical project—the possibility of philosophical praxis or existential redemption. Philosophy for the most part deals with conceptual systems and analytical descriptions. It has rarely concerned itself directly with altering our fundamental relations with the world and ourselves, although that might have been the original purpose of philosophizing. The well-entrenchedness of the image of thought is not to be disturbed easily, even when the logic of such a necessity is apparent. The existential ruts are deep that prevent thought from achieving its real potential and calling a halt to its flight from origin. Philosophical praxis therefore requires a multipronged digging into the wellspring of thought. The previous chapters in the book present four such entry points into the inner realms of thought as phenomenon. Each offers a key perspective from where the activities of thought can be observed to the point where thought and thinker can drop their usual division and move as a singularity. Each of the thinkers examined (from the point of view praxis) help perform an exegetical reading of the performance of self-consciousness—Heidegger in relating Da-sein and the world, Schelling in connecting Mind and Nature, Goethe in estheticizing formal knowledge, and Heraclitus in going from multiplicities to the singularity of being. Together they weave a new plane of possibility.

Thus we say with due caution, philosophy might be able to do with us what we have craved from the beginning of thinking: It might bring us to the door of redemptive freedom. The words of the traditions may

K. Roy, *The Power of Philosophy*,
https://doi.org/10.1007/978-3-319-96911-4_6

be simplistically co-opted here: 'Knock and the door shall be opened unto you.' Philosophical becoming within the corpus sensorium forms the womb in which redemption takes birth. Philosophy by itself is not sufficient; on the other hand, the corpus cannot awaken by itself. Their marriage may result in the transcendence of categories and raising the domain of intuitive knowledge. But this does not consist of the normal kind of philosophy that comprise descriptions, systems, and history of ideas. Rather it is of the nature of a reciprocal movement (between *corpus* and *mentis*) whose disclosure leads to a completely new space not dominated by ideas. Thus freedom is not there for the taking. One must give birth to it with philosophy as the midwife. And, not unlike biological birth, there is the necessity for a labor toward its proper birth. The birth of freedom is not ideational but ontological and transpersonal. It is the birth of a *space within space and a time within time.*

The present chapter takes a step in the direction of understanding the production of a new space and time within thought that is crucial to the praxis. To do this we take recourse to Pauline intimations in *The Bible* as well as admonitions in the *Book of Koheleth* being glimpses of thought pushed to the extreme edge of being. In a praxis of the kind envisaged here, the intuitive-psychic dimension cannot be left out as it is precisely the beginning of thinking. While impulse needs to be disciplined in a philosophical labor, thought needs a serious encounter with an Outside in order to drop the inborn piety.

We began the initial chapter with reflections on Heidegger; perhaps it would make sense to return hermeneutically to where the beginning was made. I would like to recall Heidegger's important interview with the German periodical *Der Spiegel* that was withheld from publication during his life time.[1] A small excerpt from this lengthy interview is rearranged and reproduced below that serves to pry open another layer in the 'within' of some of the major strands that have kept us underway till this point in our inquiry. The lines below show some of the deepest reflections around the crisis in thinking with which we are concerned here.

[1] Martin Heidegger, "Nur noch ein Gott kann uns retten," *Der Spiegel*, 30 (May 1976), pp. 193–219. W. Richardson, trans., "Only a God Can Save Us," in *Heidegger: The Man and the Thinker*, ed. T. Sheehan (1981), pp. 45–67.

Heidegger: [The] last 30 years have made it clearer that the planet-wide movement of modern technicity is a power whose magnitude in determining [our] history can hardly be overestimated. For me today it is a decisive question as to how any political system—and which one—can be adapted to an epoch of technicity. I know of no answer to this question.

SPIEGEL: [...] Since 1945, you have commented on the political efforts of the Western World, hence also on democracy, on a politically expressed Christian view of the world (*Weltanschauung*), even on the system of constitutionally guaranteed citizens' rights. All of these efforts you have called "half-way measures."

Heidegger: I would indeed characterize them as half-way measures, [though] because I do not see in them any actual confrontation with the world of technicity, inasmuch as behind them all, according to my view, stands the conception that technicity in its essence is something that man holds within his own hands. In my opinion, this is not possible. Technicity in its essence is something that man does not master by his own power.

SPIEGEL: Which of the [political] trends, according to your view, would be most suitable to our time?

Heidegger: I don't see [any answer to] that. But I do see here a decisive question. First of all, it would be necessary to clarify what you mean by "suitable to our time." What is meant here by "time?" Furthermore, the question should be raised as to whether such suitability is the [appropriate] standard for the "inner truth" of human activity, and whether the standard measure of [human] activity is not thinking and poetizing....

SPIEGEL: It is obvious that man is never [complete] master of his tools... But is it not a little too pessimistic to say: we are not gaining mastery over this surely much greater tool [that is] modern technicity?

Heidegger: Pessimism, no. In the area of the reflection that I am attempting now, pessimism and optimism are positions that don't go far enough. But above all, modern technicity is no "tool" and has nothing at all to do with tools.

SPIEGEL: Fine. Now the question naturally arises: Can the individual man in any way still influence this web of fateful circumstance? Or, indeed, can philosophy influence it?

Heidegger: If I may answer briefly, and perhaps clumsily, but after long reflection: philosophy will be unable to effect any immediate change in the current state of the world. This is true not only of philosophy but of all purely human reflection and endeavor. Only a god can save us. The only possibility available to us is that by thinking and poetizing we prepare a readiness for the appearance of a god, or for the absence of a god in [our] decline, insofar as in view of the absent god we are in a state of decline.

At least three themes that are visible in the above set of exchanges are clearly of consequence to us here: technicity, time, and action. Each is intimately connected with the question of learning to *think* anew; together, they represent a vitally interconnected angle in the phenomenology of thought without losing sight of the empirical context of the state of the world. Let us visit each of these themes hermeneutically so that another time and another action becomes gradually visible at the edge of thought. This means we must be prepared to come back to these points again and again without expecting some final resolution, for the very complexion of these elements change, the more we dwell on them.

Beginning with technicity, there is an allusion to a force unleashed in thought that thinking itself cannot control. Why is it the case that technicity is unable to be "mastered" by the very element which unleashes it in the first place? Thinking is never its own master despite its obsession with control. At the ontic level, thought may control the individual products of planetary technicity, but once unleashed, it cannot control the drift of technicity at the ontological level. As thinking exteriorizes its own ontological character and recuperates it at the level of apparatus by projecting it onto the world, these "maps" attach themselves to the available materiality producing peculiar agglomerates that humans begin to recognize, accept, and normalize as their objective world—the man-made world. But these exteriorizations cannot be retracted in order to move back to a previous state. There is no mechanism for doing that; the genie once unleashed can only move forward, blindly. All thinking that has disburdened itself of considering ontological essence can only move forward in a steady march toward nowhere. Weber had termed this march as the "irrationality of rationality." The occasional critical stance is directed toward particularities and never toward the underlying general drift which is long legitimized and taken for granted. Hence we witness the talismanic nature of technicity which only gathers pace with time, and with each round, the incantations surrounding it intensify, with the call toward the next level of technicity. No action within the temporality of thought can escape the effect of the talismanic incantation that surrounds modern technicity and accelerates its pace. Thinking takes its cue from it and develops a new religion whose icon is the machine. We are asked: Isn't it great that we have electricity and gas? Obviously, looking from the perspective of technological society we are pained by the possibility of the lack of either. Thinking has long become adjusted to the reality of their constant availability. But what is obscured in this kind of positioning is the fact that there are other ways of organizing life than being focused on energy consumption. Again, the question is thrown at us: Isn't it great that everything works—the trains, the flights, the highways, the Internet, and so on? Certainly everything works miraculously, but as Heidegger has observed, the fact that everything works may actually be part of the problem. The smoothness of daily life may have an anesthetic effect on us that seduces us to believe that all is well. We no longer question the direction in which all the gears mesh. We are mesmerized by the fact that they do mesh. What does it do to thinking? It makes thought lose the capacity for doubt and critical self-examination. For instance, could the fact that the technical gears of civilization mesh blind us to the possibility that there might be a totally different side of life that has been put fatally out of sight? Could it be that the idea of "success" itself is hopelessly flawed from the perspective of redemption? Could it be that ultimately success turns against itself and becomes its own enemy? There is actually enough empirical evidence for the latter. Such is the irony of this world. Without an insight into this irony, and making it part of how thought thinks about itself, thinking becomes varicose and trapped in one-dimensionality.

Next, let us take up the question of time, another theme that crops up in the dialogue above. Thought is time, mechanical time. How is that so? Time is built up through successive abstractions in consciousness till it emerges as something quite independent. First consciousness admits of a difference between day and night. Then it organizes this difference in terms of regularity of passage of bodies, that is, in terms of movement through space. In turn, these passages are organized into successive moments, and so on. Once this empty time line is established it is populated by events (past) and expectations (future). In between is placed the idea of the present, a making-present as it were. However, there is an ontological element hidden in this process, otherwise the sensation of time could not begin to be felt. Heidegger writes:

> The making present that awaits and retains interprets *itself*. And that is again possible only because, in itself ecstatically open, it is always already disclosed to itself and can be articulated in the interpretation that understands and speaks. *Since temporality is ecstatically and horizontally*

> *constitutive of the clearedness of the There, it is already always interpreted primordially in the There and is thus familiar.* The making present that interprets itself, that is, what has been interpreted and addressed in the "now" is what we call time.[2]

A certain primordiality—albeit not available to consciousness—is implicit in the very ground of possibility of comprehension and spokenness that involves time. Hence there is a kind of familiarity with naïve duration in the ordinary course of human situations. In its very reflexivity, the reflexion interprets itself in time and begins to produce progression or temporality. "But while time is 'immediately' intelligible and recognizable, this does not, however, preclude the possibility that primordial temporality as such, as well as the origin temporalizing in it of expressed time, may remain unknown and unconceived."[3] What is being contended is that immediate intelligibility of time does in no way indicate that the metaphysical nature of time has been grasped. In other words, time as such remains a mystery. Thought performs in time, produces time as vulgar temporality in that very performance, but remains oblivious of the ontological materiality of its own medium of production.

> The taking care that awaits, retains, and makes present, "allows itself" time in this or that way and gives this time to itself in taking care, even without determining the time by any specific reckoning, and before any such reckoning has been done. Here time dates itself in one's actual mode of allowing oneself time heedfully in terms of what is actually disclosed in what is taken care of in the surrounding world and in attuned understanding, in terms of what one does "all day long." The more Da-sein is absorbed in awaiting what is taken care of and, not awaiting itself, forgets itself, the more its time that it "allows" itself is *covered over* by this mode of allowing. In the everyday "living along" that takes care, Da-sein never understands itself as running along in a continuously enduring succession of pure "nows."[4]

As thought moves in the form of a principle of taking care of things, that is, in organizing matter, it constructs a series of presents or "nows"

[2] Heidegger, *Being and Time*, p. 375. Italics in original.

[3] Ibid.

[4] Ibid., p. 376.

without looking back at essence or the source of experience. This allows it to maintain a historicity in its collisions with the surrounding world like pearls on a string. Time is brought into presence in terms of what thought considers or gives itself as a "day" against the backdrop of the physical rotation of the planet. Thus we find Aristotle's definition of time: "*touto gar estin ho chronos, arithmos kineseos kata to proteron kai hysteron.*"[5] In other words, time is the rhythmic motion of that which comes before and that which follows. This is the commonsense notion of time. However, moving from one empirical now to the next, thought never has any inkling about the constituted nature of psychological time. It mistakes the physical succession of moments as inner continuity (psychological time), and hence does not inquire into an originary or primordial time.

> Thrown and entangled, Da-sein is lost in what it takes care of. But in this lostness, the flight of Dasein from its authentic existence that we characterized as anticipatory resoluteness makes itself known, and this is a flight that covers over. In such heedful fleeing lies the flight *from* death, that is, a looking away *from* the end of being-in-the-world....Looking away from finitude, the inauthentic temporality of entangled everyday Da-sein must fail to recognize authentic futurality and thus temporality in general. And if the vulgar understanding of Da-sein is guided by the they, then the self-forgetful representation of the infinitude of public time can first anchor itself. The they never dies because it is *unable* to die, since death is always my own....The they, which never dies and misunderstands being-toward-the-end, nonetheless interprets the flight from death in a characteristic way. Up to the end "it always has more time"....[Dasein] is out to snatch as much as possible from time that is still coming and "goes on." One knows only public time that, leveled down, belongs to everyone, and that means to no one.[6]

Once thrown into the world, thinking becomes engrossed in the basic common drive which is to engage with the surrounding, and becomes lost in it. Being gets caught up in the flight of time (history) and away from authentic existence. The flight *is* the denial of authentic existence. But it is also the flight from death. Mistaking the empirical sense of finitude as authentic temporality, thinking attempts to anchor itself in public

[5] Aristotle cited in Heidegger, *Being and Time*, p. 386.

[6] Heidegger, *Being and Time*, p. 389.

time, which seems endless. The succession of instants keep coming, and thinking takes them as representing privately expendable time, something that one can spend and have more of. Thus is born a key deception in the organization of thinking which no longer understands finitude, being hooked onto an external and apparently endless public time—a time of the *they*. Popular time or public time is thus essentially born of self-forgetfulness or amnesia. This public time is maintained by relatedness to an amorphous "they" or a universalized other within the dialectic of which it is anchored. In other words, just as the self is maintained by "bouncing off" experience against a universalized other, thinking as time is born of the objectivity of public instants. In turn, the "They" is used to escape the immediate facticity of temporal cessation or death; till the very end thought tries to "steal" more time, imagines it has more time. Thinking is therefore a certain kind of flight, an attempt to escape the finitude of pseudo-temporality. And in this flight from finitude-death lies the real reason why thinking is unable to comprehend things from the angle of redemption. For to truly accept death is to die psychologically to the succession of the nows, that is, to reject the time of the "they" and return to a time of the now or disjunction. To internalize and be in accordance with that line of thinking, one must be prepared to die to the old manner of being, to the old regime of public time, in order to be resuscitated into a redemptive order of thinking-being. This is what those who have confronted time, who have found another time—the prophets and the Messiahs of antiquity—tell us about *Kairos*: one must die to time in order to find Life.

For the attainment of a truly emancipatory perspective beyond the vulgar temporality and conventional action of thought in which all thinking is caught, thinking must constantly search for those openings and invitations that offer a well-considered leap into the beyond of public time. This is a possible ground or preparation for readiness toward redemptive thinking. The "preparing for a readiness" that Heidegger speaks of may be thought of as this transcendence of time as an incestuous beat of thought, and develop instead the instinct of time from the perspective of eternity. Where then shall we look for an alternative or primordial perspective that gives thinking a perch from where to examine itself in relation to time, the vulgar time in which thinking is inexorably caught and from which it is unable to extricate itself? There is a somewhat startling hint toward such action in the interview above. Heidegger refers to it in terms of a divine intervention:

"*only a god can save us.*" Obviously, Heidegger does not mean some personified god or the dramatic appearance of a savior. The reference is rather to an ontological state (Divine Innocence) that confronts thinking as it has never been confronted before. It is the considered position here that such an absolute confrontation and challenge to thought, or to thinking as it has operated conventionally, is presented by a reconceptualization of time. In other words, once again, authentic temporality or eternity must be brought back in sight and thinking oriented toward it.

There must be a way, as Heidegger indicates in *Being and Time*, to understand the production of vulgar time and distinguish it from a primordial time that is not a quantitative procession of instants. This distinction may be made along the lines of what has been known in tradition as *Kairos* or qualitative time as opposed to *Chronos* or mechanical time. This qualitative time is an opening, a sudden parting that is a 'folding back' of quantitative time as thinking knows it. The Apostle Paul writes in the letter to the Corinthians: "But this I say, Brethren, time contracted itself, the rest is, that even those having wives, may be as not having, and those weeping as not weeping, and those rejoicing as not rejoicing, and those buying as not possessing, and those using the world as not using it up. For passing away is the figure of this world."[7] The contraction of time upon itself, into a singularity, makes for phenomena to back into themselves, as it were. Each enters not merely into its opposite replacing the world of dualities by an indifference, but into a fundamentally altered relation to itself.

> The Pauline *hōs mē* [as not] seems to be a special type of tensor, for it does not push a concept's semantic field toward that of another concept. Instead, it sets it against itself in the form of the *as not*: weeping as not weeping. The messianic tension thus does not tend toward an elsewhere, nor does it exhaust itself in the indifference between one thing and its opposite. The apostle does not say: "weeping *as* rejoicing" nor "weeping as [meaning=] not weeping," but "weeping *as not* weeping." According to the principle of messianic *klēsis*, one determinate factical condition is set in relation to itself—the weeping is pushed toward the weeping, the rejoicing toward the rejoicing. In this manner, it revokes the factical condition and undermines it without altering its form.[8]

[7] I Corinthians 7:29–32.

[8] Giorgio Agamben, *The Time That Remains: A Commentary on the Letter to the Romans* (Stanford: Stanford University Press, 2005), p. 24.

Time as progression, thought as movement in time, moves forward by means of antithesis, by posing its opposite. The Hegelian dialectic's inner mechanism is precisely this propensity toward the antithesis, producing time as world history. Messianic character, on the contrary, is anti-dialectical, ahistorical. It seeks no antithesis; rather it pushes each facticity or determinate condition onto itself and cancels it by rolling it back onto itself. Thus is produced an original condition and an original time. Thus is thinking brought into contact with its origin, its essence, not as a forward movement onto an elsewhere, but in a reverse contraction that is unprecedented. Thus passes away the conventional manner of contemplating and being in this world. Thus, further, there is repudiation of some other fantastic world; instead, the very passing away of that which had arisen, or its passage not outside but within itself, generates the redemptive moment.

> In Paul, the messianic nullification performed by *hōs mē* is completely inherent to *klēsis* and does not happen to it in a second time, [...] nor does it add anything to it. In this way the messianic vocation is a movement of immanence, or, if one prefers, a zone of absolute indiscernibility between immanence and transcendence, between this world and the future world.[9]

In a powerful passage in I Corinthians, Paul explains the word *klēsis*: "... As the Lord hath called everyone, so let him walk...Let every man abide in the same calling as he was called."[10] All propensities and actional dispositions are internal to the calling (*klēsis*); they do not confer (or take away) any stature.[11] From the point of view of redemption all are at the same distance within the calling. Each arising is thus both immanence and transcendence: an origination dependent on the calling and a simultaneous subsidence that does not afford or require a separate moment or action. There is no division in the *klēsis* and in the thinking that corresponds to it. Conventionally, an idea such as freedom is linked to its opposite through the 'from': freedom *from* something. Or an idea such as justice through the 'for': justice for something or someone, etc. Thus the culmination occurs in a second or auxiliary moment besides the one

[9] Ibid., p. 25.

[10] I Corinthians 7:20.

[11] A cognate notion is found in the Upanishadic idea of *dharma*; each one must act according to their *dharma* or inner truth or a given dispensation that guides. One must act within one's *dharma*, even use it, to find truth.

in which the matter is posed. In messianic calling, on the other hand, the concept does not point toward an object or predicate. There is no means-ends relationship which is often the staple or substance of thinking. Thought normally points toward another moment in which it imagines fulfillment. Here the fulfillment is in the negation of fulfillment itself. Such is the preparation for thought in the art of negation; the positivity of thought comes up against a nothingness.

Besides, there is also the denial of ownership: "to remain in the calling in the form of the *as not* means to not ever make the calling an object of ownership, only of use [toward redemption]. The *hōs mē* therefore does not only have negative content; rather, for Paul, this is the only possible *use* of worldly situations. The messianic vocation is not a right, nor does it furnish an identity; rather it is a generic potentiality [*potenza*] that can be used without ever being owned."[12] Those "buying as not possessing" is a clear goal of not merely the dispossession of thought but rather the emptying out of thought as to even the possibility of ownership. Within messianic time there is no room for thinking to take possession of the world or any part of it, for all the mechanisms that lead to the staticity of ownership have already been pushed back onto themselves and nullified. Each situation in the world or each calling therefore is an indeterminate qualitative moment, a potential only, one that finds no moments strung together as a temporal apparatus leading to a specific finitude. Everything remains as generic potentiality without the associative tendency toward possession. Thought is checked from its innate push toward attaching or clinging to the object in time.

The alternative vision, that is, of time as *Kairos*, has a structure that is markedly different from *chronos*. Agamben notes that Paul, who was much concerned with this altered view of time, has given a particular decomposition of messianic time.

> Paul decomposes the messianic event into two times: resurrection and *parousia*.... Out of this issues the paradoxical tension between an *already* and a *not yet* that defines the Pauline conception of salvation. The messianic event has already happened...but, nevertheless, in order to be truly be fulfilled, this implies an additional time. How should we interpret this unusual scission?[13]

[12] Agamben, op. cit., p. 26.

[13] Ibid., p. 69.

Apparently the event has already occurred and yet redemption or salvation has not yet taken place. Resurrection may be understood as the radical breakdown of *chronos.* In resurrection, death, as the irrevocable-making-past of what was present, is negated or reversed; the arrow of time is turned back upon itself. And yet there is a '*not yet*,' in the sense that the timeless moment is not yet upon us. How is this antinomy to be explained? "The messianic *ho nyn kairos* [time of the now] can never fully coincide with a chronological moment internal to its representation. The end of time is actually a time-image represented by a final point on the homogeneous line of chronology. But as an image devoid of time, it is itself impossible to seize hold of, and, consequently, tends to infinitely defer itself."[14] *Kairos* has no mental representation. Hence *Parousia* cannot be guessed at from the outside; not even negatively. There is no chronological moment that may be used as a supplementary representational time in which this scission may be experienced.

In other words, there is no external perch from where this scission can be maintained or reviewed. Thinking attempts to anticipate *Presence*, but must inevitably fail, for in this gap it inserts itself as time-image that seeks a representation, which is its own continuity or the very denial of *Parousia*. Time as thought must die to itself without a second, without anticipation. But the death of thought cannot be foretold by thought.

> This is why it is important that one correctly understand the meaning of the term *parousia*. It does not mean the "second coming" of Jesus, a second messianic event that would follow and subsume the first. In Greek, *parousia* simply means presence (*par-ousia* literally signifies to be next to; in this way, being is beside itself in the present). *Parousia* does not signal a complement that is added to something in order to complete it, nor a supplement, added on afterward, that never reaches fulfillment. Paul uses this term to highlight the innermost uni-dual structure of the messianic event, inasmuch as it is comprised of two heterogeneous times, one *kairos* and the other *chronos*, one an operational time and the other a represented time, which are coextensive but cannot be added together.[15]

One must be beside oneself without ever coinciding. Therefore the situation is full of tension. This is the significant point. *Kairos* introduces

[14] Ibid., p. 70.

[15] Ibid.

irresolvable tension with respect to the *chronos* of thought. Thought's formation through time and its past knowledge of itself cannot be added to *Kairos* and hence *Kairos* remains an impossible tension. Paul expresses this as *epekteinomenos*: "Brothers, I for my part do not consider myself as having seized hold of it myself. Just one thing: forgetting what lies behind, but straining forward [*epekteinomenos*] to what lies ahead."[16] What lies behind is civilizational debris, social residuum, and the cultural products of non-redemptive thought piled up through time. What is ahead has no name, and can never be reached within time. There can only be a "straining forward" not toward a future, which is another projection of thought, but toward an indeterminateness that has no representation within thought as time. This is what thinking cannot tolerate. That word "indeterminateness" is the bane of thought. The straining forward necessary of thinking is toward the Unexpected or *Unmarked*. Thinking must silently expect the unexpected. But before it can do that thinking must go through a certain penance without which the space of silence cannot be opened up. The normal self-confidence of thought must be shattered from within so as to produce the required diffidence. Representational time, or the time in which thought puts together its self-presence, in which it creates the thinker, must be seen to be merely one part of a complex and heterogeneous temporality.

So what is to be done? In I Corinthians Paul hints at something in this direction. First: "In these things they [our forefathers] became figures [*typoi*]...and they were written for us, for our admonition, upon whom the ends of the ages are come face to face."[17] What is the relation hinted at between the *typos* or the figure (of forefathers) and ourselves? Their (worldly) actions are forbidden to us for those are continuation of the fallen state. Therefore admonition. Upon the actions of thought is a sign that is a reprimand. The relation itself looks toward an atonement; or rather, the immediate comprehension of the relation is the demand for atonement upon which *chronos* and *kairos* come face to face. Fragment no. 129 in Heraclitus simply also reads "Atonement." Atonement or 'at-one-ment' brings together the *typoi* and its other, that is, all dualities together to a point of exotic stillness. From this point on, thought does not carry on its historical actions and continuities.

[16]Philippians 3:13.

[17]I Corinthians.

At-one-ment is a radical discontinuity. In other words, rather than grope toward *Parousia*, which is impossible, thinking must contemplate its own radical discontinuity and not operate under various guises continuing to do the same things as did older patterns of thought (our forefathers). The atonement or penance gives a jolt to the psychic plexi in the corpus sensorium as a consequence of the philosophical shock that inheres in radical discontinuity. Thought lurks as a residual imprint in each cell of the body, hence its expulsion is necessarily also a corporeal act. The whole organism must be engaged in reorienting thinking and not just the mind. Admonition therefore must be understood in an ontological way meaning an action at all levels of the body-mind. Stemming from a cognate root of PIE *menyo* and Sanskrit *manas* (the matrix of thinking), admonition literally means to bring to mind in the way of restraint. To put in a restraint on thinking, that is, acquire a limit, requires the co-operation of the whole organism. Getting away from calculation, as the traditional way of the forefathers, thinking must learn to operate discretely or without psychological continuity. The sensation of a continuous subject is a superstition that is required to be rejected. Thus is arrested the psychological anxiety in thought by means of a reprimand or an admonition. Recall, the Eternal Return.

Second, in Ephesians, Paul writes: "as for the economy of *pleroma* of times [*pleromatos ton kairon*], all things are recapitulated in him, things in heaven and things on earth."[18] Here the key term is recapitulation. Under *kairos*, all thought is finally gathered together, in a kind of fulfilment of time. To think from the point of view of being gathered or swept up introduces in thinking a contemplation of totalities, or more specifically, of marginal totalities. This means that at any moment the completed cycle of thought, once reflexively grasped as complete, can potentially leap off into the Unmarked without leaving a trace, thus bringing things to a fullness and therefore to redemption. There is no separate *pleroma* or essence; there is only a holding off or deferment in which this fulfillment is denied. The subsumption within the Unmarked is the only redemption available to thought. Right away there is a philosophical shock. Thought was apparently going somewhere, to some projected destination, differentiating, breeding, becoming. But the analysis through messianic discourse shows this journey to be futile, a mere

[18] Ibid.

non-arrival. The temporality of *kairos* reveals that thinking is merely in deferment of the *pleroma*; that all thought is, in the end, a grand nullity, a one-sided production away from essence that does not bring what thought really wants, which is *Parousia*. This truth has been denied in thought for long, meaning that thinking has turned away from this truth in its attempt to create a kingdom by itself.

The perspective of redemption, and the proper understanding of *kairos* in its relation to *chronos*, thus makes nonsense of conventional philosophical thinking, since it bypasses the content of thought itself and its systems, speculations, projections, introjections, and representations. It is for this reason that this process is referred to here as philosophical shock, a shock that provides the opening for the complete review of thinking as it has conventionally operated—"one single catastrophe which keeps piling wreckage upon wreckage and hurls it in front of his feet" as Walter Benjamin put it in his famed prophetic description of Angelus Novus or the angel of history.[19] The angel of history is *chronos*: a storm is blowing from paradise (*Kairos*) and time is ripe for the ultimate contraction that has the potentiality to leave the wreckage (differentiated thought and its cultural residues) behind. The rolling back of the present upon itself is Presence or *Parousia*. Angelus Novus represents the culmination of the process of ruin in single-track thinking. For thinking to recognize its conventional and normal operations as ultimately calamitous requires courage and humility. But from the perspective of redemptive thinking nothing less would do, and the need for disciplining thinking must be realized in thinking.

Perhaps there is no single work more valuable for the restraint (admonition) of thought, as well for making it face its vanity and piety, than the *Book of Koheleth*, also known as *Ecclesiastes*. One of the twenty four books

[19] "A Klee painting named 'Angelus Novus' shows an angel looking as though he is about to move away from something he is fixedly contemplating. His eyes are staring, his mouth is open, his wings are spread. This is how one pictures the angel of history. His face is turned toward the past. Where we perceive a chain of events, he sees one single catastrophe which keeps piling wreckage upon wreckage and hurls it in front of his feet. *The angel would like to stay, awaken the dead, and make whole what has been smashed*. But a storm is blowing from Paradise; it has got caught in his wings with such violence that the angel can no longer close them. This storm irresistibly propels him into the future to which his back is turned, while the pile of debris before him grows skyward. This storm is what we call progress." Walter Benjamin, "Thesis on the Philosophy of History," in *Illuminations*, trans. H. Zorn (London: Pimlico, 1940/1999), pp. 245–255.

of the *Tanakh*, the Hebrew Bible, it looks upon all human activities as they would appear from the perspective of redemption. “Vanity of vanities, saith the Preacher, vanity of vanities; all is vanity.”[20] The word in the Hebrew Bible that is translated as vanity is ‘*Hebel*,’ which literally means vapor. This word is widely translated into English via the Greek as vanity, meaning insubstantial or transient. *Hebel* occurs 37 times in this text and sets the key-note for its central teaching. Hence it is worthwhile to pay close attention to it. For instance, it is to be noted that the word is not merely employed to qualify a state of things, rather it is speaking of the innate nature of the things themselves. It is not being claimed that all is in vain, but that all *is vanity*. This is an assertion about the ontological character of the human-made world. The word is not being employed out of disillusionment, resignation, frustration, or resentment, but as an authoritative statement of fact: that all things are such, or are in this manner, and no other. Next, the formulaic statement “vanity of vanities” (in the manner of Biblical expressions such as the ‘Song of Songs,’ etc.) indicates a superlative degree of facticity. It is employed to exclude the possibility of any exception.

However, at the same time, the things of God cannot be in vain or represent vanity; that would be against all else in the scriptures. Therefore “all” must be taken to indicate the categories of thought and perceptual relationships through which humans relate to the world. These categories are made up by thought itself and are but shadows and insubstantial. All the categories of thought, its strategies and representations, are in the end empty of true significance or meaning, and hence these are vaporous. All that thought does to achieve happiness or permanence flounders in the end due to its very ontological quality. Hence humans cannot find happiness in the shadow world of thought and its categories, howsoever real its products might seem, for these are not what they appear to be. Rather these lead to unstable and perishable things and hence to sorrow and misery. Conceit and egotism, built-up layers of ignorance and misidentification, plied with cultural reinforcements and communal reward systems, make up layered social totalities that are in the end vaporous. Nothing built on thought lasts, for its very nature is perishability. This is not to be blamed on thought as such, but on our (thought’s) misunderstanding of the nature of thought.

[20] Ecclesiastes 1:2, King James version.

The exegetical reading can also appear almost like the expansion of a mathematical tautology: All = Vanity. On the left hand side, the term 'All' might be taken to be everything that appears in consciousness, and philosophically, is made sense of through the categories. On the right side is 'vapor' or ephemeral evanescence. Again, on the left side, is 'All,' meaning totality, but totality or whole must always remain outside thought, for thinking, as we have seen, is sequential or linear, and hence can never apprehend the All or the true background against which anything lasting can be founded or understood. It can merely *pretend* to apprehend the Real. In other words, the very attempt to project thought (cognition) as giving true sense of reality must be vaporous or empty, as it has no basis even for grasping itself. Hence, the right hand side of the equation can only be filled by the vaporous; thus the tautology, Unreal = Unreal.

In the very next scriptural lines another significant question is raised as to the actual value of human labor: "What profit hath a man of all his labour which he taketh under the sun?"[21] The interrogative form suggests a strong negation. So it is important to look at this scriptural injunction carefully. The word rendered as profit in this text is the Hebrew "*Yithron*"; it means "that which remains over." Man seeks something that remains over, that is, man looks for the enduring in the labor of his thought and the toil of his body. However, nothing of the kind is available under the sun that truly endures. The phrase "under the sun" indicates a sublunary world and does not necessarily point to a different supra world. All civilizations perish and nothing remains over as the planet turns and returns. However, for many centuries now, thought has cultivated the opposite belief that humans are building permanent civilizations and the name of this effort has been called progress. The cultural metaphors and self-understandings of dominant cultures especially in the modern West are deeply invested in the projection of human labor as *the* mode of collective advancement or development that is perpetual. In his famous *Protestant Ethic* thesis Max Weber has given a genealogical account of the arising of this archetypal modern agent (*Berufmensch*) who is affirmed solely through his actions, along with the corresponding general understanding of the principle and meaning of action. The other important part played in this project of modernity is

[21] Ecclesiastes 1:3.

the systematic mastering of the outer by means of scientific and technical rationalization. Together these produce an unbroken whole that is aimed at world mastery. But just as the reflexive modern self (a specific projection of thought) is fraught with contradiction, modern science itself is a deeply nihilistic enterprise in which any scientific achievement worthy of the name *must* "ask to be surpassed and made obsolete[22]" as Weber observed, in a process "that is in principle ad infinitum," at which point, we come to the problem of *that which remains over*. Weber went on to write: "For it is simply not self-evident that something which is subject to such a law is in itself meaningful and rational. Why should one do something which in reality never comes to an end and never can?" In other words, the search for 'that which remains over' turns out to be unreachable and self-contradictory in the existing operations of thought.

But the cultural interchange necessary even to partly establish this truth about thinking is far from being secured, and consequently the "preparation for readiness" in the direction of redemption is not yet begun. Those who believe that "we" (as thought) are cumulatively acting on a largely independent reality, and bringing about positive change in the world, far outnumber and outvoice those who are skeptical about such beliefs.[23] We see a powerful example of the above in the ferocity of the attack, among other things, on Heidegger's position on planetary technicity and in the various misunderstandings that surround it.[24]

[22] Max Weber, *The Essential Weber: A Reader*, ed. Sam Whimster (New York: Routledge, 2003), p. 273.

[23] In the Indian tradition, the *Karmayogi* engages in action not in order to bring about progress in the world, but as a mode of self-awakening of the different centers of consciousness in the body-mind system as well as a means of burning out his *prarabdha* or accumulated past. Hence the famous injunction in the *Gita* to act without being attached to the fruits of action.

[24] Describing Andrew Feenberg's work, Iain Thomson writes: "Feenberg develops the critical theoretical charge against Heidegger's thought first advanced by Heidegger's former student, and Feenberg's teacher, Marcuse. In effect, Feenberg appropriates one of Marcuse's most powerful *political* criticisms of Heidegger, the charge that Heidegger succumbed to a "hopeless heteronomism," that is, he lost faith in the Enlightenment understanding of freedom as the capacity for substantive rational self-determination, the ability to direct the ends as well as the means of human life. Hence, Feenberg also expresses this Marcusean criticism in a Marxist register, accusing Heidegger of being a "technological fetishist." In the Marxist vocabulary, fetishism occurs when a "social relation between men" assumes "the fantastic form of a relation between things" (as Marx famously put it). For a Marxist (and we should not forget that "critical theory" is an interdisciplinary,

Thought "forgets" that the division between thinker and thought is its own making, and that the "sovereign actor" behind thought is none other than itself under various guises and masks. To understand this is to admit the farcical element in all of human action that arrives at no conclusion, as pointed out by Koheleth: "All things are full of labour; man cannot utter it: the eye is not satisfied with seeing, nor the ear filled with hearing."[25]

The word *dabar* in Hebrew can mean both 'word' and 'thing,' and so the first part could be interpreted as all things are tediously and ceaselessly in movement ("full of labour"), or as word-thought wearisomely moving in circles without coming to any meaningful conclusion. Besides, the word *yaged* also means suffering, apart from weariness. In other words, there is great suffering in this ceaseless movement that bestows no clarity or insight about its own nature. Bible commentary tells us:

> The idea…is this – Man's life is constrained by the same law as his surroundings; he goes on his course subject to influences which he cannot control; in spite of his efforts, he can never be independent. This conclusion is developed in succeeding verses. In the present verse the proposition with which it starts is explained by what follows. All things have been the object of much labor; men have elaborately examined everything; yet the result is most unsatisfactory, the end is not reached; words cannot express it, neither eye nor ear can apprehend it. This is the view of St. Jerome, who writes, '*Non solum do physicis, sed de ethicis quoque scirc difficile est. Nec sermo valet explicare causas natu-rasque rerum, nec oculus, ut rei poscit dignitas, intueri, nec auris, instituente doctore, ad summam scientiam pervenirc. Si enim nunc 'per speculum videmus in aenigmate; et ex parte*

post-Marxian development of Marxism), to *fetishize* something is to detach it from the human labor that produced it while continuing nevertheless to project human meanings on it, thereby mistaking these projections for an independent reality. The fetishist's unconscious anthropomorphic projection endows a humanly created thing with the magical appearance of possessing a *telos* independent of human ends. Heidegger's substantivism "fetishizes" the essence of technology, then, insofar as it treats a human creation as if it were beyond human control." Iain Thomson, *Heidegger on Ontotheology*, p. 50. But Heidegger's criticism of the technologization of being has little to do with fetishism. It concerns the "progressive technologization of intelligibility" and is focused on the nature and consequence of one-track thinking. Thought's projections recovered as material processes or objects are not distinct from thinking itself. Hence, in truth, the real reason why thought cannot control that to which it has given birth (technology, in this case) lies in its ontological character.

[25] Ecclesiastes 1:8.

> *cognoscimus, et ex parte prophetamus,' consequenter nec sermo potest explicate quod nescit; nec oculus in quo caecutit, aspiecre; nec auris, de quo dubitat, impleri.*' Delitzsch, Nowack, Wright, and others render, 'All things are in restless activity;' i.e., constant movement pervades the whole world, and yet no visible conclusion is attained.[26]

Nature is incessant movement, restless activity. Aggregates are formed, breaking down again to form yet other aggregates. That which is born, dies, meaning disorganizes after a period. Organization and chaos follow one another relentlessly from one cycle to another without moving toward any final resolution. There is no stasis. While all of this is true, the real point may however may be deeper than that.

> The intention of the author is to show that man, like nature, is confined to a circle from which he cannot free himself; and though he uses all the powers with which he is endowed to penetrate the enigma of life and to rise superior to his environments, he is wholly unable to effect anything in these matters. Man cannot utter it. He cannot explain all things. Koheleth does not say that man can know nothing, that he can attain to no certitude; his contention is that the inner cause and meaning elude his faculties, that his knowledge is concerned only with accidents and externals, and that there is [a] depth which his powers cannot fathom. The eye is not satisfied with seeing, nor the ear filled with hearing. Use his eyes as he may, listen to the sounds around him, attend to the instructions of professed teachers, man makes no real advance in knowledge of the mysteries in which he is involved; the paradox is inexplicable.[27]

The human aggregate is also caught up in the tumult of nature, that is, in movement and change. It attempts to penetrate the mystery of perpetual change and arrive at some enduring meaning at the core but fails. It tries to look beyond the change and rise above it, but it cannot. It can certainly acquire a lot of data about the formation and transformation of matter, but no matter how much empirical knowledge is gathered through the senses, the labors of thought do not arrive. In other words, as the chatter of thought joins the restless world of matter like the wind

[26] Biblehub, *Commentary on Ecclesiastes*, Retrieved from http://biblehub.com/commentaries/pulpit/ecclesiastes/1.htm.

[27] Ibid.

and the tides, it merely goes round in circles without penetrating to the core or bringing about any definite knowledge about inner cause, purpose, or the meaning of activity.

Through activity we cannot find the source or meaning of activity. What is the root of this conundrum? We find some light on this in Ecclesiastes 7:29: "Lo, this only have I found, that God hath made man upright; but they have sought out many inventions." The human being was made in alignment with that which is morally right (*yasbar*) and true, but instead thought has chosen to seek out and construct various apparatuses (*chishshebonoth*) that it regards as the superior instruments of navigation in life. The consequence is that thought's activities do not bring emancipation; these remain as deeds and nothing else. To put it differently, man lacks for nothing, he was made complete in and of himself, and yet, for obscure reasons, thought has sought new instruments that bedevil it. Bible commentary has it:

> Of one thing he was sure, which Koheleth proceeds to specify - he has learned to trace the degradation to its source, not in God's agency, but in man's perverse will. That God hath made man upright. Koheleth believes that man's original constitution was "straight," "right," "morally good," and possessed of ability to choose and follow what was just and right (Genesis 1:26, etc.). Thus in the Book of Wisdom (2:23) we read, "God created man to be immortal, and made him an *imago* of his own nature (ἰιότητος). Nevertheless, through envy of the devil, came death into the world, and they that are his portion tempt it." But they (men) have sought out many inventions (Chronicles 26:15), where the term implies works of invention, and is translated "engines," i.e., devices, ways of going astray and deviating from original righteousness. Man has thus abased his free-will, and employed the inventive faculty with which he was endowed in excoriating evil (Genesis 6:5). How this state of things came about, how the originally good man became thus wicked, the writer does not tell. Koheleth knows from revelation that God made him upright; he knows from experience that he is now evil; and he leaves the matter there.[28]

When thought is in alignment with essence there is no puzzlement. Action born of such alignment does not lead the human astray. However, envy born of misalignment leads thought astray, and now thinking seeks "inventions" in order to come into possession of the

[28] Ibid.

material world and its secrets as in the case of Faust in Goethe. Although empirically it is obvious that thinking has gone astray, thought in general cannot, does not, admit the wickedness of its doings. Instead, unredeemed thought glorifies all its actions upon the world and sees its own engineering as advancement toward truth. Whereas, it is evident from Koheleth that all the engineering of thought is in vain and leads only to vexation of the spirit, thought is completely taken up by the inventive faculty. This can only lead to vexation for that which is complete cannot be made more complete; the only task before it is to recognize its completeness. Unmoored from essence, thinking comes in contact with its surroundings, and attempts to "overcome" its surroundings through the invention and deployment of various apparatuses and devices. But it merely succeeds in complicating its situation and generating a new set of conundrums. The equation of thought and thing (*dabar*) in the earlier lines is highly suggestive. Thinking is reciprocally mirrored in the formulation of the thing but separates itself from the thing as discovered in Shelley earlier. The spectacle of differentiation in thought that begins to appear as independent reality is thus seen to be the main problem that cannot be solved by thinking.

Further, each cycle of complication adds a layer to the "world" further obfuscating and alienating thinking from its metaphysical roots, that is, from the sense of wholeness. Nevertheless, once the point of departure from *yasbar* is recognized and acknowledged, we are underway. It becomes possible to imagine the situation in which thinking retraces its steps to the point of separation. It is possible to imagine this because the point of separation is a singularity and not a description or representation; each instant retains the possibility of retreating to the ontological singularity, to *Kairos*. But there is something that stands in the way. Let us return once more to Heidegger's assertion that "Only a god can save us. The only possibility available to us is that by thinking and poetizing we prepare a readiness for the appearance of a god, or for the absence of a god in [our] decline, insofar as in view of the absent god we are in a state of decline."[29] This "god" or ontological insight is deemed necessary because having spun a world out of its own threads, thought is unable to retreat to the essence. Its path is blocked by terror. Using the "poetizing" that is left to us, we must get to the root of this terror in which thought lives. This terror is akin to the terror of the creature in

[29] Heidegger interview in *Der Spiegel*.

Kafka's brilliant unfinished work *Der Bau* ("The Burrow") who ceaselessly burrows deeper into futurality in the hope of finding that final security, but at the same time somehow realizing that it will never come. The currency of thought is thought: thinking fabricates and uses its own broken off tendrils to "solve" problems of its own making in the process of burrowing into time, into futurality. But this is sheer inflation: thought's real (ontological) assets have little correspondence with the hyper-inflationary world it has built. It has inflated the world out of all proportions to its actual possibility and is now called upon to back it up which it is unable to do. Thus it becomes bankrupt. It strains to prevent collapse of this bubble each instant. The terror is the product of the threat of imminent collapse. Thought stares at the bubble it has created in incomprehension and confusion, its response to crisis is to pump more air into the balloon which is already in a hyper-blown state. Poetizing in this overblown state, in part, implies letting the air out of the system in a guided and thoughtful manner. It is negative activity. The organic substratum must be cooled, must be emptied of its projections and introjections.

Such is the action of *Kenosis.* The latter word occurs in Paul's letters. In Philippians 2:7, Paul writes, "[Christ] emptied himself, by taking the form of a servant, being born in the likeness of men [*ἀλλὰ ἑαυτὸν ἐκένωσεν, μορφὴν δούλου λαβών, ἐν ὁμοιώματι ἀνθρώπων γενόμενος*]."[30] The word *ekenosen,* from *kenoo,* means 'emptied.' The Christ emptied himself of divine content to be born among ordinary humans. But from the other end, in order to meet the Christ, that is, in order to recognize essence, the ordinary human being must engage in negative action and empty themselves of the productions and projections of thought. In other words, metaphorically speaking, the cranial fluids must be drained and the cerebral balloon collapsed before one can reawaken the instincts necessary to turn toward essence. One must be reborn as nothing just in the same way as the essence took birth as nothing. Only nothing can adequately meet nothingness. It is thus that thought's original function as thanksgiving can be rediscovered. The negation of cerebral inflation will come as a philosophical shock to conventional thinking that has been used to, for so long, believing in such elaboration as the path to emancipation. But we have tried that route and failed comprehensively and for reasons already discussed.

[30] Philippians 2:7, Standard English Version.

The ontological route is radically different. It requires not elaboration of any kind. Rather, it requires shedding and divestiture. The more thinking sheds its pretensions, the more it sees the truth of what it has done. The more the world shrinks in terms of projections and psychological elaborations, the more the truth of things become apparent. The singularities reappear in the partings of the cultural debris and civilizational residuum. We are able to look beyond the Angelus Novus back toward paradise, as it were.

However, this can never be reduced to a formula or to some culture-wide phenomenological practice. The new restraint in thought accompanying the philosophical shock could potentially enter into thinking at any possible thought moment. The question is never 'how much' or 'how many.' Rather, the issue is 'whether'; that is, *whether* thinking wants to revise its posture at any nodal point, for then, the new angle as hermeneutic effort is immediately underway. We must not make the error of individualizing the problem, nor should it be thought of as a problem of the collective. The circulation of thought in ontological terms is beyond both the categories of individual and collective. Both are constituted and not constitutive. So when thought poses the question 'who is going to do this?' one can immediately sense the staging of escape by shifting the burden. Thought cannot legitimately ask the question, for to pose such a question implies the admission of some new imaginary category besides thought, which is necessarily a deception. Thus are all escape routes closed till thought faces itself naked and immobilized. And how do we get here? Little by little each of thought's projections are slowed down and eventually stalled by means of a hermeneutic phenomenology we have been discussing that strips away the outer masks or camouflage under the cover of which thinking dupes itself as the proliferation of diverse formulations. It populates the world through *dramatis personae*, which, in each case, is none other than itself, projected as observer and observed, particular and universalized, victimizer and victimized, glorified and demonized. The slowing down of projections creates the possibility of a sudden parting in the curtain of thought. The wisdom literature tells that it's always a remainder that is redeemed, but thought cannot know in advance what constitutes that remainder. The point is that it does not matter, for thinking contains in it all of thought; what affects the part affects the whole.

There is one final point to be made here to which we shall turn now. It pertains to the nature of the error to which thinking is prone as it strides along on a straight line believing that it is constructing high civilization. In his famous essay on St. Francis, G.K. Chesterton makes an important observation:

> Viewed merely in an external and experimental fashion, the whole of the high civilization of antiquity had ended in the learning of a certain lesson; that is, in its conversion [to faith]. But that lesson was a psychological fact as well as a theological faith. That pagan civilization had indeed been a very high civilization. It would not weaken our thesis, it might even strengthen it, to say that it was the highest that humanity ever reached. It had discovered its still unrivalled arts of poetry and plastic representation; it had discovered its own permanent political ideals; it had discovered its own clear system of logic and language. But above all, it had discovered its own mistake. That mistake was too deep to be ideally defined; the short-hand of it is to call it the mistake of nature-worship. It might almost as truly be called the mistake of being natural; and it was a very natural mistake. The Greeks, the great guides and pioneers of pagan antiquity, started out with the idea of something splendidly obvious and direct; the idea that if a man walked straight ahead on the high road of reason and nature, he would come to no harm; especially if he was, as the Greek was, eminently enlightened and intelligent. We might be so flippant as to say that man was simply to follow his nose, so long as it was a Greek nose. And the case of the Greeks themselves is alone enough to illustrate the strange but certain fatality that attends upon this fallacy. No sooner did the Greeks themselves begin to follow their own noses and their own notion of being natural, than the queerest thing in history seems to have happened to them. It was much too queer to be an easy matter to discuss. It may be remarked that our more repulsive realists never give us the benefit of their realism. Their studies of unsavoury subjects never take note of the testimony they bear to the truths of traditional morality. But if we had the taste for such things, we could cite thousands of such things as part of the case for Christian morals. And an instance of this is found in the fact that nobody has written, in this sense, a real moral history of the Greeks. Nobody has seen the scale or the strangeness of the story. The wisest men in the world set out to be natural; and the most unnatural thing in the world was the very first thing they did. The immediate effect of saluting the sun and the sunny sanity of nature was a perversion spreading like a pestilence. The greatest and even the purest philosophers could not apparently avoid this low sort of lunacy. Why? It would seem simple enough for the people whose poets had conceived Helen of Troy, whose sculptors had carved the Venus of Milo, to remain healthy on the point. The truth is people who worship health cannot remain healthy on the point. When Man goes straight he goes crooked. When he follows

> his nose he manages somehow to put his nose out of joint, or even to cut off his nose to spite his face; and that in accordance with something much deeper in human nature than nature-worshippers could ever understand. It was the discovery of that deeper thing, humanly speaking, that constituted the conversion to Christianity. There is a bias in a man like the bias on a bowl; and Christianity was the discovery of how to correct the bias and therefore hit the mark. There are many who will smile at the saying; but it is profoundly true to say that the glad good news brought by the Gospel was the news of original sin.[31]

Chesterton is making a case for ethical consideration without which "perversion spreads like pestilence." Reason by itself is not enough however high it might have flown. And, contrary to Kantian beliefs, rational thought cannot be the source of ethics, for thinking by nature is fragmentary and one-track, requiring a limiting principle that will correct its "bias." The true source of ethics and morality is therefore revelation or direct perception, and it's only the understanding born of revelation that can act as a check on thinking. Although creatively of the highest quality, Greek thought's error lay in the implicit belief in its own powers. It therefore had to pay the price of hubris. The strange thing about the empirical world is that even the highest capacity of thought in the end is unable to reach fulfillment, and begins to degenerate at some point.

But there is something equally important that is missed by Chesterton. While it is true that the "news of original sin" provided the necessary correction to runaway thought, it is equally true that historically thought seized upon that "news" to spin out of it a complex new web complete with an innovative theology, and eventually an exclusive religion with unprecedented liturgical apparatus. In other words, the old error was repeated in a new way. It appears that thought cannot leave truth (insight) alone; before long it must seize, organize, amplify, secure, and exploit it. For this, the unsettled insecurity at the core of thinking is to be held responsible. For as we have seen earlier, thought represents only one side of things. It requires the other side to bring it to proper dis-*closure*. In other words, thought must turn to essence in order to complete its purpose. But turning to essence does not mean organizing essence. Philosophical praxis of the kind proposed here consists precisely in grasping the ontological limits of thought and holding it to that limit.

[31] G.K. Chesterton, *St. Francis of Assissi* (London: Hodder and Stoughton, 1983), p. 4. The entire contents of this book are in the public domain.

Summary

There is an irreducible distance between *pleroma* and *chronos*. Essence will not reveal itself in time. So what is to be done? There is a suggestion that only a God (revelation or insight) can save us, or help us get out of this tension. The chapter suggests a philosophical labor or praxis that bids thinking to voluntarily accept limits on its activity, recognizing and acknowledging its ontological structure. The hypostasis of thought has sunk the entire being figuratively into a 'hole' from which being is now to be retrieved not as ontological category but as a facing-toward-origin. A systematic regression to pre-conceptual or meditative thinking becomes necessary in which thinking acquires the necessary immanent limits. It must sort through the vast archeological data to pick out the moments of insight refraining from the desire to organize. It must learn to *wait*, without being seduced by the incessant movement that is nature. The waiting is not a passive idling. It is an active waiting that requires thinking to remain ever watchful against crossing its limits. Through this active waiting, *chronos* slows down and time as thought annuls itself, making room for the new. Thought as time opens out to an indeterminateness that is the beginning of intuition. There is a stirring that is not of the usual binary energy of thought. The composite which had aligned itself exclusively behind thought as its guiding light, realigns itself on a balance between insight and representation. This new composite strains forward toward a preparation without engaging in the usual activities of thought which is measuring and calculating, recalling and projecting. Instead there is a watching over the sea of thought, its arising and subsidence, bringing the composite closer and closer to the point of origin that lies at the center of activity. The watchful waiting is not expectation of the usual kind, but toward expecting the unexpected. This is one part of philosophical praxis.

References

Agamben, Giorgio. *The Time That Remains: A Commentary on the Letter to the Romans*. Stanford: Stanford University Press, 2005.

Benjamin, Walter. "Thesis on the Philosophy of History." In *Illuminations*, edited by Hannah Arendt and translated by H. Zorn. London: Pimlico, 1940/1999.

Biblehub, *Commentary*. http//:www.biblehub.com.

Chesterton, G.K. *St. Francis of Assisi*. London: Hodder and Stoughton, 1983.
Heidegger, Martin. "Nur noch ein Gott kann uns retten." *Der Spiegel* 30 (May, 1976): 193–219. Translated by W. Richardson as "Only a God Can Save Us." In *Heidegger: The Man and the Thinker*, edited by Thomas Sheehan. New Brunswick: Transaction Publishers, 2010.
The Bible, Standard English Version.
Thomson, Iain. *Heidegger on Ontotheology: Technology and the Politics of Education*. Cambridge, UK: Cambridge University Press, 2005.
Weber, Max. *The Essential Weber: A Reader*, edited by Sam Whimster. New York: Routledge, 2003.

CHAPTER 7

Beyond the Inner Daguerreotype

One last discussion remains in this attempt to find entry points in a philosophical praxis that makes thought unsentimental toward itself, questionable to itself. This relates to the manner in which thinking attaches itself to the subtle and gross reward system in its vicinity and empirically creates an outline of an inner image that gradually takes charge of thinking. Once solidified, this inner daguerreotype or the image of thought is not easy to dislodge, for social proceedings as well as the inner directions of pleasure and pain occur with reference to this image. Nevertheless, this nucleus of introjections needs to be reabsorbed in thought so that thinking can get a new direction. Some propositions that follow help us denaturalize this peculiar phenomenon which, although obvious, is not easily graspable.

The foregoing chapters have aimed at creating a minimum critical environment toward the development of transformative praxis wherein thinking can turn to face itself—something it is not used to doing or has been unwilling to do—dropping all images and defensiveness, going beyond cultural programming and socialization, pondering an organic negation by which it might return hermeneutically to its origin after each departure. The ontological basis of its own movement remains obscure to thought, a condition that needs to be remedied in any serious attempt to think. From multiple angles we have looked at the preoccupations of thought as it refuses to think, that is, refuses to think what most needs to be thought about, which is its own condition of possibility. Given this backdrop, next we obtain some deductions in the form of a propositional

K. Roy, *The Power of Philosophy*,
https://doi.org/10.1007/978-3-319-96911-4_7

arrangement, a deliberately chosen format, that allows us to survey what thinking can disclose to itself about itself. The contents take this form in order to take forward the leads developed in earlier chapters in a pointed and succinct fashion. The propositional form helps gather the various strands into singular tresses. The "explanation" that follows each proposition offers associated matter developed elsewhere in the book. The inner daguerreotype is suggestive of the pre-critical self-image of thought that is built up through memory. So long as thought remains invested in the daguerreotype, it remains divided against itself incapable of truly thinking—the self-image is a schism in thought maintained through and by division, as we have seen earlier. By means of these propositions the attempt is to deconstruct and go beyond the daguerreotype so that new light is thrown on the operation of thought. We begin with simple observations drawing our means from the four main thinkers discussed in the foregoing sections.

Proposition I There is poverty of thought.
Commentary: How can we say that we are poor in thinking? Is this not an age wherein thought has triumphed in every direction? Has it not sent humans into space and cracked open the "atom"? But let us imagine a balloon that is expanding indefinitely. The expansionism of thought has no other reference point than thought itself. There is no way of knowing that the extravaganza of thought is on the whole beneficial in the sense of being in tune with its own true interest. Kant's critique of judgement is inconclusive in this regard since it fails to explain the anomaly of the thinker. The expansionism is thus "poor" because it is simply the result of rarefication of the existent line. It expands what is already given; it does not touch the real quality of anything inside the balloon, other than accelerate the effects of expansion itself. From this crudest of analogies we might understand why the expansion in thought projects do not lead to any qualitative change in conditions or in the direction of thinking. In fact, the expansion results merely in growing thoughtlessness since thought permits itself no time to gather itself.

> The flight-from-thought is the ground of thoughtlessness. But part of this flight is that man will neither see nor admit it. Man today will even flatly deny this flight from thinking. He will assert the opposite. He will say—and quite rightly—that there were at no time such far-reaching plans, so many inquiries in so many areas, research carried on as passionately as

today. Of course. And this display of ingenuity and deliberation has its own great usefulness. Such thought remains indispensable. But—it also remains true that it is thinking of a special kind.[1]

Expansionist thinking is calculative or instrumental thinking that moves from plan to implementation to evaluation without pausing to consider the meaning of all this activity, and whether it truly helps to enhance the ecological and aesthetic form of existence. It does not see fit to ponder the question whether this is the true purpose of thinking. Expansionist thought is thought without con-science or deep reflective capability.[2]

Proposition II There is instrumental thought and reflective or meditative thinking.
Commentary: There are two kinds of thinking. Thought which is *techne* or which reflects the activity of planetary technicity is considered in Proposition I. There is a different kind of thinking that reflects the ingathered-ness of thought. In-gathered thought is thought turned toward its origin or its condition of possibility.

[1]Martin Heidegger, *Discourse on Thinking* (New York: Harper and Row, 1966), pp. 45–46.

[2]Theodor Adorno wrote: "The only philosophy which would still be accountable in the face of despair, would be the attempt to consider all things, as they would be portrayed from the standpoint of redemption. Cognition has no other light than that which shines from redemption out upon the world; all else exhausts itself in post-construction and remains a piece of technics. Perspectives must be produced which set the world beside itself, alienated from itself, revealing its cracks and fissures, as needy and distorted as it will one day lay there in the messianic light. To win such perspectives without caprice or violence, wholly by the feel for objects, this alone is what thinking is all about. It is the simplest of all things, because the condition irrefutably call for such cognitions, indeed because completed negativity, once it comes fully into view, shoots [*zusammenschiesst*] into the mirror-writing of its opposite. But it is also that which is totally impossible, because it presupposes a standpoint at a remove, were it even the tiniest bit, from the bane [*Bannkreis*] of the existent; meanwhile every possible cognition must not only be wrested from that which is, in order to be binding, but for that very reason is stricken with the same distortedness and neediness which it intends to escape. The more passionately thought seals itself off from its conditional being for the sake of what is unconditional, the more unconsciously, and thereby catastrophically, it falls into the world. It must comprehend even its own impossibility for the sake of possibility. In relation to the demand thereby imposed on it, the question concerning the reality or non-reality of redemption is however almost inconsequential." Theodor Adorno, *Mimima Moralia: Notes from the Damaged Life* (London: The New Left Press, 1974), p. 4.

> This meditative thinking is what we have in mind when we say that contemporary man is in flight-from-thinking. Yet you may protest: mere meditative thinking finds itself floating unaware above reality. It loses touch. It is worthless for dealing with current business. It profits nothing in carrying out practical affairs....Yet anyone can follow the path of meditative thinking in his own manner and within his own limits. Why? Because man is a thinking, that is, a meditating being. Thus meditative thinking need by no means be "high-flown." It is enough if we dwell on what lies close and meditate on what is closest upon that which concerns us, each one of us, here and now; here, on this patch of home ground now, in the present hour of history.[3]

Calculative thinking is important in its own way for practical affairs. But it is one-sided; it gets carried away in the drift of causal relations that come within its ambit to which it attaches itself claiming knowledge. The only reason we even begin to suspect and feel that this kind of thinking is inadequate is because to begin with we are primarily a thinking-reflecting being. Hence we must not think that meditative thinking is an exclusive affair that is restricted to some particular kind of disposition. No high ideas or ideals are necessary for the latter kind of thinking. It is enough if we train ourselves to be reflective of what lies closest to us. Each thing turns us back on ourselves when meditated upon, melting the hardness of isolation, helping us to be underway. Meditative thought does not deny or negate the need for the other kind of thinking, but itself moves from singularity to singularity without any expansion. It does not manufacture concepts or cling "one-sidedly to any single idea," but remains ceaselessly bound to its own process inwardly.

Proposition III Thought does not understand the significance of the increasing dominance of technology and hence its own attitude. It is simply caught in it.
Commentary: We cannot avoid the involvement with technology nor escape the use of technical devices. But we must learn to use them with a wary watchfulness carefully avoiding fixation. In other words, we must not allow technology to dominate us and corrupt our inmost nature. To put it differently, we must retain an ambivalence with regard to this phenomenon. There must be a demeanor toward technology that is one of

[3]Heidegger, *Discourse on Thinking*, pp. 46–47.

simultaneous affirmation and negation. Having this dual vision we no longer view all of existence in a technical mode.

> We let technical devices enter our daily life, and at the same time leave them outside, that is, let them alone, as things which are nothing absolute but remain dependent upon something higher. I would call this comportment toward technology which expresses "yes" and at the same time "no," by an old word, releasement toward things. There is then in all technical processes a meaning, not invented or made by us, which lays claim to what man does and leaves undone. We do not know the significance of the uncanny increasing dominance of [ ] technology. The meaning pervading technology hides itself....But if we explicitly and continuously heed the fact that such hidden meaning touches us everywhere in the world of technology, we stand at once within the realm of that which hides itself from us, and hides itself just in approaching us. Releasement toward things and openness to the mystery belong together. They grant us the possibility of dwelling in the world in a totally different way. They promise us a new ground and foundation upon which we can stand and endure in the world of technology without being imperiled by it.[4]

The meaning of technology does not lie within technology. This is the most important philosophical realization here. This means that the use of technology or technical devices is not to be regarded as innocent and consequence-free, without significance at an altogether different level. It means that each time we use technology or calculative thought something is enjoined upon us over which we have no control, and of which we have no understanding. Nevertheless the concealed effect is there. The hidden meaning of technology is not available to us but it touches us everywhere. Although we do not know its meaning or significance we must continually heed the fact that such hidden meaning is there and affects all we do and fail to do. Hence we must become ambivalent, an attitude Heidegger calls *Releasement toward things*. This attitude also opens us to the mystery of things. This alone can protect us from being overwhelmed and overcome by technicity that makes us forget that there are other ways of thinking and being that are closer to the essential nature of the human.

[4] Ibid., pp. 54–55.

Proposition IV Thinking also presents the problem of the thinker. But the absolute present contains no thinker for it has no cognitive content. Commentary: The present is indivisible; it is not a succession of moments. Therefore the present always remains unlived, forever out of reach of thought. The thinking self wants to *become contemporary*, or to enter the present, without success. It fails because it belongs to the past, to time as succession. The past can never be the present, which always slips out of grasp. The present is always *Kairos*, or the time of the now. The present is chronologically indeterminate, outside history or eschatology. Precisely because of this we cannot think our way into the present. The Present lives through us, and outlives us, as the Unlived. What then is the relation of thought to the present? We live without Presence, facing forever a future. Speaking of the difference between chronological time and *Kairos*, Giorgio Agamben writes:

> In every representation we make of time and in every discourse by means of which we define and represent time, another time is implied that is not entirely consumed by representation. It is as though man, insofar as he is a thinking and speaking being, produced an additional time with regard to chronological time, a time that prevented him from perfectly coinciding with the time out of which he could make images and representations. This ulterior time, nevertheless, is not another time, it is not a supplementary time added on from outside to chronological time. Rather, it is something like a time within time—not ulterior but interior—which only measures my disconnection with regard to it, my being out of synch and in noncoincidence with regard to my representation of time.[5]

Thought is *chronos*, or time. But *Kairos* or the time within time is not produced by thinking; it is the connection to the *sub specie aeternitatis*. The turning away from chronological time is the first step toward redemptive thinking. This timeless time has no representation within the *saeculum* or secular time, hence the reference to a messianic time that brings time to an end. When a sequence of thought breaks down or dissipates, there arises the possibility of an intuition toward *Kairos*. An intuitive awareness within thinking of *Kairos* is essential in order to turn toward what needs to be thought.

[5] Giorgio Agamben, *The Time That Remains: A Commentary on Paul's Letter to the Romans* (Stanford: Stanford University Press, 2005), p. 68.

Proposition V Thought becomes isolated when it is without the activity of the senses.

Commentary: The isolate that is instrumental thought has clearly learnt to dominate and even colonize the senses. Whereas the awakened senses in their interconnected movement become alive to a universal rhythm, isolationist thought uses senses for material extraction or for territorial advantage. In the *Nicomachean Ethics*, Aristotle is seen as saying:

> He who sees senses [*aisthanetai*] that he is seeing, he who hears senses that he is hearing, he who walks senses that he is walking, and thus for all the other activities there is something that senses that we are exerting them [*hoti energoumen*] in such a way that if we sense, we sense that we are sensing, and if we think, we sense that we are thinking. This is the same thing as sensing existence: existing [*to einai*] means in fact sensing and thinking. Sensing that we are alive is in and of itself sweet, for life is by nature good, and it is sweet to sense that such a good belongs to us. Living is desirable, above all for those who are good, since for them existing is a good and sweet thing. For good men, "con-senting" [*synaisthanomenoi*, sensing together] feels sweet because they recognize the good itself, and what a good man feels with respect to himself, he also feels with respect to his friend: the friend is, in fact, an other self [*heteros autos*]. And as all people find the fact of their own existence [*to auton einai*] desirable, the existence of their friends is equally—or almost equally—desirable. Existence is desirable because one senses that it is a good thing, and this sensation [*aisthesis*] is in itself sweet. One must therefore also "con-sent" that his friend exists, and this happens by living together and by sharing acts and thoughts in common [*koinonein*]. In this sense, we say that humans live together [*syzen*], unlike cattle that share the pasture together...[6]

The importance given to the senses relative to thought is striking. Instead of considering thought as principal, throughout this important passage, Aristotle finds the senses as the intuition of the good. The true acknowledgment of the other (*heteros autos*) lies in "con-sent" or in sensing together, not merely in thinking together. One can live fully only by, at the same time, appreciating the life of another. Existence becomes beautiful and sweet through sharing. Thus we produce a life together in con-sentience.

[6]Aristotle, cited in Giorgio Agamben, *What Is an Apparatus and Other Essays*, trans. David Kishik (Stanford: Stanford University Press), pp. 32–33.

Further, in this connection, the noted thinker Ivan Illich observes something relevant and interesting with respect to Christian liturgy:

> The Eucharistic gathering in the very first Christian centuries explicitly claimed to establish a new "we," a new plural of the "I." This "we" was not of this world. It didn't belong to the world of politics in the Greek sense, or of citizenship in the *urbs*, in the Roman sense. These guys got together for a celebration which had two high points, one of them called *conspiratio*, and the other one *comestio*. *Conspiratio* mustn't be translated into English as conspiracy because *spiritus*, spirit, ghost, the supreme form of inwardness, Holy Spirit, was the meaning which informed the word *conspiratio* and not the sense we give it today of a bunch of rebels trying to subvert the political community. What is established in the *conspiratio* is, in the strictest sense, non-worldly, in spite of its somatic, its bodily depth. It is a celebration of the statement, 'You are in this world but not of this world.'[7]

This is remarkable, and a vital clue as to the place of thought. *Conspiratio* literally means to breathe together. Redemption has to overcome the fragmentation in thought, and hence the phenomenological practice of breathing together in order to discover and overturn the process of division. Learning to think must recalibrate thought's relation to the senses and to the sensorium in general in order that they might work together toward redemptive thinking. The sensation of the goodness of life is the primary object that is often impeded by "senseless" thought. Philosophical bilingualism requires con-sensuality that proceeds alongside thought.

Proposition VI Thinking must learn to loosen the (imagined) nucleus of permanence.
Commentary: Thinking tends to obscure the point that it is thought and no other than thought of which issues forth the "I" or "We." In other words, the formulation of the "we" is in the language of thought whose foundation is obscure or unknown. The objectification of thought in a pronoun leads to its peculiar exaltation ignoring the fact that its basis is not sovereign but contingent. The greatest scandal of thought is this forgetfulness through which it manufactures magnificent consciences

[7] Ivan Illich, *The Rivers North of the Future* (Toronto: House of Anansi Press, 2005), p. 161.

and grandiloquent images. It also crucifies. Albert Camus once wrote: "Through a curious transposition peculiar to our times, it is innocence that is called upon to justify itself."[8] Innocence is precisely that which is untouched by thought. Having exchanged ethics for rationality and trumped all other modes of perceiving, thought now sits on judgement about that which is beyond its purview. In being underway, thinking must be made to renounce its dubious knack for what Marx had called the confounding of the opposites (what is truly useful is made to appear useless, and the useless is granted value). It must also sacrifice the tendency toward encroachment. Whenever thought is found to indulge in paeans, immediate suspicion is warranted. The cunning of thought creates "benignity" which it then draws upon for the maintenance of various truth games. Thinking dresses itself up in various images of the benign or respectable soul that, in fact, has mastered many duplicities. Thought gives kudos to itself—in a congratulatory mood it confers upon itself various blessings that are nothing but cover-ups for lives lived without a deeper ethic of life. The time is upon us now to unmask our thinking, which is nothing but ourselves. For example, "we the people" is no less a theatrical portraiture of the dense calculations of thought than "we the rulers," two sides of the division of thought. Those with intuition about the nature of thinking do not live benignly but with a hardened self-consciousness, watchful, intolerant of deception. They are not swayed by the pious projections of thought.

Proposition VII Thinking colonizes the corpus sensorium.
Commentary: What characterizes a human being is the possibility innate in her/his constitution of *auto-poieisis* or self-production. But this production is not only in thought but lies in sensuous activity that might include thought as one element. Thinking must acknowledge the conjoint production of sensation, intuition, and corporeal action, otherwise there is takeover instead of *poieisis*. One-dimensional thought prevents the flowering of the other dimensions of the composite called human.

> Marx thinks of man's being as production. Production means praxis, 'sensuous human activity.' What is the character of this activity? While the animal, writes Marx, is immediately at one with its vital activity, *is* its vital activity, man does not confuse himself with it; he turns his vital activity

[8] Albert Camus, *The Rebel*, trans. Anthony Bower (New York: Knopf, 1956).

> into a means for his existence. He produces not unilaterally but universally. 'It is for this very and only reason that he is a being belonging to a genus [*Gattungswesen*].' Praxis constitutes man in his proper being: it makes a *Gattungswesen* of him. The character of production, then, is to constitute man as a being capable of a genus; it is to give him the gift of a genus (*Gattung*). Yet Marx adds immediately afterward: 'Rather, [man] is a conscious being, that is, his life is an object for him, precisely because he is a *Gattungswesen*, a being belonging to a genus.' Man, then, is not a *Gattungswesen* to the extent that he is a producer; on the contrary, it is his quality as a generic being that makes a producer of him. Marx reasserts this essential ambiguity when he writes that, on the one hand, 'the practical creation *of an objective world*, the *transformation* of inorganic nature, is proof that man is a *Gattungswesen*' but that, on the other hand, 'precisely in the transformation of the objective world man proves himself for the first time a *Gattungswesen*.' We face here a real hermeneutic circle: on the one hand, production, man's conscious vital activity, constitutes him into a being capable of a genus, but on the other hand it is his capacity to have a genus that makes a producer of him.[9]

The circularity is easily understood when we understand that *Gattungswesen*, or arising into genus-essence, is not something individual; rather we are inserted into an ongoing universal process. It is the unconscious participation in a process that endlessly circles onto itself in an *eternal return*, each instant, while keeping open the possibilities given unto the composite. It is a process that is anterior to and independent of the thinking or doing of any thinker or doer. But the conscious participation of thought in *Gattungswesen*, or in bringing forth the genus-essence, or receiving the gift of genus, depends on the humility of thought. One does not achieve genus; *one frees it* by the right kind of struggle and attitude. Freeing the gift of genus or *Gattung* is the main task before the human, and for that there must be decolonization at all levels. As we have seen in Heraclitus, this freedom is brought about by "driving everything through everything." In other words, this is not some one-sided mental-intellectual-institutional achievement. The oscillations that have settled into the corpus sensorium, including the matrix of thought as different spatial congealments, must again be disturbed and loosened, thus driving the erotic energies surging against

[9] Giorgio Agamben, *The Man Without Content*, trans. Georgia Albert (Stanford: Stanford University Press), p. 23.

one another, achieving a new plasticity as well as porosity. Only then the composite called human can retrieve the possibility of coming-into-being. This is the true sensuous activity, the productive curriculum of the human. A clearer representation or composite picture of what this phenomenological or corporeal praxis means is not easy to give but the different facets of it have been under continuous discussion throughout the present text. A progressive intuition attends upon us once one is underway that cannot be foreseen or mapped ahead of time.

Proposition VIII Thinking unaware of the condition of its possibility turns pathological.
Commentary: Compulsive and mechanical thinking is always getting away from itself, filling the empty horizon of time with various clutter including events and their apparent causal chains. Thus legitimated by its own mechanism thinking proceeds additively believing this additive process as positive evolution. But real thinking involves bringing this entire process to a momentary seizure so that a philosophical shock can result. Marx had observed: "The reform of consciousness consists entirely in making the world aware of its own consciousness, in arousing it from its dream of itself, in explaining its own actions to it."[10] Rewriting it in terms of thought, redemption in thinking would consist in making thought aware of the net of its self-produced cognitive latticework that results in a peculiar sensibility. The false autonomy granted to this latticework needs to be acknowledged in terms of a delusion that is closely tied to historicism or the temporal progression of events as offering meaningful significance. What historicism forgets to examine is the action of thought in the extraction of significance. Thought can neither grasp the totality of the present state of things nor predict where things are going, as Karl Popper had pointed out in *The Poverty of Historicism*. And yet social thought draws its legitimacy precisely from these two defunct assumptions. Instead, thinking must learn to accommodate within itself a counter-movement of self-abnegation coming out of the realization that thought cannot be reasonable as long as it is part of a world that is unreasonable, as the Frankfurt School theorists had long noted.

[10] Karl Marx, *Early Writings*, trans. Rodney Livingstone (New York: Penguin Books, 1992).

> Historicism justifiably culminates in universal history. Nowhere does the materialist writing of history distance itself from it more clearly than in terms of method. The former has no theoretical armature. Its method is additive: it offers a mass of facts, in order to fill up a homogenous and empty time. The materialist writing of history for its part is based on a constructive principle. Thinking involves not only the movement of thoughts but also their zero-hour [Stillstellung]. Where thinking suddenly halts in a constellation overflowing with tensions, there it yields a shock to the same, through which it crystallizes as a monad. The historical materialist approaches a historical object solely and alone where he encounters it as a monad. In this structure he cognizes the sign of a messianic zero-hour [Stillstellung] of events, or put differently, a revolutionary chance in the struggle for the suppressed past. He perceives it, in order to explode a specific epoch out of the homogenous course of history; thus exploding a specific life out of the epoch, or a specific work out of the life-work. The net gain of this procedure consists of this: that the life-work is preserved and sublated in the work, the epoch in the life-work, and the entire course of history in the epoch. The nourishing fruit of what is historically conceptualized has time as its core, its precious but flavorless seed.[11]

The additive history of liberal historicism is useless from a liberationist perspective. Strings of events, howsoever truthfully recounted, organized, or periodized, do not bring about the leap necessary for emancipation from history itself. Normal history has time as its lubricant; it is precious but useless from the point view of redemption. A different viewing of history involves not the procession of facts, but looking for the "zero hour" of thought, where thinking grinds to a halt confounded by contrary pulls out of which it sees no way out. Into this zero hour is born a messianic moment that promises a new direction in thought. From this messianic zero hour alone thinking can begin anew with a break from the past. This is true revolution in thought. It is not another revolution that is the product of thought, but is a revolution within thinking itself, within the manner in which thinking has conducted itself so far. Thought, exploded out of content-based thinking, for an unconditional moment floats as free energy toward redemption, toward essence.

[11] Ibid., p. 258.

Proposition IX The propensity of thinking toward the abstract and the virtual, and the retreat from the sensual-phenomenological, is a primary source of its contradictions.

Commentary: Pure abstraction is pure sign without the limitation of a referent. Thought bids for the pure sign in a bid for absolute power. Cut loose from the obligation and the necessity of thinking about its source or essence, thinking moves from abstraction to abstraction inventing newer and newer spaces from which to recuperate value. This is the inexorable movement toward the virtual. The discarnation of thinking or its divorce from anything sensual is the imagined deliverance freed from *ensarcosis.* But in most traditions the essence has reappeared to man in the carnal form or as *in-carnate*. Ivan Illich explains why it is important to let the gaze rest on the material figure and not optically retreat from contact with the embodied:

> [W]hat impresses me so much is the speed with which, during the second part of my life of seventy years, virtual spaces, images and other objects presented in virtual spaces, have spread. There are quite a few serious thinkers now who claim that, among the most profound changes of the last twenty-five years is the ubiquity of virtual spaces from which we are asked to derive our knowledge. Perhaps it's now becoming clearer why I spoke at such length about icons. The icon was conceived as a threshold to a super-reality into which only faith could lead. The virtual space asks you to look into a nowhere in which nobody could live. The icon, I would argue, cultivates my ability to see the misery of a slum, or to be present on a bus, or during a walk through the streets of New York. It allows me to shed, through my gaze, some light from the beyond on those whom I touch. Experiences in the virtual realm, on the other hand, lead me to see what is virtual and disembodied about others. They become clothes hangers so to speak for the abstract "programming" which I bring to my encounter with them. Antique optics is concerned with preparing a virtuous way of seeing and making you aware of the pitfalls into which your visual ray can fall. I think that a contemporary optics ought to do the same — to make me aware of what happens when I establish the habit of consorting with the seductive nonentities that are constantly being conjured up all around me and of how this preponderance of the virtual affects my everyday intercourse with others. And this is especially critical because many of the younger people with whom I have had to do during the last seven or eight years really believe that they have a binocular camcorder in their skulls, and

> can only conceive the training of the gaze in terms of technical improvements in their rate of digital digestion.[12]

The digitalization of consciousness is one of the profound characteristics of late modernity that cuts off thought even more effectively from its source. The retreat from the actuality of the objects of the senses, that is, from tactility, is simultaneously an abandonment of the wholeness of being. Thinking isolated from the limits and contingencies of the flesh attempts to create a pure virtual world where it can perpetuate itself undisturbed by the sensuous-nature. The eschatological limits built into the possibilities of thought are transcended by erecting "seductive non-entities" that can be made to do in virtual spaces what the embodied cannot. The apparent limitlessness of cyberspace and its promised fantasy-utopia is a projection of thought, a turning inside out of thought that exteriorizes its inner emptiness projecting it as a novel space of discovery and action. But the imaginary bubble-space thus created is in reality a self-imposed quarantine and internment from which the only release is realization and recoil. Learning to think might propose deliberate activities at the phenomenological level, such as walking through the streets while being observant of the inner and the outer, or engaging in ordinary things seriously such as turning the soil for growing a patch of something, and so on. The re-contact is of critical consequence that challenges and helps slow down the rate of digital digestion. The withdrawal from everyday intercourse with others by resorting to the virtual and its repercussions must be understood in all its dimensions so that the great danger of virtuality is disclosed at the phenomenological level.

Proposition X Thought remains in denial of death.
Commentary: Calculative thought faces the future privately as a never-ending series of moments "borrowing" from the apparent inexhaustibility of collective or public time. It sees death distantly and not as something intimate and immediate. It approaches the finality of death practically as a problem to be overcome. Thus a great part of the effort of thought turns to prolongation and perpetuation.

[12] Ivan Illich, *Rivers North of the Future: The Testament of Ivan Illich* (Toronto: The House of Anansi Press, 2005), p. 93.

> I found out that at around the same time that German philologists began to claim that education meant "to lead out into freedom," the Hippocratic Oath was being redefined. Traditionally it had been understood to say that I, as a medical man, will have nothing to do with death, implying, I will neither procure it nor fight against it. Now it became, I will do everything I can to prolong the patient's life. I became aware that throughout history in all cultures there had been people, from witches to masseurs to acupuncturists, who had tried to relieve pain, to make discomfort bearable, and to help and encourage people to face reality; but never had anyone spoken of *killing* pain until the middle of the nineteenth century, when, as I learned from an historical dictionary of Americanisms, various concoctions began to be sold in the United States under the name of painkillers. That's the first reference to the idea that you can kill pain without killing a person. And the term has stuck, although you still can't use it in any other language. At the same time, people began to have diseases, rather than to be sick. After I wrote *Medical Nemesis* I thought I would find help in understanding how this ghastly world could come about in which most people are convinced that they should do everything possible to prolong their own lives, and those of their relatives, and consequently need Ronald Dworkin's "Philosopher's Brief" and the Supreme Court of the United States to decide if they may be administered death as they are administered life.[13]

That the great machinery of thought should be turned toward extension of life of individuals is no surprise, when one grasps the truth that the limits within which thinking had been placed, were undone by thought itself. The expansionism and self-aggrandizement naturally saw death as an affront that had to be dealt with. The perceived organic substratum of thought, the body, now needed official attention, and various laws began to be enacted that began to re-organize life as a medical problem. Frequent pronouncements in the media proclaim how someone or other is "battling" some terminal disease or other that receives a round of social applause. Heart and liver are routinely "harvested" and sent over long distances to "save" lives. Great advancements are claimed by thought in "conquering" some disease or other. Thought has devised official guidelines for everything. But thought never confronts the question whether these so-called advancements and attempts toward deferment of death have brought about a qualitatively better life in general or a more healthy society. Instead, the general fear of ending has been

[13] Illich, op. cit., p. 96.

successfully tapped toward legitimizing the official administration of living and dying. This over-administered society is something that Max Weber had called the "iron cage" and had wondered about the kind of human that would ultimately live in it. The question therefore arises: Has thinking then merely proliferated as proliferation, its sole justification being the value attached to the acceleration of its own proliferation?

The propositions show the way to a kind of negation within thinking that removes the illusory personal element from the condition of thought and brings it out into the open as a common process. The pulse of thought that attaches itself to specific bodies and speaks through the individuated daguerreotype is, for the first time, observed correctly. This correct observation is praxis. Action that proceeds from accurate and unsentimental observation is without contradiction. And life without contradiction is the ultimate task of philosophy.

References

Adorno, Theodor. *Mimima Moralia: Notes from the Damaged Life*. London: The New Left Press, 1974.

Agamben, Giorgio. *The Man Without Content*. Translated by Georgia Albert. Stanford: Stanford University Press, 1999.

Agamben, Giorgio. *The Time That Remains: A Commentary on Paul's Letter to the Romans*. Stanford: Stanford University Press, 2005.

Agamben, Giorgio. *What Is an Apparatus and Other Essays*. Translated by David Kishik. Stanford: Stanford University Press, 2009.

Benjamin, Walter. *Illuminations*. Translated by Harry Zohn, New York: Schocken Books, 1969.

Camus, Albert. *The Rebel*. Translated by Anthony Bower. New York: Knopf, 1956.

Fisher, Ernst. *The Necessity of Art: A Marxist Approach*. Translated by Anna Bostock. Harmondsworth, UK: Penguin Books, 1963.

Heller-Roazen, Daniel. "Editor's Introduction." In *Potentialities: Collected Essays in Philosophy*, edited by Giorgio Agamben. Stanford: Stanford University Press, 2009.

Illich, Ivan. *The Rivers North of the Future: The Testament of Ivan Illich*. Toronto: House of Anansi Press, 2005.

Marx, Karl. *Early Writings*. Translated by Rodney Livingstone. New York: Penguin Books, 1992.

CHAPTER 8

Epilogue

Philosophical bilingualism faces toward knowledge and away from it simultaneously, affirming and negating at the same time, generating a space of "enigmatic solitude" that accompanies thought everywhere. The self-knowledge of thought is primordial; its reference point is not history, and thus marks out a time within time. The notions presented here must by no means be regarded as a general denunciation of thought; that is not its spirit or intention. Rather it is an attempt to nudge thinking toward its true potential, to a redemptive fullness not available in logistical or calculative thinking. When that which is essentially a (morphological) passage mistakenly attempts to build the permanent, whether civilizationally or individually, we have a problem. There is deception, chaos, and ultimate downfall, the result of misalignment with *what is*. The principal effort of thinking is not to be directed at endless calculation, whether with respect to self or with respect to society. The principle of subject-object reciprocity makes nonsense of the permanent—it returns things to their original state ontologically, randomizes, to begin again. The philosophical task of thinking instead is to meditate on the conditions of its possibility and therefrom to ask the question whether there is a necessity from which thought itself springs. There is no ready or easy answer to that question. It depends on the extent to which thought is willing to set aside its habits and modes of operation. It depends on this sacrifice. And it depends on the hermeneutic-phenomenological work that we are willing to do.

Thought cannot think its way to freedom. No system may overcome itself by itself. It may only *prepare for a readiness*, that is, 'stretch toward'

K. Roy, *The Power of Philosophy*,
https://doi.org/10.1007/978-3-319-96911-4_8

(*epekteinomenos*) something that might be called redemption. The foregoing pages have attempted a phenomenological hermeneutics that spirally tightens the noose around thinking till it is left with no escape route but to face itself. Thinking must learn to confront itself in all its nakedness shorn of the camouflage, trappings, and pious pretensions—the various guises under which it pretends to be something other than what it is, and someplace other than where it is. It is the infinite capacity of thought to invent and reinvent itself in events, personalities, processes, calamities, and glorifications that are, in actuality, its own projections, introjections, phantasies, and denials that populate the world with what appear to be independent things, dialectical developments, and autonomous capacities. But the critical deactivation (*katargesis*) of thought cannot be a whimsical affair. It has to be assiduous and unremitting. Besides, all the plumage must be shed voluntarily through intellectual insight.

When thought loses its plumage through the exposure of artifice, its immediate response is to grow new ones; new oppositions and truth games emerge to cover up the breach. Preparation for a readiness, on the other hand, is to maintain the breach, holding the defensive reaction in abeyance for insight to be able to occur. Insight alone can result in the reform of thinking taking it past the piety of thought. Who or what has insight? Obviously no one. Insight is complete unto itself, non-dual, free of agentic superstition. Insight is whole, without the subject/object division that is the usual substance of thought. When two thoughts are punctuated by insight, there is an injection of the unknown between two knowns. A minor death occurs; thought is disoriented, an ontological uncertainty enters the conventional certainties of thought. The consequence is a slowing down. Thought's hitherto unproblematic circulation now includes a certain hesitation.

A new atmosphere emerges: linear sequential crowding gives way to pauses and small silences. Continuities are disturbed. A question mark appears over thinking itself that, until this hour, covered the entire surface of consciousness. There manifests in thinking, a nascent realization of itself as phenomena, and not as the special consciousness of defined individuality coinciding with a particular organismic contour. The self-image of thought consisting of its habitual association with a specific body is displaced by a new kind of openness that is progressively free of sentimental clutter. Heraclitus thought of it as drying of the soul, that is, getting rid of dampness that obstructs the inner fire. The transcendent categories have been displaced by an immanence that is the preparation for a readiness. But readiness for what? For a leap into the beyond, or beneath, of assumed categories and false temporal continuities. This leap is by no means the abandonment of reason understood as the search for a life beyond contradiction. Instead, the fatal confusion of reason with the piety of thought is reversed.

The conditions for such a possibility are neither impossible nor easy to meet. Nor can it be the result of any sequential activity of thought as time. The road to redemption necessarily involves a new perception of and relationship with time in the absence of which thought measures the future with the same yardstick with the help of which it had spun existing relations of the present.

> The kingdom of truth will almost certainly never come, and in the final aim set before itself by the republic of scholars will, in all likelihood, never be attained. Nevertheless, the unquenchable interest in truth that burns in the breast of every *thinking man*, will demand, for all eternity, that he should combat error with all his power and spread truth in every direction, i.e., behave exactly *as if* error must some day be completely extirpated and we might *look forward to a time* when truth will reign [with] undisputed sovereignty. This indeed is characteristic of a nature like that of man, designed to be forever approximating to unattainable ideals.[1]

First, who or what is this so-called "thinking man?" It is thought itself in its anthropic guise, is it not? The writer refers to a thinker that aims for truth. Biographical thought in association with archival memory marks itself with a pronoun. This is the game that thought has played for centuries, as it has progressively turned away from its source or essence. The self-same element that blocks the flow of being by its splitting, and the denial of essence, "burns" for truth, apparently. The Cartesian thinker above "combats error" unmindful of the fact that it is itself the very source of error. This tilting at the windmills of the Quixotic form sets up the dramatis personae of the thought factory and perpetuates the Cartesian division between thinker and thought. Next, the looking "forward to a time when truth will reign" is a projection and phantasm of

[1] Hans Vaihinger, *The Philosophy of 'As If': A System of the Theoretical, Practical, and Religious Fictions of Mankind*, trans. C.K. Ogden (London: Routledge & Kegan Paul, 1935), p. 145.

thought uncomfortable with what it has produced as reality. The positing of a future time is an extension of *chronos*, of public time that cannot cross over to *Kairos*. But the reason for this does not lie in idealism or any characteristic nature of "man" as Vaihinger above imagines, but in the distinct ontological characters of the respective temporal realms. Nothing in this world will make *chronos* attain to *kairos*; no carefully laid mental or psychical trap will yield that possibility. Thought as time must withdraw to its initial position and stay there, and let the fact of its being *sub specie aeternitatis* do the rest. All claims on behalf of thought must be relinquished in thinking, for all "truths" of man are but projections from the ontological perspective.

In other words, to be underway, toward the preparation for a readiness, thinking must voluntarily renounce power. A certain kind of deliverance from Power or *Katargethemen* [de-activation], mentioned several times in the letters of Paul, may be thought of as a critical weakening of the force of thought.[2] As long as thought believes in and lives by its own power, it continues to make the same blunders of elaboration and expansion. A de-activation of thinking does not however mean thoughtlessness, but rather, it means the forswearing of the immense projections of thought and its inter-linkages that cover consciousness from end to end. The beatitudes had declared that "the meek shall inherit the earth." The meek does not however mean the docile or the subdued, but those in whom the arrogance of thought had dissipated, and who were thus become open to the new in spirit. And "inherit," incidentally, did not refer to ownership of the land, but complementary trusteeship. But even more, the meek, or those who have seen and abjured, are conveyed to the principle of eternity. In 2 Corinthians we find Paul's testimony: "*And he said to me, My grace is sufficient for you; for my strength is made perfect in weakness.*" Paul goes on to say that "when I am weak, I am strong."[3] This kind of messianic inversion is a classic manner of negation of the force of habit and conventionality of thought. But taken literally, it means that true potentiality is realized when thought dethrones itself as the proper guide of action, that is, in ἀσθενείᾳ or weakness. The word weakness must be understood properly. When Heidegger admits in the interview with *Der Spiegel* that philosophy cannot bring about

[2] Romans 7:5. *The Bible*, New International Version.

[3] 2 Corinthians 12:9–10. *The Bible*, New International Version.

redemption by itself, there is the proper realization of the necessity of weakening in the stance of thought.[4] In making thought inoperative in its usual mode, there is a preparation for a readiness for Grace or redemption.[5] Each instant's relation to eternity or Presence (*Parousia*), and fulfillment (*Pleroma*), cannot be mediated by thought. It also must be delinked from any global process such as the system envisaged in Hegel. This is not the defeat of reason, but the expulsion of the 'as if' from the content of thought.

Further, there is a darker side that we must simultaneously deal with, using Apostolic language as datum. I refer again to the letters of Paul, whose words serve to reveal much about thinking when read ontologically. Paul writes to the Thessalonians:

> He will oppose and will exalt himself over everything that is called God or is worshiped, so that he sets himself up in God's temple, proclaiming himself to be God....For the secret power of lawlessness is already at work; but the one who now holds it back will continue to do so till he is taken out of the way. The coming of the lawless one will be in accordance with how Satan works. He will use all sorts of displays of power through signs and wonders that serve the lie, and all the ways that wickedness deceives those who are perishing. They perish because they refused to love the truth and so be saved.[6]

It is clear that the "He," whatever it might be, cannot but present itself in thought in order to be operative, for "he sets himself up" in the place of the highest faith. Hence it is also not wayward to pitch for a

[4] "If I may answer briefly, and perhaps clumsily, but after long reflection: philosophy will be unable to effect any immediate change in the current state of the world. This is true not only of philosophy but of all purely human reflection and endeavor." Heidegger interview, *Der Spiegel*, op. cit.

[5] We find in John Chrysostom: "This is the meaning of *katergeitai*, and he [Paul] made it clear to us in the words which follow. After you heard him say *katergeitai*, he did not wish you to think of this as complete dissolution but as an increase and advancement to something better. So after he had said *katergeitai*, he went on to add: "Our knowledge is imperfect and our prophesying is imperfect. When the perfect comes, then the imperfect will be rendered inoperative [*katargethesaz*]." So the imperfect no longer exists, but the perfect does ... This is because the rendering inoperative [*katargesis*] is a fulfillment [*plerosis*] and advancement to something better [*pros to meizon epidosis*]." Cited in Agamben, *The Time That Remains*, p. 99.

[6] 2 Thessalonians 2:4, 7, 9 & 10. *The Bible*, New International Version.

correspondence or an equivalence between the "He" and thinking itself: thought is shaped by its "secret power." In other words, the "He" and its operations and seductions become manifest in thinking so that anomie begins to operate. All the "displays of power" and "signs and wonders" are perfect descriptions of the innovations of thinking itself, of the technology of thought, about which we have been warned earlier. Thought replaces essence (God), and "lawlessness" begins from that moment on. The display of power is the central deception that blinds thought to truth and to its own self-nature.

The Day of Judgement is nothing other than the revelation of the true nature of thought to itself. Thought has taken the place of God; has pretensions to infinite capacities. But these capacities merely serve to increase anomie since they ultimately oblige the appetites of power which is the road away from the truth or essence. Power, control, domination of the earth, subjugation of nature, technologization of being, all of these are satanic in the sense of being vanities and vexations that are doomed from the start, being sources of conflict, conflagration, and contradiction. These are contra-being, and must be acknowledged to be so at the deepest phenomenological level toward the preparation for a readiness. Redemptive thinking, as we have seen earlier, thus begins and ends in the renunciation of Power, including that of the inventive power of thought (as noted by Koheleth discussed earlier). The epistemic categories must be thought of as helping us deal with the everydayness and practicality, and no more, given the nature of the world into which we are thrust. It is important therefore not to misunderstand or misplace the epistemic content of thought, and at the same time, always to hold keenly in mind the ontological status of thinking, that is, the inquiry into the process and medium of its arising as well as its subsidence. Thus, philosophical bilingualism must keep its feet in two worlds simultaneously.

Let me turn next to an intellectual for whom I have immense respect, one who was never deceived by thought, and one who had the capacity to bring together intellect and Eros in a manner that could halt the triumphalism of thought like few I know: that thinker is Ivan Illich. Writing about the fifteenth century Florentine monk and reformer Girolamo Savonarola, Illich says:

> Let me tell you about Savonarola's last day. He was condemned as a heretic. No proof of heresy was offered beyond the fact that he would not desist from his claim that he was a prophet who spoke under divine

> inspiration… On the day of his burning, in the morning at Mass, he speaks in a beautiful prayer of how sadness has invaded him, of how his friends and everything he sees depress him. He comments on the Miserere and speaks of the abysm of his misery at having declared the day before under torture that he was not divinely inspired when he preached. I take it back, he says. I lied out of fear of torture, and I want this to be known publicly. Let the abysm of my sinfulness dissolve in the abysm of your mercy.[7]

How shall we interpret this data ontologically? Organized thought (the Church, in this case) identifies an aberration, a threat to itself when experience of Essence or revelation is declared or claimed. The grand delusions, aggrandizements, and apotheosis of thought are challenged and disturbed by one who speaks not the crafty formulations of thought but avows divine inspiration. But there is a deeper melancholy attendant upon the situation in the present case. Before his burning, and under sustained physical torture, Savonarola had recanted. Embodied thought had withdrawn the claim of Presence. This now returns to haunt the situation; but at the same time, it teaches one how to die to thought. While the recanting itself is recanted, reversed, set aside, thinking is rolled back upon itself. Torture is the marking of time on the body. Its principal threat is the positing of a future of pain; the instants grow out of the possibility of suffering. The anticipation or projection of imminent pain is time as fear, or its equivalence. But when the future is refused, *Presence* brings time and thought to an end psychologically. The point of realization is that thought as time is also thought as fear. Redemptive or liberatory thinking consists of the ability to grasp the materiality of fear, not in order to struggle with it or overcome it, but to merge with what is. The self-image is displaced by an immanence, which is to die to conventional thinking toward a readiness.

But there is a different transcendent stance that masquerades as immanence in modernist thinking without examining which the present text is incomplete. It is the cybernetic vision, a contemporary stance of thought—of the input/output view of societal formations and in-formations—that Illich examines so closely.

[7] Ivan Illich, *Rivers North of the Future: The Testament of Ivan Illich* (Toronto: House of Anansi Press, 2005), p. 118.

> There are two entirely different, and, I think, irreconcilable interpretations of our present predicament. In my writings of the 1960s and 1970s, I spoke of the modernization, or professionalization, of the client. I tried to show how the client forms his self-perception by interiorizing, as one so easily says, the school system, for example. You classify yourself, and submit to classification by others, according to the point on the curve at which you dropped out. In the same way you internalize your need for health care by claiming your right to diagnosis, painkilling, preventive care, and medicalized death. Or, by swallowing the car you paralyze your feet and have to jump into the driver's seat to go to a supermarket. But sometime in the 1980s I began to think about these things differently. I realized that people were being absorbed or integrated into systems in a way that went beyond what I had at first thought...What of the person who has himself been swallowed by the world conceived as a system, a world represented or made present to his fantasy in a disconnected but seductive sequence of visiotypes? Fantastic talk about life as a subsystem with the ability to optimize its immediate environment takes on a gruesome meaning when it is used by someone who has been swallowed by the system to express his self-consciousness.[8]

A distinction is being drawn between an earlier stance of thought in which self-perception or reflexivity is brought about through the interiorization of various apparatuses and organizations and a subsequent "systemic" attitude. Different dimensions of the person are drawn from various "needs" and responses to those needs. In this there seems to be a residual distinction between actors and needs that could potentially be the ground for self-criticality. But an important change follows in recent times as observed by Illich. The earlier ground seems to have disappeared, and now the language of systems has swallowed up the person without the true benefit of an immanent perspective. Illich uses the word "visiotypes" to refer to certain signifiers which have been emptied of linguistic content or meaning, and now operate on the social plane as "self-evident" visual markers. Signifiers such as "cyberspace" or "virtual reality," etc. have attained a peculiar solidity that apparently require no reflection. They point away from themselves to self-justified pathways for negotiating reality as well as adjusting to it.

All thought is contortion on an unknown matrix. This central realization requires a point of view that is immanent, that is, a practice of seeing things as they would appear when looked at from within thinking itself,

[8]Ibid., p. 12.

as it were. This means, obviously, loss of the transcendental viewpoint of the subject. Now the greatest danger of the loose "systems" talk outlined above is that there is no immanent perspective; instead, the transcendental subject uses this uncritical systems mode cynically to express and be expressed in terms of an enlarged self-interest. Systems talk thus becomes a convenient camouflage to hide systematic exploitation of various hues and kinds, and helps in naturalizing these under grand titles and nomenclatures. The task is therefore always to unmask these nomenclatures at each moment, and under all circumstances. That is the only way forward in a domain where there is no way forward, for all ways forward have already been anticipated by the cunning of thought and been mapped or territorialized in advance. Only the acute observation of the form of thought and thoughtlessness discloses what is in need of disclosure.

Once unmasked, there is the perception that something liquid moves beneath all the various veneers and disguises—*terror*, the basic building block of self and society. It is worth noting, in the view held here, that there is no real opposition between the two (i.e., self and society), despite the conventional belief to the contrary. The opposition itself is an artifice, a product of thinking. But the question we must grapple with now is 'what is fearless thinking?' Once we are under way, as we have attempted through the length of the present text, it is not difficult to grasp the basic answer to this question: thought, as it recoils and retreats (rolls backward) into its unknown matrix, produces fearless thinking. That is to say, thought in reverse contains the possibility of shedding fear. Forward moving, rampaging thought, notwithstanding its bluster and fulminations, is still driven by terror. The retreat or deactivation (*katargesis*) is not some final act but a daily phenomenological and hermeneutic practice that somehow links up the corpus sensorium with the organicity of thought. The wholeness of this mysterium alone can counter the terror of isolationist thinking and misapprehension, and thereby present a fresh dimension.

The deepest perception that an inquiry like the present one can presume to touch is that the 'I' thought must revert onto the AM-ness of things; that is to say, the 'AM' or being is prior to any thought process, which is but a derived evanescence whose primary obligation is to face the AM-ness or essence. Otherwise thinking is reduced to a hovering phantasm that is an emanation out of the self-referentiality of thought itself. In other words, it has no reality of its own, and hence no positivity or possibility of redemption. The permanence associated in experience with this emanation is the result not of any intrinsic ontological attribute but the consequence of a lack of awareness or critical observation of its ephemerality. Since most of individual life and social life, over time, becomes based on the fears and drives of the 'I' thought, most of civilizational disasters can be seen to be the product of ontological non-awareness. Hence it becomes supremely important to inquire into this process without mystifying it further or reifying it in terms of ego, superego, etc. These terms do not bring us any closer to the phenomena themselves but merely add another layer of perplexity. Redemptive thinking is the capacity to observe the activities of thought without any presumptions or categories. It leads thinking, eventually, to directly and phenomenologically realize the basic mystery of its possibility.

Once the basic mystery and wonder is admitted in thought, the path becomes open for a new kind of thinking to emerge—a philosophical bilingualism. This thinking is 'concerned thought' that leaves a reflexive trace in the heart-mind whenever it moves. It is slow, weighty, and watchful, half-turned toward itself, and does not accumulate semi-digested experiences as memory. At its center is a silent question mark that remains unresolved about its own purpose and ground. This is the preparation for a readiness. It engages in social function from a primeval, atavistic ground without the pretensions of novelty. The ever-changing frames of the shadow world of thought are revealed to itself as principally the Same, notwithstanding its novel modes and contours. The opacity and piety that surrounds conventional thinking is gradually replaced by a constant see-through-ness that strips thought of all masquerades. The newly developed transparency is a preparation for redemption. Philosophy thus no longer misses the moment of its realization. It does not because it is no longer caught in *chronos* or mechanical time. Intellectual insight liberates philosophical labor from time, making it aware of an unexpected dimension. Liberated labor or praxis, in turn, frees thought from incessant calculation, turning it toward its own mystery. The waiting we have spoken of earlier is not a waiting in time, but a slow *turning-toward* in which intention plays no part. The esthetics of waiting is realized in the perception that no-one is waiting (psychologically), meaning that, there is no subject behind the waiting. Then the waiting takes on a new significance, because 'waiting' is really a superior relaxation of the tension of thinking, a letting go of the suffering of thought. At the end of the day, the rivers are still rivers and the mountains still mountains, but their relation with the thought composite has changed forever. Phenomena arise and subside within a non-resistive attention. Thought indefinitely awaits a new *klesis* without anxiety, even without the knowledge that it awaits. For it is not the old kind of waiting that lies-in-wait with anticipation, but a negative waiting which transforms the very waiting itself. It brings us unto the Open.

One last thing in the lines that remain. Yesterday's insights are no good for today, however powerful, just as the memory of yesterday's sun is no good for lighting up the world today. Each instant thought must make a new beginning with the kind of philosophical bilingualism spoken of as its mode of action. It cannot do so with the burden of memory which holds it back in the throes of time, history, and contradiction. There is no cumulative wisdom in thinking as such. The mystery of the Open demands that all accumulation be laid aside for they arise within the existing culture of thought which we know does not bring redemption. The *kenosis* or emptying of the one-dimensionality leads to a new condition of philosophical bilingualism in which there is no necessary opposition between intuition and intellect or *mythos* and *logos*.

References

Agamben, Giorgio. *The Time That Remains: A Commentary on Paul's Letter to the Romans*. Stanford: Stanford University Press, 2005.

Illich, Ivan. *The Rivers North of the Future: The Testament of Ivan Illich*. Toronto: House of Anansi Press, 2005.

The Bible, New International Version.

Vaihinger, Hans. *The Philosophy of 'As If': A System of the Theoretical, Practical, & Religious Fictions of Mankind*. Translated by C. K. Ogden. London: Routledge, 1935.

Index

K. Roy, *The Power of Philosophy*,
https://doi.org/10.1007/978-3-319-96911-4

R

Printed by Printforce, United Kingdom